The Mwindo Epic

Mr. Candi Rureke, during the performance of the
Mwindo Epic, holds a rattle (*right hand*) and a mock *conga*-scepter (*left hand*),
one of the main magical attributes of the hero Mwindo.
The young men standing behind him
participate in the songs.

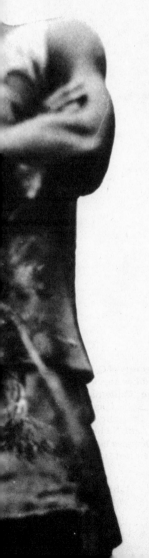

The Mwindo Epic

FROM THE BANYANGA (CONGO REPUBLIC)

EDITED AND TRANSLATED BY DANIEL BIEBUYCK
AND KAHOMBO C. MATEENE

UNIVERSITY OF CALIFORNIA PRESS
BERKELEY   LOS ANGELES   LONDON

University of California Press
Berkeley and Los Angeles, California
University of California Press, Ltd.
London, England
Copyright © 1969 by The Regents of the University of California
Library of Congress Catalog Card Number: 68–28370
Designed by W. H. Snyder
Printed in the United States of America

ISBN 0-520-02049-9

PREFACE

In April, 1956, I organized a field expedition of several weeks into one of the most remote forest areas of Nyanga country, an area then known as *groupement Kisimba* in Belgian administrative circles. I had been actively engaged in field research among the Nyanga since April, 1954. The Nyanga had known me since late 1952 when, working among the Bembe and the Lega, I had on several occasions visited them in order to plan for future research projects.

By the time of my trip to Kisimba, I had acquired a broad knowledge of Nyanga culture, I had a good grasp of the language, I was well accepted by the people, I knew all the key informants, and I had been able to recruit an excellent team of collaborators. These included two categories of people: on the one hand, Mr. Amato Buuni and Mr. Stephano Tubi, two young men born and raised in the Nyanga milieu, who had finished their junior high school studies and whom I had trained in field methods since late 1952; on the other hand, two older Nyanga, Sherungu and Kanyangara, who had not been to school, but who possessed an admirable knowledge of Nyanga culture and who held important ritual and political offices in the Nyanga political system. Whereas Mr. Buuni and Mr. Tubi acted as clerks, writing down texts and various types of supplementary information, Mr. Sherungu and Mr. Kanyangara were readily available, first-class informants and *hommes de confiance* who could critically advise me on data obtained from my other informants in the various villages.

By the time I was planning my Kisimba trip, I had already visited large sections of Nyanga country, making routine ethnological investigations and writing down, with the help of Mr. Buuni and Mr. Tubi, hundreds of tales, narratives of events and dreams, and thousands of proverbs, riddles, songs, prayers, incantations, and praise formulas. I knew for a long time that the Nyanga had a longer, more expanded type of story, classified by them under the special name *kárisi*. On a couple of occasions I had received fragments of such stories from select informants, but I had never been successful in getting a complete and coherent text, either because the narrator was too old and too confused or because he did not remember the complete text (or had never known it), or because the narrator was simply uncooperative and apprehensive of the necessity to sit day after day with me and my collaborators to painstakingly narrate—indeed narrate over and over again—the various passages of his *kárisi*-story.

Then, on my Kisimba trip, while doing the routine work of taking village censuses, writing down genealogies, collecting information on descent groups, on kinship patterns, on political structure, on religion, and the like, I met Mr. Shé-kárisi Rureke in the village of Bese. Very cooperative and understanding, very lucid and intelligent, Rureke sat down with us for twelve days, singing, narrating, dancing, miming, until the present text was completely written down.

These days represent a great and memorable time in my life, one of the highlights of my long fieldwork in the Congo. We would begin to work early in the morning and, with a few short breaks, continue well into the night. Large crowds of people from Bese and from surrounding villages and hamlets would come to listen to the narration, to participate in the refrains of the songs, to dance. There was an atmosphere of joy and relaxation in this village where, as in the other Nyanga villages, life had become increasingly dull and joyless as a result of the various pressures introduced from the outside.

Rureke himself was inexhaustible in words, in movements, in rhythm, even though he became very tired physically (during the last days, his voice became increasingly hoarse and I was compelled to treat him regularly with some European ointments and mouthwashes). Very excited by the stimulus he received from his audience, very self-confident about his knowledge, and very proud about his achievements, Rureke was able to maintain from beginning to end the coherence of his story and the unusual richness and precision of language, as well as to capture the essence of Nyanga values.

Because of a variety of other duties and commitments, this great narrative has remained hidden in my files for a long period. In 1956 and 1958, I published in Dutch translation small fragments of it in a periodical, *Zuiderkruis*, which was published in Léopoldville. In 1964, thanks to a generous grant from the Alumni Foundation of the University of Delaware, I was able to bring to the United States one of my former students in Léopoldville, Mr. Kahombo C. Mateene, Nyanga by birth, trained in African linguistics and anthropology at the universities of Lovanium (Congo), Delaware, and California (Los Angeles). In close collaboration, we have worked on the definite establishment of the Nyanga text, on the translation, and on the notes.

I am pleased to present here, as the fruit of long and painstaking travail, this Mwindo epic in the Bantu text and in English translation. This epic is certainly a tribute to the rich content of Nyanga culture and to the creative talent of Mr. Rureke and his predecessors.

My sincere thanks go to my Nyanga informants and collaborators, particularly to the narrator himself, Mr. Shé-kárịsị Rureke, for their loyal assistance in helping me to save from oblivion part of so great a cultural tradition. I want to express my appreciation for the unfaltering encouragement and sponsorship I received during my fieldwork in the Congo from the Belgian Research Institute, Institut pour la recherche scientifique en Afrique centrale, and, in particular, from its former secretary-general, Dr. Jean-Paul Harroy, and its former director-general, Dr. Louis van den Berghe. The University of Delaware and the African Studies Center of the University of California, Los Angeles, have kindly provided me with the grants necessary for permitting Mr. Kahombo C. Mateene to work with me on this project. Finally, I want to acknowledge the dedicated work done by Mrs. Lorraine Przywara in Delaware and Miss Andrée Slaughter in California in the typing of the manuscript and in the improving and correcting of the English text.

In the field, the epic text was recorded in writing (with tonal indication) jointly by Amato Buuni, Stephano Tubi, and myself. The preface, introduction, and notes in their present form are entirely my responsibility. The definite establishment of

the Nyanga text and the method of word division are the work
of Mr. Mateene. The translation is the result of intensive collaboration by Kahombo C. Mateene, Amato Buuni, Stephano
Tubi, and myself.

D. B.

CONTENTS

Miréngé esímbănge băte
Ná barjmj bátásibéyo.

The tunes [voices] that we sing
The uninitiated ones [the ignorant ones] cannot understand them.

*

FROM THE MWINDO EPIC

INTRODUCTION

THE NYANGA[1]

The 27,000 Bantu-speaking Nyanga live in the mountainous rain forest area of Walikale territory in the former Kivu Province, in the eastern part of the Congo Republic, Kinshasa. The ethnohistorical traditions are weakly developed and are primarily concerned with the establishment and distribution of the Nyanga in their present habitat. All these traditions, however, point to origins in East Africa and more particularly in Bunyoro and Toro (Uganda). Migrating from East Africa, the Nyanga settled for some time in the grasslands and on the mountain slopes on the Congo side of the Lake Edward region, where several remnant groups of this migration are found today. Moving southwestward from there, the Nyanga gradually infiltrated the rain forest. Nyanga oral traditions explicitly state that in the rain forest their forefathers met with small, scattered groups of at least three different ethnic units: Pygmies, called Twa or more specifically Remba; Tiri-Asa of Kumu ori-

[1] For further general information on the Nyanga see the following studies by D. Biebuyck: "De mumbo-instelling by de Banyanga (Kivu)," *Kongo Overzee*, XXI (1955), 441–448; *De Hond by de Nyanga: Ritueel en Sociologie* (Brussels: Académie royale des Sciences d'Outre-Mer, 1956), 168 pp.; "L'organisation politique des Nyanga: La chefferie Ihana," *Kongo Overzee*, XXII (1956), 301–341; XXIII (1957), 59–98; "Mwéndo de Zwoeger: Een heldedicht van de Banyanga," *Zuiderkruis*, I (1956), 77–80; III (1958), 35–45; "Les divisions du jour et de la nuit chez les Nyanga," *Aequatoria*, XXI (1958), 134–138; "Six Nyanga Texts," in W. H. Whiteley, ed., *A Selection of African Prose* (Oxford: Clarendon Press, 1964), I, 55–61; "Prières des chasseurs Nyanga," in G. Dieterlen, ed., *Textes sacrés d'Afrique noire* (Paris: Gallimard, 1965), pp. 135–143; *Rights in Land and Its Resources among the Nyanga* (Brussels: Académie royale des Sciences d'Outre-Mer, 1966). A broad selection of Nyanga texts is ready now and will be published in 1967 under the title *Anthologie de la littérature orale nyanga* by the Académie royale des Sciences d'Outre-Mer, Brussels.

1

gin; Mpamba of Lega affiliation. Smaller remnants of Pygmies and Lega, and larger groups of Tiri-Asa (Kumu), are still found in Nyanga country. All are culturally closely interwoven with the Nyanga. Among them, the biologically miscegenated groups identified as Pygmies play a most significant role. They are attached by strong political and ritual bonds to the Nyanga sacred chiefs: they are the chief's hunters, they hold various ritual offices connected with the chief's enthronement, they provide the chief with one of his ritual wives (whose firstborn son holds the ritual position of *mwǎmitwá*, lit., chief Pygmy), and they are traditionally the chief's bards, experts in narrating and singing the longer epic tales. To the entire Nyanga population, they stand in some sort of joking relationship in that, for example, they are allowed to freely harvest plantains in all banana groves.

The impact of Pygmy culture on the Nyanga has been very strong. This is visible, for example, in some of the techniques and beliefs associated with hunting and food-gathering, and in the cult system, where the Nyanga worship, among other divinities, Měshémutwá (Meshe the Pygmy). The Nyanga assertion that their great epic texts, like the one presented here, originally flourished with those Nyanga groups that were most intimately associated with the Pygmies, contains an important culture-historical reference and points to the possibility that these epics or at least their basic themes originated with the Pygmies. I did not, however, find any special awareness of this fact among the so-called Pygmies whom I met in this region between 1956 and 1958.

Above all, the Nyanga are trappers, food-gatherers, and cultivators, but they also hunt and fish. Nyanga economy and diet are based on the complementary relationship among these various activities, which may receive different degrees of emphasis owing to limited local specialization. Dive-fishing, for example, or big-game hunting by highly esoteric corporations of hunters is found only in certain select Nyanga villages. As is revealed in rituals, taboos, legal principles of distribution and sharing, principles of land tenure, and as is also clear from the events and values suggested in hundreds of tales, trapping is the single most significant economic activity in Nyanga society. Agriculture is centered on the growing of the plantain banana. The system of cultivation is very extensive and informal and is based on the "slash without burning technique." Over the years, new banana groves are added to the existing ones in a cyclic shifting pattern; the banana groves, nevertheless, yield for many years, the duration of productivity depending upon the degree of maintenance. The Nyanga also traditionally cultivate a variety of grain and root crops, which are planted either in or on the edge of the banana grove. The sowing or planting of some subsidiary crops requires the partial burning of grasses and branches accumulated in patches of the banana grove.

The ideology of descent, inheritance, and succession is patrilineal. The descent groups themselves are thought to be patrilineal and are built around a nucleus of *de facto* or *de jure* agnatically related kinsmen. But membership in these patrilineally focused descent groups is not determined merely by unilineal male kinship bonds. In order to understand this feature of the Nyanga social structure, it is necessary to distinguish between two basic types of marriage. First is the more classic form of marriage based on the transfer in stages from the man's group to the wife's group of a fixed number of matrimonial goods which establishes for the husband and father the right to affiliate children born of that marriage with his own descent group. Second are the marriages between women and spirits, which are decided upon by the agnatic relatives of the women as a result of dreams, oracles, and so on. These spirit wives are permitted to live in what are usually prolonged, stable unions with married or unmarried "lovers" of either their own or their agnates' choice. These "lovers" have sexual rights to and various domestic and economic claims on the women, but cannot legally affiliate with their own descent groups the children born of these unions. In other words, spirit wives—who are found in large numbers throughout Nyanga society, in all descent groups—procreate children in the name of the agnatic descent groups of their fathers, brothers, and paternal uncles. In the course of time these uterine relatives are identified in genealogical recitations, as well as in the actual kinship nomenclature, with the male agnatic nucleus of the descent groups of their mothers; that is, they are treated as descendants of their unmarried mother's brothers.

Some descent groups are named after a male eponymous

3

founder, others are known by nicknames and epithets. The known genealogical charts are shallow in depth and subject to considerable manipulation. The descent groups themselves are dispersed units consisting of several small localized corporate units composed of one or several agnatically related extended families. Each of the descent groups has a core area or a cradle area with which, before the colonial policy of resettlement was introduced, at least one of its localized family units is associated as *miné* (owner, lord, legally and mystically linked with . . .).

Politically the Nyanga are organized into autonomous petty states, each ruled by a sacred chief *(mwǎmí)*. The chiefs are recruited in only a limited number of descent groups, some of which are considered to be agnatically related to one another, a practice that makes provision for special bonds of cooperation or at least of friendship among several autonomous chiefs. The sacred chiefs, surrounded by nobles *(barúsí)*, counselors *(bakungú)*, and ritual officeholders *(bandirabitambo)*, have directly under their control the different village headmen whose villages lie within the limits of the state. In other words, each petty state is territorially subdivided into a number of villages and hamlets; there exists no other intermediate territorial grouping.

Ancestral cult is little developed among the Nyanga: people occasionally pray to a dead agnatic relative (father, paternal grandfather, or paternal aunt) but there are no shrines nor is there an intensive worship of the ancestors. The entire cult system is built around a number of divinities, most of whom, like Muisa, Kiana, Hángi, Měshé, Nkángo, Kahómbó, are said to live together with the dead in the Underworld *(kwirúngá,* a place identified with the craters of the active and extinct volcanoes that are found east of Nyanga country, on the boundaries of the Congo and Rwanda) under the leadership of Nyamurairi, god of fire.

Some other divinities which are actively worshiped, such as Kéntsé (Sun), Nkúbá (Lightning), Iyúhu (Wind), Kibira (Leopard), Musóka (Water Serpent), are said to have left the Underworld to live in the sky, on earth, or in the water. All these divinities, together with the ancestors, are known under the generic term *bashumbú.* Shrines are made and plantains are grown for them, women are dedicated and married to them, sheep and hunting dogs are consecrated to them, prayers are said to them, and distinctive cultual paraphernalia for each of them are kept by their adepts. They manifest themselves in dreams and oracles and are responsible for good and evil in Nyanga life. The earth is further peopled with the land-dwelling dragon Kirįmu, the forest specter Mpacá, and the Binyanyasį (restless spirits of those Nyanga who committed suicide or died, stigmatized as sorcerers, as the result of a kabį-ordeal), and by the water-dwelling, rather friendly monster Mukįtį. The Nyanga formulate several ideas about Ongo, God, who is said inter alia to be the "heart of the earth," to have created everything, to be the giver of life (buingo), to have given man the knowledge that he possesses. Finally, the Nyanga have elaborate boys' circumcision rites. They also possess a wide variety of semisecret associations (membership in which is mostly restricted to certain descent groups) none of which has a tribe-wide adherence or distribution.

The profusion of Nyanga oral literature stands in contrast to the fairly limited, though highly efficient, technology. The Nyanga possess an impressive variety of fishing, trapping, and hunting devices, but the wickerwork, plaiting, ironwork, pottery, and carving are simple. Wooden dishes and pots are decorated with incised designs. Plastic art is practically unknown in world collections, although the Nyanga make decorative masks of antelope hide, a rare type of anthropozoomorphic wooden statue used in the mumbirá-initiations and very rare bone and ivory carvings for the mbúntsú association.

NYANGA ORAL LITERATURE

The small Nyanga tribe possesses a highly diversified oral literature, rich in content and style. There are innumerable situations and occurrences that occasion the recitation, singing, or narration of the traditional texts. The Nyanga live in an isolated and largely undisturbed environment where social relationships among individuals, families, and larger groups of kinsmen are intensive and intimate. Daily, after returning from work in the forest, small groups of men—agnates, affines, friends—sit together in the men's meeting place to eat, drink, smoke, discuss the day's events, assign the next day's tasks, analyze patterns of behavior and action, scrutinize personal and familial problems, instruct the children in the social mores, criticize misconduct. These routine gatherings, which often extend long into the night, are a major occasion for narrating tales, quoting proverbs, solving riddles, not merely as a form of entertainment and fun, but also as a means of clarification of ideas, of interpretation of events, and of enhancement of existing values.

In their own domestic sphere, the women of the village also gather, in small groups of three or four in the company of their younger children, to eat, chat, and instruct. Like the men, they narrate stories, recite proverbs, and solve riddles, which, though similar in content and theme to those of the men, are commonly different in conclusion or explanation. Adolescents, too, males and females living in their own spheres, daily participate in dances for sheer entertainment or in games, an intrinsic part of which are traditional songs, riddles, proverbs. In addition to these regular daily activities, there are the hundreds of special occasions—rites, initiations, statewide councils, specialized dances—which are inconceivable without narrated, sung, recited texts, oral texts that either belong to the common patrimony or are the possessions of specialized groups and specific categories of people.

All Nyanga know a certain number of texts; some are able to narrate, sing, or recite them coherently and completely, others are confused narrators, able only to communicate the essence of their content. The expert narrators or singers do not make a profession of or derive a special social status from their skill. They may be in demand and thus receive much food, banana beer, and small presents. They may be famed and praised for their art, but they are not looked upon as a group of specialists, nor can they make a living of it. The expert narrators and singers may know a fairly large number of texts, but rarely does their knowledge approach the unusually high level and competence of that of Mr. Sherungu Muriro, one of the great Nyanga informants, who gave me 21 very long tales, 82 "true" stories, 43 interpretations of dreams, 268 riddles, 327 songs (some mere proverbs, others long and complex concatenations of aphorisms and personal reflections and remembrances).

6

The Nyanga musical instruments, inseparable from the dances, initiations, and gatherings of which the oral literature is an integral part, cover the following range. There are three types of funnel-shaped drums of different sizes (*ioma, mukíntsa, kandúndú*, beaten with two hands, two drumsticks, one drumstick, respectively); the percussion stick (*nkwángátiro*); the antelope horn (*kahanda*); the small reed or bamboo flute (*kaféréré*); the calabash or wickerwork rattle (*ishengo*); the music bow (*kimpúrenge*); the two-stringed zither (*ntsentse*); the three types of zanzas (*kantsambi, ikimbi,* and *kasái,* the last of recent introduction); the anklet bells (*ntsumbo*) made from nutshells or iron.

Any type of text, except prayers, can be narrated, recited, and/or sung with the accompaniment of some of these musical instruments or of simple handclapping, but certain dances, initiations, or narratives require specific instruments or combinations of instruments. Praise songs for chiefs, headmen, and mountains, for example, may be accompanied by only two rattles, two drums, and the small flute.

We have prepared for publication an anthology of Nyanga oral literature[2] in which selected samples of the various forms of this literature are given. A brief description of these forms as they are classified by the Nyanga follows.

mushúmo. This category comprises proverbs, maxims, and other terse statements that represent part of the Nyanga code of values. Almost all teachings and precepts given in the course of initiations are presented in the form of proverbs that are sung or recited. Most of the so-called songs (*rwímbo*) consist of nothing but concatenations of proverbs intermingled with reflections improvised by the singer. In legal contexts and in a very wide range of discussions and arguments, proverbs are currently quoted. All Nyanga proverbs are to be thought of as a form of poetry. The majority of them are composed of two verses, separated by a caesura. Quite often, the Nyanga reciter formulates only the first verse, leaving the task of either thinking or actually phrasing the second one to his audience. The structure of these verses follows definite quantitative patterns

---

[2] To be published in 1968 in the *Collections* of the Académie royale des Sciences d'Outre-Mer, Brussels.

(e.g., number of words and syllables) as well as qualitative patterns (e.g., rhyme, alliteration, assonance, reduplication). Frequently, the normal tone pattern is changed to enhance the qualities of rhythm. Both men and women know proverbs, but men make the most extensive use of them.

inondo. These are riddles that are most commonly used by adolescents and women. More restricted in their range of applicability, the riddles are less rich in content than the proverbs. They are sung or recited and accompanied by handclapping, gestures, rhythmic movements. Like the proverbs, most Nyanga riddles are a form of poetry consisting of two verses. The first verse contains a statement, a proposition, a compound personal name, rarely a purely onomatopoeic form, and may or may not be introduced by a verbal expression meaning "Tell me," "Teach me," "May I know," or "Beware." The second verse provides the answer, which may be a single word, but usually is a sentence containing the justification of the answer or a partial repetition of the proposition. It is often introduced by a verbal expression meaning "It does not surpass," "It is not difficult."

mubikiriro. Prayers, which again are a form of poetry, are recited slowly and distinctly, the reciter pausing after each verse to permit the other celebrants to answer *aé* (yes) or to mumble *um*. Prayers are composed of many repetitious statements, which identify the names and epithets of the divinity or divinities invoked, give praise to the spirits, contain implorations for help, strength, good luck, good health, and success in hunting, and they make promises. They are recited by men—generally elders, headmen or other officeholders—without musical accompaniment, on various occasions, for example, before and after the hunt, at the blessing of departing relatives and of hunting dogs, during the dedication of persons or animals to divinities, on state occasions, and throughout the course of offerings and libations.

musinjo. Eulogistic recitations for chiefs, headmen, and mountains are given on state occasions by elders who are prominent in the political structure as headmen and officeholders and who are leading adepts of certain cults. The recitation, without musical accompaniment, is made in a staccato manner (words are split by the reciter into syllables or groups of two

8

or three syllables) after which there is a short pause to permit participants to murmur *aé* or *um*. The content is monotonous and consists mainly of names, but the ethnohistorical knowledge and data about land and territorial divisions to be gained from them are very rewarding. The most impressive aspects of the eulogistic recitations, however, are to be found in the rhythm, the gestures, and the intense solidarity or *esprit de corps* manifested by the members of different groups.

ihamuriro. Stereotyped formulas, used in divination and medicinal practices, with highly esoteric overtones, are enunciated extremely quickly by specialists (diviners and medicine men) while interpreting oracles or preparing and applying medicine.

rwîmbo. These are songs; all Nyanga songs are a form of poetry. As formerly mentioned and as revealed by those that occur in the Mwindo epic, the songs are basically concatenations of proverbs, improvised, terse statements made by the singer about his personal experiences, remembrances, as well as abstracts of tales. According to the social or ceremonial circumstances, highly different interpretations may be given for identical songs and only twin songs are among the more specialized ones. Both short and long songs are interspersed in the tales.

uano and *mushîngá*. The first is a tale in general, the second a tale where the supernatural element, produced by the intervention of divinities, celestial bodies, monsters, and forest specters, stands in the foreground. Countless minor and major variants of the same tales are known, and everybody from adolescence on is able adequately to narrate or at least to summarize some of these tales. The dramatis personae in the tales are animals—all kinds of animals, but particularly the Duiker antelope, the turtle, the hunting dog, and the leopard. It is striking, however, that the most sacred animals, like the pangolin, the hornbill, the flying squirrel, the dendrohyrax, the bongo antelope, and the potto, are *never* included in these stories. In the tales there are human beings (particularly individuals who stand in a kinship or friendship relationship to one another, or chiefs and Pygmies). There are personified abstract characters (e.g., Shébuhányá, the Calamitous; Shéburongú, the Generous; Shébushú, the Man-of-Hatred). There are also extraordinary

9

awe-inspiring beings like Kirịmu, the Dragon; Mpacá the Forest Specter; Mukịtị, the Water Serpent. Much more rarely are divinities or ancestors mentioned in these texts. Semideified celestial bodies and the elements (e.g., Moon, Star, Rain, Hail, Cloud) occasionally appear as principal or secondary actors in the tales. Tales are narrated, partly sung, mimed, and partly dramatized on a great variety of domestic, legal, ritual occasions to entertain, to instruct, to explain, to moralize. It would be inexact to isolate for any given tale a single one of these functions. Most, if not all, Nyanga tales simultaneously perform recreational, pedagogical, etiological, and moralizing roles, but specific situations may demand special emphasis on a single function.

nganuriro. These are "true stories" about partly imaginary, partly real events. Men, particularly trappers and hunters, are the experts in telling this type of story. In a terse style and a somewhat laconic tone, always speaking in the first person (singular or plural), men tell about things that happened to them or to their close relatives (the stories invariably begin with either "I (we) have seen . . ." or "I (we) have heard . . ." or "We were astonished . . ."). The occurrence of unusual events, the apparition of strange beings, the development of abnormal situations, or the ascription of extraordinary powers and skills to *known* persons are all depicted as real happenings. In this kind of "true stories" which are told in the men's meeting place, the embryos of new tales are found in the reports on long hunting or trapping expeditions or on a prolonged journey to a distant kinsman.

There are many other texts, which are generally not classified as literature, but which, as far as the Nyanga are concerned, fall into well-established categories according to content and style. They are the following:

mwanikiro. These are meditations, reflections expressed in a concise style. Many traces of these well-stated personal thoughts which are given in men's discussions are found in the songs. As already stated, Nyanga songs are essentially concatenations of proverbs and of such concisely formulated personal reflections.

kishámbáro. Discourses on or systematic coherent treatments of the problems of the country or state uttered by the elders, headmen, and chiefs.

įhano. Instructions; teachings made to the youth about customs, skills, techniques, patterns of behavior. The texts are short, conceived in an easy, informal conversational style, and are generally introduced by the formula "we are accustomed to do. . . ." The stereotyped description and analysis of good and bad omens (*mwangiriro; kihunda*) and of taboos, prohibitions, and injunctions (*mutándo*) would also fall under this category of teachings and counsels.

kárįsį. These epic texts are few in number and are known to only a small number of men. The central hero in the Nyanga epics, as in the text presented here, is Mwindo. Mwindo is currently given as a personal name, in the family unit, to a male who is born after a number of girls. The Nyanga also see a relationship between the name and the verb *uindo*, to fell trees, thus emphasizing physical strength. Mwindo has several epithets, such as *Kábútwa-kénda* (the Little-one-just-born-he-walked) and *Mboru* (etymology unknown to the Nyanga). He is considered to be a small being, as is indicated by the diminutive prefix *ka-* by which he is designated throughout the epic. He is human, although he is not conceived and born as a normal human being (in some versions, he is a product of parthenogenesis; in other versions, he is born from sexual intercourse, but through his mother's medius). He is the son of a chief, rejected in some versions by his father, but ultimately he becomes chief; accepted by his father in other versions, he becomes chief after a partition of the state. He has fabulous gifts (he can move on land, in water, underground; he has the gift of premonition); he has powerful human, animal, and supernatural allies (paternal aunt, spiders, bats, lightning); he possesses by birth powerful magic objects (e.g., a *conga* flyswatter made from antelope or buffalo tail) which permit him to escape the worst difficulties. He is the destroyer of evil forces, the savior of people, a generous leader.

Kárįsį is the generic term for the long epic narratives that celebrate Mwindo's feats, but, interestingly, in one version of the epic, *Kárįsį* is also the name of a chief, who is married to the divinity of good fortune (Kahómbó) and whose son, born of parthenogenesis, is Mwindo. For a small group of individuals, those who participate in the performance, transmission, and preservation of the epic form of literary tradition, Kárisi is a male spirit. When asked why he learned the epic, a Nyanga bard replies that he did so as the result of a compulsory message received in dreams from Kárisi. This can be easily understood in the following terms. The patterns of transmission of epics are, of course, determined by kinship and friendship. Young men who are agnatic relatives, affines, and/or blood friends of the accomplished bard learn the epic in an informal way by accompanying him as helpers whenever he goes to recite. They are usually about three in number, but not all these young men will ultimately be expert in narrating the epic. It is likely that only one of them—the more energetic, intelligent, assiduous, better-liked one—will be fully instructed by the bard in the performance of the epic in all its complexity. If one of the bard's companions falls sick or suffers other frustrations (ill-fated hunting parties, death of near relatives, personal injuries), the oracles will surely ascribe his misfortune to Kárisi's anger and dissatisfaction about the slowness and negligence with which he has been learning the epic. The cause of this evil fate can be removed only by appropriate devotions to Kárisi. These devotions are accomplished in two ways: first, the accelerated learning of the epic text and its subsequent performance; second, the erection, behind the house, of a small table-like shrine (busuni) on which offerings and libations of banana beer are made. The bard and his colleagues and friends ceremonially drink banana beer, through an otherwise rarely used reed tube, from a gourd placed on the shrine.

The main emblems of the cult are an iron bell and a butenge-spear with copper rings fixed around the shaft. These objects are said to be carried by the spirit Kárisi when, dressed in royal paraphernalia, he reveals himself in dreams. During offerings, the spear is planted near the shrine and the bell is attached to the gourd. During narration, the spear stands near the bard, while the bell may be fixed to his ankle. The bards themselves are called Kárisi, which indicates, as is clear from other similar cultural practices, that they are devotees of the spirit Kárisi or Shé-kárisi, a name constructed like any teknonym, signifying that he is the "father of . . . ," "possessor of . . . ," "in control of . . . ," or "maker of . . ." an epic story.

As shown by the translated text, the epic is said to be

cárwǐmbo, the song par excellence. Episode by episode, the epic is first sung, then narrated. While singing and narrating, the bard dances, mimes, and dramatically represents the main peripeties of the story. In this dramatic representation, the bard takes the role of the hero. The normal musical accompaniment consists of a percussion stick (*nkwángátiro*) which, resting on a few little sticks so as to have better resonance, is beaten with drumsticks by three young men (*bashénkwángátiro*). These men regularly accompany the bard when he performs; they are recruited among the members of the bard's own descent groups and/or his close affines (e.g., sororal nephew) or blood friends. They know large fragments of the epic, and, whenever necessary, help the bard to remember and to find the thread of his story. Eventually, one of them will acquire full knowledge and mastery of the text and be the bard's successor. The narrator himself shakes the calabash rattle (containing little seeds or pebbles) and carries anklet bells (*ntsụmbo*). The percussionists and members of the audience sing the refrains of the songs or repeat a whole sentence during each short pause made by the bard. In this capacity, they are called *barịsị̈ya* (those who agree with . . . ; those who say yes). Members of the audience also encourage the reciter with short exclamations (including onomatopoeia) and handclapping or whooping.

The Nyanga epic is not a text performed only at certain times or on highly esoteric ceremonial occasions. There is nothing secret about it; it is to be heard and enjoyed by all the people. Normally a chief or headman or simply the senior of a local descent group, in order to entertain his people and guests, would invite the bard to perform a few episodes of the epic in the evening, around the men's hut in the middle of the village. Large crowds of people, male and female, young and old, would come to listen or rather to be participant auditors. The bard and his collaborators would receive food and beer. During the performance, they would receive, not only from the host, but also from many auditors, *masabo*-gifts consisting mainly of small amounts of *butéá*-money, beads, and armlets. They would also receive, like any good musician or dancer or singer, the praises of the crowd, praises expressed in words and in gestures (symbolic drying of sweat, adjusting of the clothing,

INTRODUCTION

pulling of the fingers, and straightening of the back of the dancing narrator). There would not be any special fees paid to them at the end of the performance, although the bard might receive, like any other respected guest, a special farewell gift (ikósórwa). If excitement ran high and beer and food were plentiful, the narrator would be invited to continue parts of the narration on the following evening. The interesting point is that the narrator would never recite the entire story in immediate sequence, but would intermittently perform various select passages of it. Mr. Rureke, whose epic is presented here, repeatedly asserted that never before had he performed the whole story within a continuous span of days.

The epic incorporates most literary forms known to the Nyanga, in both poetry and prose: rigidly stereotyped enunciations and improvised remarks, songs consisting of proverbs, improvised reflections, riddles and abstracts of tales, songs that have the characteristics of praises, prayers, and blessings. The protagonist is a human hero (murai), but he is surrounded by almost all categories of dramatis personae found in the tales: human beings (chiefs and officeholders, Pygmies, kinsmen, friends, and followers); animals (insects, fishes, birds, mammals), some of them his allies (spiders, bats, hawk) and some his enemies (fishes, crabs, aardvark); fabulous beings (the Water Serpent Mukíti and the Dragon Kirímu); divinities (Kahómbó, Muisa, Nkúbá); personified, and sometimes semideified, celestial bodies and the elements (Moon, Star, Rain, Hail, Cloud). The content of the epic is a rich survey of customs, institutions, activities, behavior patterns, values, material objects that are of main significance to the Nyanga. It is, in fact, a synopsis of Nyanga culture. Functionally the epic is many things: entertainment, moralization, an explanation of causes, and an interpretation of existing customs; it is a paideia.

Finally, what is presented here as a piece of oral literature is much more than that. It is music, rhythm, song, dance, movement, dramatic entertainment. It is feasting and gift-giving (those who present the gifts dance and gesticulate). It is group solidarity and mass participation. For the bard himself, the act of narrating the story has religious significance. He believes that Kárìsì, deified, wanted him to learn the epic; to perform the drama adequately makes the narrator "strong," protects

14

him against disease and death. The narrator believes he will find in his songs the force that Mwindo himself, the hero of the epic, derives from them.

THE NARRATOR, MR. SHÉ-KÁRĮSĮ CANDI RUREKE

I met Mr. Rureke, narrator of the Mwindo epic, in Bese. Extremely isolated, far away from roads, located in a dense forest area that is infested with big game and intersected by numerous rivers, Bese is famous for its hunters, trappers, and fishermen, and for its great tradition of blacksmithing. Composed of sixty-four huts and nine outlying hamlets, the village is fairly large in size. Male representatives of not less than sixteen different descent groups live in the village which is traditionally placed under the headmanship of a member of the Bacira descent group. Bese is part of a small traditional state called Rare or cŭo cáBana-Kabákį, which, as is common among the Nyanga, consists of only a couple of villages and their outlying hamlets. The state is ruled by one of the few surviving sacred chiefs, Mwanankuyu. As a result of repeated and systematic regrouping and resettling of people by the Belgian administration, this and other petty states in the northwestern part of Nyanga country were merged into a single administrative unit, known as *groupement Kisimba*. A region of exceptionally dense rain forest called Ihímbí cuts across the boundaries of the Rare and other states. This region, which ecologically is but a southeastward extension of the huge rain forest that covers the adjoining territories of Lubutu, Bafwasende, Mambasa, and part of Lubero, was originally occupied by Pygmies, few of whom remained in the area because of emigration or absorption into Nyanga ranks. According to Nyanga traditions, the first peoples to encounter the Pygmies in these areas were collectively known as Bahímbí. These Bahímbí are part of a cluster of peoples living in areas adjoining Nyanga country and are known in ethnographical records as Bapiri, Bamate, Batįrį. Nyanga groups, immigrating from the east (Rutshuru territory), later settled in this area and established political control over it. As a result of this contact, the Bahímbí, who were already strongly influenced by the Pygmies, were culturally assimilated by the Nyanga. Nyanga culture predominates among the few

groups still known as Bahímbí, but they differ from most other
Nyanga in that they are heavily specialized in big-game hunting. Mr. Rureke, by his kinship origins, belongs to such a
group.

As shown in the first lines of this epic, the region of Ihímbí
forms the setting within which the action takes place. In his
last song, the narrator even praises Ihímbí: *MwiHimbí
kwítú nongóbo/in Ihimbi, in our country it is fine*. The fact,
then, is that Rureke possessed a house in the village of Bese and
that he resided there, but Bese was not his home village. A
member of the Bana-nkurí descent group, Rureke was born in
the village of Koutu which was located in the heart of Ihímbí
before it was abandoned in about 1931, both as the result of
boundary disputes and of administrative resettlement of scattered groups. Before the colonial era, Koutu had been the
center of a petty state called cǔo cáBana-Koumbo. The male
members of Rureke's descent group were classified as the perpetual maternal uncles of the local ruling line of Baruko chiefs.
The abandonment of Koutu resulted in the dispersal of its
descent groups. Rureke, his two uterine junior brothers, Butinda and Muhiirwa, and two members of the Baruko group
settled in Bese.

It would be incorrect to think of Rureke as a "stranger" in
Bese village, for he was linked by various ties to many of its
inhabitants. First, there had always been close political ties
rooted in kinship between the rulers of Kouto and Rare.
Second, Rureke's maternal uncles (the Baherí) and his in-laws
(the Bafúyá or Babúyá) were established in Bese. Third, Rureke
had personal relationships, founded in distant kinship and in
friendship, with two men of considerable influence in the
village. Both men, Risaki Kangakora (the senior son of the
village headman) and Butinda (a son of the headman's senior
brother) of the Bacira group, were classificatory sororal neph-
ews of the Baruko. Rureke, as a member of a group that stood
in a perpetual relationship of maternal uncles to the Baruko,
was automatically considered to be a classificatory grandfather
of both men. This relationship was enhanced by some special
form of *esprit de corps* arising from the fact that all three men
had been working for European concerns, located not too far
from Nyanga country.

Rureke, a youthful-looking man about fifty years old, was not wealthy, nor did he hold any political or ritual office. In contrast with his junior brothers, he had only one wife; she was sick and resided with her two children in the hamlet of Bese, which was occupied by members of her own descent group, the Bafúÿá or Babúÿá. Rureke depended for his food on the wives of his junior brothers and of his two friends. In his youth, Rureke had been a skillful maker of mats and baskets and that is how he got his name (which literally means basket). Then he had become a helper of Kanyangara of Bese, who was an expert narrator of the Mwindo epic. Kanyangara, who belonged to the Bafúÿá or Babúÿá descent group, had blood brotherhood relationships with Rureke's father; Rureke's father also selected a wife for his son from this group. On several occasions, Rureke refers in the songs to the fact that he has learned his story from the Babúÿá (his pronunciation of Bafúÿá), thus paying tribute to his teacher:

> Twanánge múano
> We are telling (from) the story
> Rwánángá Babúÿá
> That the Babuya have told (long ago).

and

> Tuané kwaruano
> Let us recite from the story
> Runaáná Babúÿá
> That the Babuya are used to reciting.

Rureke knew only that Kanyangara had learned the epic from a certain Bishusha whom he could not further identify.

From Rureke's social background it is clear that the epic he knew had its roots in a region where three cultural traditions (Pygmies, Bahímbí, Nyanga) had been intimately integrated with one another. The Nyanga insist that the Pygmies were at one time great bards who performed kárisí-like stories for their chiefs. They do not, however, say that these stories originated with the Pygmies. On the other hand, it is interesting to note that Rureke, the only great performer of the Mwindo epic alive in Nyanga country in the mid-fifties, had, through his kinship origins, very deep roots in an area that all Nyanga agree was once occupied by Pygmies. It is also significant that

Rureke learned the epic from a member of the Bafúyá (Babúyá) whose original name they themselves assert was Bana-Mutwá (an appellation that contains the word for Pygmy).

Throughout the epic Mwindo is designated and designates himself as a small creature (systematic use of the *ka-* diminutive prefix). Given the fantastic attributes of the miraculously born hero, there is no reason that he could not have grown rapidly or have been born to full size. This fact may also indicate Pygmy influence.[3] The Pygmies figure in Rureke's epic as the hero's loyal hunters; in other, but shorter or fragmentary, versions of the Mwindo epic, the role of the Pygmies is elaborated upon much more. In one of them, Mwindo is represented as a great hunter, going on fabulous expeditions with his fourteen Pygmies and two dogs.

According to P. Schebesta, the Kibira-speaking Basúa Pygmies and also the southern Efe Pygmies have a divinity known by the name of Kalisia.[4] It is tempting to see a connection between this name and the Nyanga Kárịsị (which is, as we have stated, the generic term for epic, the name of a chief said to be the father of Mwindo in one version of the epic and the name of a divinity worshiped only by the bards). The Pygmy Kalisia is characterized as the lord of the forest and of game, as the protector of hunters who guides their search for animals and helps in killing them. He also appears in dreams, giving counsel about trails of animals and places to set up hunting camps. During the ceremonies of the cult, a spear is planted near the offering pole.[5] The elements of dream and spear are also present in the Nyanga worship of Kárịsị. Moreover, the hero Mwindo himself possesses the basic characteristic that the Pygmies ascribe to Kalisia: in Nyanga, Mwindo is a *minéntsí*, a master of the path, a leader who knows in advance of things to come.

The customs, institutions, values, behavior patterns described and suggested in the Mwindo epic are consistently Nyanga; however, epithets and recurrent detailed descriptions of physical traits and emotions are infrequent in the rest of

---

[3] According to Schebesta, the Pygmy Tore, divinity, ancestor, culture hero, is also small (P. Schebesta, *Les Pygmées du Congo Belge* [Brussels: Académie royale des Sciences d'Outre-Mer, 1952], p. 305; see also H. Tegnaeus, *Le héros civilisateur* [Uppsala, 1950], p. 165).

[4] Schebesta, *op. cit.*, pp. 303–306.

[5] *Ibid.*, pp. 303–306.

Nyanga literature. The contention is not that the Mwindo epic originated with the Pygmies, but that the Nyanga incorporated several themes, dramatis personae, and functions that they adopted and adapted from the Pygmies and also possibly from the Bapiri-Batįrį-Bamate cluster.

THE MWINDO EPIC

The text presented here is by far the longest, most comprehensive, most coherent, most detailed, and most poetic of all versions of the Mwindo story which I heard in Nyanga country.[6] The themes of the epic are typical, but neither exclusive nor exhaustive of the feats generally ascribed to the hero Mwindo. In other words, there are, according to the different versions of the epic, variations in the hero's alliances and struggles and in the details of his life story. The miraculous birth into the chief's family, the conflict with the father (though usually less circumstantially analyzed), the aid of the maternal uncles and the maternal aunt, the alliance with animals, the friendship with the Pygmies, the Herculean tasks imposed by the divinities, the *wiki*-game, the ascent and/or descent of the hero to the supernatural realm—all are common themes. In some versions, however, the Pygmies play a much more active and significant role throughout the epic, more of the story moves in the supernatural realm, there is a larger number of imaginary beings (normally absent from Nyanga tales and religion) such as Ukanga (Big Rock), Kabaraka (alleged brother of Lightning), Musero (White Rock), Itembe (Wild Banana Tree). Elsewhere, Mwindo has a sister Nyamitondo who is married to Lightning and who sometimes assumes the role played by the paternal aunt here. In still another version where the temporary metamorphosis of human beings and divinities into hunted animals is a constant theme, Mwindo is a great hunter and is exposed by the god of fire to a number of tests. In this version, too, Mwindo gets help, not from his living paternal aunt, but from her spirit.

---

[6] I have recorded five other versions of the epic: one is a complete story but is half as long as this text; the second is still shorter and confused (the old narrator did not adequately remember the text); the three others are fragmentary.

In our version of the epic, Mwindo identifies himself in dialogues and songs as *Kábútwa-kénda* (the Little-one-just-born-he-walked), but there is one version in which Mwindo and *Kábútwa-kénda* are two different persons, related to each other as half brothers, Mwindo being the false hero. In that version, *Kábútwa-kénda* is born by parthenogenesis, whereas Mwindo is born of the chief's ritual wife in normal fashion. *Kábútwa-kénda*, described as a great singer and musician liked by women, wins all battles against Mwindo, yet is generous, providing his brother with a wife and a village and bringing him back to life after he died. After *Kábútwa-kénda*'s death, the astute Mwindo usurps the throne destined for his paternal nephew Buingo wa-Ngoma. In his unwillingness to return power to his nephew, as stipulated by the oracles, Mwindo causes the death of his own child. The dead child, however, obtains the death of its father (Mwindo) after his arrival in the Underworld.

In our epic, a synthesis is made of all the feats and attributes of Mwindo and *Kábútwa-kénda* and all are ascribed to Mwindo: he is astute, strong, miraculously born; he is wronged by his father; he has the help of certain animals, of his maternal uncles, and of his aunt; he is a great singer whose songs have a magic force; he is successful in battle; yet, he is not a perfect hero, since without his magic scepter, the help of Lightning, the help of his aunt and uncles, the help of certain animals (hawk, sparrow, spiders, bats, hedgehog), the help of his *kahombo* (good fortune), he would not be able to confront all his opponents; ultimately he changes in character from a boaster to a wise, generous, benevolent ruler.

The Nyanga have no titles for their tales or subtitles under which to indicate the various episodes of the epic narrative. We have, therefore, presented the text as one continuous entity. In order to give a better idea of the various actors and their functions, of the various themes and situations described, I present a synoptic table of contents.

I. THE SETTING

A. Temporal and spatial

The events take place in remote times in a known place, the state of Ihímbí, the village of Tubondo (which, as its name indicates, is a place of many raphia trees and, as is implied elsewhere in the epic, is located on a hill or mountain). The main action takes place in the village of Tubondo; it is there that the epic begins and there that it ends; it is the place to which the action returns at the four turning points of the epic. The sequence of locations in which the events take place is:

Village of Tubondo
Pool or dwelling place of the Water Serpent Mukiti
Village of Tubondo
River dominated by Mukiti's allies
Village of Tubondo
Subterranean world of Muisa, Ntumba, Sheburungu
Village of Tubondo
Deep forest
Village of Tubondo
Celestial realm of Lightning, Rain, Hail, Moon, Sun,
    Star
Village of Tubondo

The spatial plan of the epic corresponds closely to the Nyanga conception of the division of the universe into four spheres: *butú* (sky), *mwanyá* (atmosphere), *oto* (earth), *kwirúngá* (underworld). The actors move and the actions take place in these four spheres: Star puts the hero in the sphere of *butú*; the contacts with Lightning bring him to the less distant sphere of *mwanyá*; the subterranean journey to Muisa, Ntumba, Sheburungu is in the *kwirúngá* sphere; the rest of the action takes place on earth, the *oto* sphere. Earth itself has four subdivisions: *kumbúka* (the village; the inhabited world), *kubusará* (the deep forest), *kumundura* (the forest, clearings, fields near the village), *kundúsi* (the water). Action occurs in all these places, but it is centered in the village.

B. The key dramatis personae
Chief Shemwindo and his seven wives (among whom are a preferred wife and a despised one); the chief's sister, Iyangura, paternal aunt of the unborn hero; the hero, whose name is not mentioned in the beginning, but who is already known as Mwindo because of the teknonymic name by which the chief is called.

21

As the action moves on, a great many other actors are drawn in besides the inner circle of kinsmen. They fall into six categories.

1. Humans
Unnamed group of nobles, counselors, and commoners, of midwives, of old and young people
Maidservants of Iyangura
Drummers and singers of Mwindo
Pygmies of Mwindo

2. Animals
On the hero's side: the Spiders, the Bats, the Hedgehog, the Sparrow
Opposed to the hero: the fishes, prominent among them Kasiyembe (the guardian of the hero's aunt); the cricket
Ambiguous: the Hawk
Semideified, enemy of the hero: Ntumba or Aardvark

3. Divinities
Inimical to the hero: Muisa and Sheburungu
Friend and ally of the hero (but in the earliest stage of the epic working against him): Nkuba
Ambiguous: Kahindo, daughter of Muisa; Musoka, sister of Mukiti
Friendly, but not allied: Kentse, Sun; Mweri, Moon

4. Semideified elements
Friendly, but not allied: Rain, Hail, Cloud, Star

5. Fabulous beings
Hostile, but never in direct conflict with hero: Mukiti, the Water Serpent
Enemy of the hero's Pygmies, destroyed by hero: Kirimu, the dragon

6. Mystical objects that help the hero in his struggles
Conga: scepter made from buffalo or antelope tail, to which hero owes in final instance all his power
Bag of good fortune
Rope
Axe

C. The intentional and simultaneous pregnancies of the chief's seven wives

D. The unmotivated interdiction and threat by the chief that the seven wives should not bear males

II. INTERLUDE: THE MARRIAGE OF IYANGURA, THE HERO'S PATERNAL AUNT, TO MUKITI, THE MYTHICAL WATER SERPENT

The action takes place both in the village of Tubondo (courtship, marriage negotiations, gift exchanges, transfer of valuables) and in the village of the Water Serpent (exposé of marriage plans, accumulation of matrimonial goods, actual marriage ceremony). This very beautiful and poetic interlude, which is absent from other versions of the epic, gives a fairly accurate description of marriage customs, and strongly emphasizes the basic Nyanga values of generosity, hospitality, and refinement in social relationships. The passage is full of unusually rich imagery, rarely, if ever, found in the rest of Nyanga literature, suggesting the beauty of both Iyangura and Mukiti and the intensity of their mutual passion. The interlude contains at least three elements of main significance for the development of the epic. First, it gives a justification for the absence from the village of the hero's aunt, a person who in Nyanga practice could have exercised strong pressures against her ill-inspired brother. Second, it gives special status and power to Iyangura, because she is depicted as Mukiti's ritual wife (*mumbo*); from many points of view, the ritual wife has the powers and privileges of the chief. Third, because as a ritual wife she lives in separation from her husband (a normal Nyanga practice), the freedom of decision and action which she shows throughout the story is fully justified.

III. THE HERO'S MIRACULOUS BIRTH; HIS ATTRIBUTES AND FIRST EXPLOITS

The action takes place in and around the village of the hero's birth, Tubondo.

A. As prescribed by the chief, six of his (the chief's) seven wives bear daughters.

B. The preferred wife does not give birth; she is mocked by the people and is anxious about her fate.

C. The unborn hero performs several domestic tasks for his mother (brings firewood, water, vegetables).

D. In meditation, the unborn hero decides upon the time and manner of his birth; he appears through his mother's medius, but his mother has the pains of child delivery.

E. Complot of the midwives: they refuse to reveal the child's sex to the chief and his counselors.

F. Naming of the child: Mwindo (boy following a series of girls).

G. Betrayal of child's sex by cricket.

H. Apparition of the hero's father as a villain and the hero's reactions.

Father throws spear into the hut, but hero's word has magic force: "May this spear end up at the bottom of the house-pole. . . ."

Father has his counselors bury the hero, but the latter, in the grave, warns his father of his own coming sufferings; at night a strong light is visible from the grave, and the hero escapes to go back to his mother's hut.

In the middle of this passage, the narrator has inserted the enumeration of the mystic objects and supernatural gifts with which the hero was born (*conga*-scepter, adze, bag of good fortune, rope, capacity to speak and laugh from birth on).

Father has his counselors make a drum, imprison the hero in it, and throw him in a pool (the realm of Mukiti); there is rain and hail for seven days, also famine.

The hero's mother is despised by her husband.

I. Meditations of the hero in the drum.

J. In a song, the hero reveals to the young maidens of Tubondo his coming journey and his goal to find his paternal aunt.

K. In another song, the hero repeats for his father and his father's counselors his plan of action.

IV. THE HERO'S AQUATIC JOURNEY
IN SEARCH OF HIS PATERNAL AUNT

The action takes place in a river that is the realm of the mythical Water Serpent Mukiti. The hero travels in the drum beneath the surface of the water and, at one moment, in the sand underneath the riverbed.

A. By means of a magic song, the boasting hero subdues the various species of fishes and crabs which, as Mukiti's allies, block the road. For the first time, in this song, the hero gives himself the epithet of *Kábútwa-kénda* (the Little-one-just-born-he-walked).

B. Encounter with the snake divinity Musoka, identified here as the junior sister of Mukiti. Mwindo speaks in a soft voice to this woman, who, uncertain about her role, asks her brother for advice. Finally, Mwindo is compelled to avoid her barrage by traveling past it underneath the riverbed.

C. The hero's encounter with Mukiti "at the knot where Mukiti was coiled up." Mwindo identifies himself as Iyangura's child; maidens at the wading place bring the news to Iyangura.

D. Encounter with Iyangura: informed by the maidservants, Iyangura, following a path bordering the river, goes to see for herself. Mwindo reveals himself and his goals in a song, but Iyangura, to be more sure about his identity, exposes him to tricky questioning. When she identifies him "as the sororal nephew of the Bats," the drum leaves the water and Iyangura slashes the membrane and Mwindo is freed. He appears as "multiple rays of the rising sun and of the moon."

E. Betrayal by Hawk: Kasiyembe, the guardian of Iyangura, is informed by Hawk about the encounter of Mwindo and Iyangura.

F. Encounter of the hero with the villain Kasiyembe, "the man of hatred."

Kasiyembe challenges Mwindo; Hedgehog informs Mwindo about the traps set for him by Kasiyembe and builds a tunnel that will permit the hero to avoid the traps and go directly to his aunt's house.

Mwindo takes up Kasiyembe's threat and sends his aunt home, inviting her to warn Kasiyembe.

Spider builds bridges across the traps.

Mwindo arrives in his aunt's house through the tunnel.

Iyangura's duplicity: although she knows about her husband's deceitful plans, she does not permit Mwindo to eat, but urges him to dance, as requested by Kasiyembe.

Mwindo's successful dance above the pits and his provocative song; during this dance, for the first time, the hero agitates his *conga*-scepter, which with the help given by the Spider's bridges gives him a double immunity.

Kasiyembe implores Nkuba for help, but Mwindo's words again have force and Nkuba strikes in vain.

By sheer volition, Mwindo sets fire to Kasiyembe's hair; those who try to extinguish the flames can find no water, not even saliva.

At Iyangura's imploration, Mwindo wakes Kasiyembe by means of a song and his *conga*-scepter.

Kasiyembe praises and blesses Mwindo.

V. THE HERO'S RETURN TO HIS NATAL VILLAGE TUBONDO; HIS FATHER'S FLIGHT; THE DESTRUCTION OF TUBONDO

The action consecutively takes place in Iyangura's hamlet, on the trail leading to Tubondo, in the village of the hero's maternal uncles, in a glen facing Tubondo, and in Tubondo itself. Mwindo is no longer a lonely traveler; he is accompanied by his paternal aunt and her maidservants who are joined in the course of the trip by Mwindo's maternal uncles, the Bats.

A. Mwindo announces his plan to return to his home village to fight with his father.

B. His aunt is skeptical about the issue, yet decides to accompany him together with her servants.

C. Songs are sung along the way in which the boasting hero warns his father about his coming.

D. The hero stays overnight in the village of his maternal uncles; his body is forged by them at his own request. Skeptical about Mwindo's fight, they decide to accompany him.

E. Mwindo and his followers are compelled to spend the night in the glen below the mountain on which Tubondo is built. It is cold and rainy; the people are hungry. Again sheer volition and a long, compelling song permit Mwindo to provide his followers with shelter, food, and implements. In this passage there is a succinct inventory of Nyanga material culture provided by a long song in which Mwindo compels all objects and animals in his father's village to join him in the glen.

F. Mwindo sends his uncles to fight in Tubondo; all but one, who brings the news about the catastrophe, are wiped out.

G. Mwindo alone sets out to Tubondo "to find out the reason why my uncles are all wiped out," leaving his bag, his axe, and his rope to his aunt.

H. Arriving in Tubondo, he wants to dance, but is not allowed to do so and is insulted. In a long song, he again explains his grievances, then asks for Lightning's intervention.

I. Lightning destroys Tubondo, wiping out all its inhabitants, but Shemwindo manages to escape underground through the root of a *kikoka*-fern.

J. Mwindo gets his aunt and her servants, establishing them in Tubondo; he brings his maternal uncles back to life and wills all animals, implements, foods back from the glen.

VI. MWINDO'S SUBTERRANEAN JOURNEY IN SEARCH OF HIS FATHER

The action takes place underground, where the Nyanga locate the larger number of their divinities. Alone, because all others "are used to eating terrestrial foods," Mwindo enters the Underworld through the root of a *kikoka*-fern and travels into the realms of Muisa ("place where no one ever clusters around the fire"), of Ntumba, Aardvark, and of Sheburungu (one of the epithets under which the supreme divinity of fire, Nyamurairi, is known).

A. Mwindo, by some form of clairvoyance, knows that his father has fled to the realm of Muisa.

B. He takes leave of his aunt, but maintains contact with her by means of the rope with which he was born.

C. Sparrow points out the *kikoka*-fern at whose root Shemwindo entered the Underworld.

D. Encounter at a wading place with Kahindo, daughter of
   Muisa, covered with yaws.

   Mwindo explains his intentions.
   He gets magic formulas from her which will permit him to
   escape Muisa's tricky invitations to sit down, to drink banana
   beer, and to eat banana paste.
   He heals the yaws of Kahindo.

E. Encounter with Muisa.
   Mwindo successfully escapes the tricky language of Muisa.
   He rests and eats in Kahindo's house.
   Muisa imposes upon him the Herculean task of clearing the
   forest, cultivating and harvesting bananas in a single day.
   Mwindo successfully carries out the various tasks, but, about
   to return with the bananas to Muisa's village, he is subdued by
   Muisa's magic belt, then saved by his own *conga*-scepter.
   Mwindo comforts his aunt, who, feeling the rope become
   still, thinks he is dead.
   He sends his *conga*-scepter to smash Muisa, then arrives with
   the bananas in the village and awakens Muisa at his daughter's request.
   Muisa, revivified, sends him out on honey-harvesting and
   again, seeing his success, has him smashed against a tree by
   his magic belt, but Mwindo is brought back to life by his
   conga-scepter and brought down from the tree by Lightning.
   Muisa now sends a boy for Shemwindo, even though he has
   permitted Shemwindo to flee.
   Hawk informs Mwindo about Muisa's betrayal and Shemwindo's flight.
   Mwindo has Muisa smashed by his *conga*-scepter and leaves in
   search of his father.

F. Encounter with Aardvark (Ntumba).
   Mwindo explains his plans in a song; he asks for the help of
   lightning.
   While Mwindo is unable to enter Ntumba's cave, Ntumba
   has Shemwindo flee to Sheburungu.
   Lightning destroys Ntumba's cave.
   Hawk informs Mwindo about Shemwindo's flight.
   Mwindo curses Ntumba ("May you never again find food in
   this country of yours"), but does not otherwise act against him.

G. Encounter with Sheburungu.

The hero meets hungry little children at the entrance of the village; he asks for and receives food from his distant aunt.

Mwindo plays the *wiki*-game with Sheburungu; he stakes and loses everything; when, however, he wagers his *conga*-scepter, luck turns in his favor.

At that very moment, Sparrow and Hawk inform the hero that his father is again trying to flee.

H. Encounter with father.
"They" (unspecified) lay hold of him.
Restraint and moderation on Mwindo's part: no insults, no violence.

VII. MWINDO'S SUBTERRANEAN JOURNEY HOME IN THE COMPANY OF HIS FATHER

Again, the villages of Sheburungu, Aardvark, and Muisa are the setting, until the hero emerges from the underground realms at the root of the *kikoka*-fern. It is unclear whether Mwindo carries his father during this trip or whether he is simply with him, for the verb *nirị̣te* used in this context has a double meaning: lit., "I am carrying," but fig., "I have, I possess," as when one says in Nyanga that he has (carries) a wife or matrimonial goods.

A. Mwindo returns to Sheburungu all goods won from him in gambling: Sheburungu blesses him.

B. Mwindo informs his aunt about his coming return.

C. Mwindo relates his own life story to Ntumba, who has rebuilt his cave; he is blessed by Ntumba.

D. In a song, Mwindo reminds his aunt of his coming return.

E. At Kahindo's request, Mwindo awakens Muisa; he reveals the mystery of his birth to Muisa.

F. Mwindo reminds his aunt of his coming return.

G. Mwindo rejects Muisa's proposal that Mwindo marry his daughter Kahindo.

H. He emerges at the root of the *kikoka*-fern.

VIII. MWINDO AS RULER OF TUBONDO

The setting is the village of Tubondo, first in its state of destruction, inhabited only by Mwindo's aunt, maternal uncles, and helpers, and then as rebuilt and revivified by Mwindo with its seven descent groups. The circumstances are solemn: big statewide gathering of people and enthronement rites.

A. Mwindo is greeted on arrival by his aunt and maternal uncles and seated by them on many spearheads.

B. In a long song, Mwindo narrates his feats.

C. Hospitality is given by Mwindo to his father: the father is accommodated in a guesthouse, and receives a goat and rice. Mwindo has abandoned his boasting; in a calm and dignified tone, he simply points out to his father that he made a big mistake.

D. For three days, Mwindo, at Iyangura's request, brings all the people of Tubondo back to life, dancing to drums beaten by his maternal uncles and waving his *conga*-scepter. All the people of the village come to life pursuing the same activities as they were when they died.

E. At Iyangura's insistence, Shemwindo calls together a big council.

F. Solemn opening of the council: apparition of the "three radiant Stars," Iyangura, Mwindo, Shemwindo; their installation on copper chairs suspended from the sky by Nkuba; invocation for strength and praise of the participants by Mwindo.

G. Speeches by Shemwindo, who publicly recognizes his errors; by Iyangura, who justifies her departure from Mukiti's's village and criticizes her brother; by Mwindo, who in a merciful mood asks for harmony and peace.

H. Decision to split the state into two parts to be ruled by Shemwindo and Mwindo.

I. Enthronement of Mwindo.

J. Departure of Iyangura; the blessing of Mwindo.

IX. THE DRAGON HUNT

The action takes place in the forest and in the village. The actors are the Dragon (Kirimu), the Pygmies, and Mwindo. Most versions known to me describe the fight with the Dragon.

Numerous Nyanga tales deal with this theme: the Dragon is represented as a ruthless, man-eating, but somewhat stupid monster, which is sometimes killed by a little child.

A. Mwindo's Pygmies on a hunting party are swallowed by Kirimu, except one, Nkurongo, who brings Mwindo the news.

B. Mwindo overcomes the Dragon with a song of defiance and with his *conga*-scepter.

C. Mwindo's *conga* flies through the air to collect people to carry the monster back to the village.

D. The Dragon is carried to the village, cut up, distributed (with the injunction that every part be eaten); many people are liberated from the monster's belly.

E. Finally, the eyes are roasted and from each, as it bursts in a splatter, come a thousand people.

F. Lightning, who without Mwindo's knowledge had made a blood pact, smells the roasting eyes and decides to put his ally Mwindo to the test.

X. MWINDO'S CELESTIAL JOURNEY

The action takes place in space that is successively represented as a desolate place of severe cold and of extreme heat. The duration of the journey, rarely explicitly indicated, is one year.

A. Mwindo, singing and confident about the outcome, is lifted into the sky by Lightning. "Here there is no room for his heroism"; the hero is reduced to a passive, suffering subject, exposed to icy winds, great heat, and thirst. He is successively taken into the realms of Lightning, Rain, Hail, Moon, Sun, Star. Before being permitted to return to earth, the hero receives the order never again to kill an animal and to accept Lightning as his guardian.

B. Mwindo is returned to earth by Lightning.

C. He relates in a song and a speech his celestial experiences. Joy and life come back to the village which had been mourning ever since Mwindo's departure.

XI. MWINDO'S GLORY

    A. Mwindo announces his message of prosperity and gives his commandments for an ordered life (no quarrels; no adultery; no mockery; awe for the chief; respect on the part of the chief for his subjects; solidarity; fertility).

    B. Mwindo, a well-settled chief, rules in peace over his country and receives the allegiance of many strangers.

XII. THE NARRATOR'S CONCLUSIONS

    A. "There is nothing bad in what God has given to man."

    B. Excess leads to destruction.

    C. Everybody needs advice.

    D. Solidarity and mutual help save the people; there is no true authority without these.

    E. There is no absolute power.

Few personality traits are explicitly mentioned in the text. The epithets themselves generally bear on physical characteristics or on political status of the actors: for example, the water serpent Mukiti is *mịné-márịba*, lord of the pools; Shemwindo is *nyeré-kurwábo*, master of their (country, village); Nkuba, the divinity of lightning, is *mirábyo*, flashes. The principal epithet of Mwindo himself, *Kábútwa-kénda*, stresses his capacity to walk from birth on. At least three physical traits are explicitly mentioned for Mwindo. He is small: *kabóntsóbóntso*, a small baby; *mwăna wémwịyoroyo*, just yesterday's child; *ubútwăyo tété-tétéyo*, just born a while ago. He is beautiful; for example, when his aunt opened the drum in which Mwindo was imprisoned, she saw "the many rays of the rising sun and the moon. That is the beauty of the child Mwindo." He is a virile man; that is, he can act and talk like a full-fledged adult male. Different characters call him *wábŭme*, a man of poise (a concept that emphasizes his full manhood), or *wábŭme ukeráá byăra*, a man who has (his) nails cut (a concept that stands in opposition to the image of the ill-inspired, pernicious forest specter Mpacá, whose nails are never cut). For Hawk, Mwindo is *kárí ná mishịnga kakị́rị*, with stories (feats) great; for Mukiti he is *wátáriké tu*, he surpasses all expectations; for Musoka, he is *mutáre*, a hero.

The context of the story implicitly indicates many other traits of Mwindo's personality. On the one hand, he is an excessive boaster, intrepid, arrogant, verbose, highly self-conscious, and ruthless, and, as such, he is largely unacceptable and somewhat unreal to the Nyanga, for truly great men (chiefs, headmen, great hunters) avoid boasting about their strength and skill. On the other hand, Mwindo is generous, magnanimous, and righteous. Although verbose, he rarely misuses words (e.g., to curse or to slander; he does so only when Muisa exaggerates in testing him: "stay like that, you dog"). Although threatening, he rarely is truly angry or irreconcilable (he first destroys his enemies, then permits them to live again; contemplating his destructive work, he remarks that "he would heal him when he would be back from where he was going"). Although ruthless in his search for his father, he bears him no grudge. Although often hard, his attitude toward his mother is tender (she is referred to as *nya-mwako*, mother of the cradling rope, an honorific term) and his attitude is pious toward his aunt and his father. The first Mwindo is evident as long as the search for his father lasts; the second one is best revealed after his father is found. But, even at the climax of his boisterous arrogance, Mwindo occasionally shows tenderness (for his aunt) and generosity (for the hungry children and for a suffering female spirit). Even at the peak of his generosity (when he brings people back to life, returning all the goods won in games), Mwindo still gives proof of his excessive ruthlessness by killing three people who criticized him. The hero achieves his full fame and glory, *nkúrú*—his full acceptability in Nyanga eyes—only through catharsis in the celestial realm where he is a mere passive and suffering subject.

Mwindo's father is depicted as an ill-advised coward and weakling, the opposite of what a chief should be; Mwindo's aunt is talkative and insecure, but outspoken and fair in defending her nephew's cause and full of solicitude for him.

Several key Nyanga values are, directly or indirectly, stressed in the epic. The value of restraint and moderation is emphasized in the conclusions drawn by the narrator; there is a passage in which Mwindo's aunt explicitly asks Mwindo to practice restraint (sịcá émutíma: bring down your heart); Mwindo achieves full glory only when he has gone through a catharsis that frees him from all excesses. This value runs like a leitmotiv through much of Nyanga thinking, indeed through much of the thinking of several other populations of the Kivu Province (e.g., the Lega, among whom it is the basic theme of all precepts given in the teachings of the bwami-association). Nyanga tales relate the episode of the aquatic bird bishóbịshó, which had its nest built in the reeds near a lake and claimed to be the only important being in the world. The lake swallowed the bird's nest and eggs; the oracles taught the bird to say: "I am important but only in the company of the lake." Mwindo achieves full karamo (life force) and nkúrú (fame and force) only when he has definitely abandoned his boisterous, megalomaniacal behavior. So long as he is not purified of it, he is not an absolute hero; he is protected owing to the presence of his aunt or because of his conga-scepter or bag of good fortune or song (Mwindo is not strong, but the song itself is powerful, as when in other tales weak creatures escape severe dangers because of the force of their song). The values of hospitality and generosity are strongly emphasized (there is much reference to providing visitors with a house in which to sleep, with food and gifts); Mwindo is generous toward his aunt, his uncles, young children, and even his enemies. Kinship solidarity (reflected in the relationships between Mwindo and his aunt, Mwindo and his maternal uncles, and ultimately in the relationship between father and son) and friendship (e.g., Mwindo's reliance upon his friend Lightning) are constantly placed in the foreground. Poised and well-informed leadership is also of great importance (Shemwindo's hatred against his son causes nothing but destruction and misery for himself and for his people and allies; Mwindo's poise and wisdom ultimately produce happiness and glory). Against a background of many boisterous threats, there is insistence on the choice usage of words (e.g., in the highly select and precise usage of reciprocal kinship terms, honorific epithets, euphemisms, and extremely rare verbal curses).

The idea of good life is synthesized by the term karamo, often used in the text, which means good health, strength, force, salvation, good life (karamo is derived from irama, to recover,

to heal). *Karamo* is the current greeting among the Nyanga;
it is also a central theme in invocations, prayers, and other
cultual practices. When, at the end of so many peripeties and
successes, Iyangura returns to her husband's village, there is
nothing left for her but to wish that her nephew may be in
full possession of *karamo*. To have *karamo* means to be
healthy, to be wise, to be free of passions, to have many children, to be successful in hunting, to entertain smooth social
relationships.

The Mwindo epic is a coherent, well-balanced, well-
constructed story told in a rich language, enhanced by the
poetic talent of the narrator, Mr. Rureke. It incorporates all
the literary styles known to the Nyanga. It contains a succinct
survey of many basic institutions and customs, some described
in detail, others merely suggested or implied (e.g., kinship
terminology, patterns of behavior between kinsmen, marriage
customs), aspects of political organization (e.g., local groups,
political hierarchy), ritual, and religion. It provides a broad
inventory of Nyanga material culture, and gives succinct references to basic techniques of agriculture and honey-harvesting.
The epic also tries to account for the origin of certain institutions (cult of Lightning, fission of political entities, hunting
taboos imposed on chiefs). It further provides a synopsis of
basic Nyanga values. And finally, it permits us to enter the
personal world of the narrator, who inserts many of his own
reflections and meditations.

THE SYSTEM OF TRANSCRIPTION

I. THE SYMBOLS USED IN THE NYANGA TEXT

A. Vowels

	Degree of aperture
i̧, u̧	1st
i, u	2d
e, o	3d
a	4th

In the English translation we have not maintained this distinction; i is used to represent the Nyanga i̧ and i, u is used to
represent the Nyanga u̧ and u.

B. Semivowels

1. There are two front semivowels y:
   y corresponding to i̧ as in i̧ya: to come
   ÿ corresponding to i as in i̧ya: to kill
2. There is only one back semivowel w.

C. Consonants

The characters of the Roman alphabet are used with the following specifications:

1. The nasal onset consonant cluster ns is represented as nts.
2. The nasal palatal ɲ (I.P.A.) is represented as ny.
3. The voiceless palatal fricative ʃ (I.P.A.) is represented as sh.
4. The voiceless palatal affricate tʃ (I.P.A.) is represented as c (pronounced as in the English "church").

D. Tones

high tone: ′   rising tone: ˇ
low tone: no sign   falling tone: ^

E.

Capital letter in the middle of a word, preceded or not by a hyphen or apostrophe, to indicate the beginning of a proper noun, for example, Bana-Muki̧ti̧ (those of Mukiti's group).

F.

Apostrophe. Used to indicate elision of final syllable vowel or of the initial semivowel, or, in some cases both:
wamaki̧nd'ibinga for wamaki̧ndá ibinga (he had finished marrying)
kumbo'érŭsi for kumbo wérŭsi (downstream of the river)
mwi̧r'ani for mwi̧ra wani (my friend)

G.

Hyphen. Used to indicate the compounding of a bound morpheme and a word (e.g., shé-Mwindo: father of Mwindo) or the reduplication of morphemes (e.g., iki̧á-kia, to do often; lit., to do and do, from ikia, to do).

II. WORD DIVISION IN THE NYANGA TEXT

The principles of word division followed in the transcription of the Nyanga text are outlined in great detail in a forth-

coming study by Mr. Kahombo C. Mateene.[7] The nominal and
verbal forms, the locative *hó, ko, mo*, the possessive and de-
monstrative pronouns, the invariables, such as *nti* (then), *ngí*
(it is), *ntí* (it is not), *mbu* (that, saying that), the associative
particle *na* (and, with, etc.), and so on, are treated as words.

NOTES ABOUT THE TRANSLATION

We have tried to be as literal as possible, yet produce a readable
text. We often draw attention to an interpreted translation in
the notes. One of the greatest difficulties rested in the common
occurrence of what could be called a mixed form of discourse
(direct and indirect). A simple instance of this procedure is
given in the following sentence:

> *básúbie Mukįtį mbu bó báshįmá, ǒngo Mukįtį, múkinwa cábé,
> íyé wendaa kánonka . . . nti íyé ǒngo'nonkéngi bó.*

translated as:

> They answered Mukiti saying: we are satisfied, (you) Mukiti,
> because of your word; now you will go to win valuables . . .
> from now on you win them for us.

Literally the Nyanga sentence reads:

> They answered Mukiti that *they* were satisfied, *you* Mukiti,
> because of *your* word, now go to win valuables . . . from now
> on you win (them) for *them*.

It would have been simple to put this sentence completely in
the form of direct discourse by changing *bó báshįmá* into *băte*
(we) *twashįmá* (we are satisfied) and *ǒngo'nonkéngi bó* into
ǒngo'tunonkéngi. This grammatical procedure is surely inspired by euphemism on the part of the narrator who, in songs
and in gestures, tends to identify himself very strongly with
the hero, and yet, whenever he can, tries to conceal this fact.
The narrator treats the dialogues both as a distant witness
and as a fully involved participant. The element of euphemism
involved in the usage of direct, indirect, and mixed forms of

---

[7] Under the title "Nouvelles considérations sur la délimitation des mots
dans une langue bantoue," to be published in *Cahiers d'Etudes Africaines*
(Paris), nos. 25, 26.

discourse was clearly revealed to me in a tale, where the narrator began a dialogue between the hero of his story with *é titá* (oh! my father), and then immediately corrected himself, interrupting the dialogue by *ishé kuti naménda kwishámbaka we* (my father . . . !—no—his father, so that I would not go to attribute him to myself [i.e., to compromise myself by saying *my* father]).

There are also many terse or figurative expressions that are difficult to translate exactly. A few examples:

> *bákié mbu básisimuké* . . . , lit., when they woke up, and translated as "in fixing their attention," but it is difficult to decide whether the narrator wants to express the idea of "the next morning" or of "suddenness," as if they had been daydreaming and had suddenly come back to reality.
>
> *wákárísha bana-cé biÿo bĭngĭ*, translated as "he had his people prepare much food," but the verb implies an order for preparing food to be used as a counterpresent.
>
> *súnga búmĭnĭrengi ani kumongo . . . niseéngi na múmatema*, translated as "see how I am dancing, my back (shivering) . . . and my cheeks contain my laughing," but the text literally says "see how I am dancing on the back; and I am laughing in the cheeks." (For young men good dancing is determined by the movements of the shoulder blades; a "laughing in the cheeks" is a standard expression for strong but contained laughing which makes the cheeks swell.)

The vocabulary is exceptionally rich and precise; there are many poetic and figurative uses of words to which attention is frequently drawn in the notes. The Nyanga language is very much concerned with repetitions indicating place, relative time, and circumstance:

> "There was a river in which there was a pool and in that pool there was in it Mukiti, Master-of-the-pools. In his dwelling place in the pool (lit., where he was seated, established, located in the pool) Mukiti. . . ."
>
> "When the night had become daylight, in the morning. . . ."
>
> "After the divers, swimmers, had been found, they took . . . ; when they arrived at the pool . . . the swimmers entered into the pool, they asked. . . ."

Although these repetitious statements are cumbersome in reading, they are a typical expression of Nyanga thought patterns and have therefore been left as they are.

The square brackets in the translation refer to words that are in Nyanga but make the translated sentence cumbersome. The parentheses in the translation refer to words that are absent from Nyanga but are necessary for a better understanding of the translated text.

The Mwindo Epic

TRANSLATION

Long ago there was in a place a chief called Shemwindo.[1] That chief built a village called Tubondo, in the state of Ihimbi.[2] Shemwindo was born with a sister called Iyangura.[3] And in

---

[1] *mwami/chief*: traditionally, the Nyanga have no paramount chief. They are politically organized into petty states, each ruled by a sacred chief. Each chiefdom is autonomous, but the rulers are often linked by the recognition of a common agnatic origin or by affinal and friendship ties. *shé-Mwindo*: a typical construction for a teknonymic name, *shé-* (his father) followed by the name of the child. The chief's name here already foreshadows the name of his son to be born.

[2] *ubúngú/village*: concept refers to a fairly large village (some 75 to 100 people on the average) occupied by members of more than one kinship group, in opposition to *kantsari*, a hamlet. *kuTubondo*: the Nyanga frequently name their villages after a dominant phytogeographical aspect of the area where they are located. *kabondo* means little raphia palm tree. Raphia palms are extremely important in Nyanga technology (in basketry and plaiting and in the making of traps and snares, money). Village names and other place-names always occur in Nyanga in conjunction with a locative prefix, mostly *ku-* (cl. 17). *cúo/state*: the generic concept with which the Nyanga designate the petty chiefdoms into which they are subdivided. This term is then followed by a connective and by the specific name of the chiefdom to which reference is made. *Ihimbi*: not a legendary place, but one of the most isolated regions of Nyanga country, located in the Kisimba administrative unit of Walikale territory. The people inhabiting this region are said to be Bahímbí, outstanding hunters of big game among whom the Pygmy cultural impact is very strong. Most Nyanga speak about this place as a region of mystery and danger.

[3] *wabútwá ná/was born with*: the forms used here do not indicate that Shemwindo and his sister were twins, but clearly show that they were full siblings. *mwísí'ábó/a sister: mwísí* means girl; used with a possessive pronoun in the singular, it designates a daughter; used, as here, with a possessive pronoun in the plural, it refers to a sister, real or classificatory. *Iyangura*: a very uncommon personal name. Some of my informants related it to the verb "to arbitrate," meaning that she received this name because of her father's qualities as an arbiter; others tended to see a con-

that village of Shemwindo there were seven meeting places of
his people.[4] That chief Shemwindo married seven women.[5]
After Shemwindo had married those [his] seven wives, he sum-
moned together all his people: the juniors and the seniors,
advisors, the counselors, and the nobles.[6] All those—he had
them meet in council.[7] When they were already in the assembly,
Shemwindo sat down in the middle of them; he made an appeal, saying: "You my wives, the one who will bear a male
child among you my seven wives, I will kill him/her; all of you
must each time give birth to girls only."[8] Having made this

nection with the verb relating to the performance of twin-birth ceremonies. In this epic, Iyangura acts as a kind of arbiter in the conflict that
opposes her brother, Shemwindo, to his son, Mwindo.

[4] *ndushú/meeting places*: oval-shaped huts with two doors which serve
as the meeting places for daily as well as ceremonial activities of the male
members of a small, localized kinship unit. It is also used to designate that
kinship group itself. *sirínda/seven*: the number here is purely symbolic;
rarely, if ever, are there seven kinship units to the village in Nyanga
society. In Nyanga thinking, seven is a perfect number; constant reference
to it is made in some ethnohistorical traditions and in certain ritual practices. The number seven is frequently used throughout the epic: the chief
has seven wives; he hurls his spear seven times; it rains for seven days;
the hero asks for seven strokes of lightning, and so on.

[5] *bomína/women:* the term *bakárí,* spouses, wives, is appropriate when
all matrimonial prescriptions have been fulfilled. When speaking about a
chief's wives, the term *bowé* would be more adequate.

[6] The suggestion is made here that all people, young and old, male and
female, officeholder and commoner, are called together. This is, of course,
an unusual procedure, since normally only male *bakwákare* (seniors and
officeholders) participate in such councils. It is to be noted that every
petty chiefdom is a politically autonomous entity with its own apparatus
of political officeholders who are basically of two categories: *barúsi,* members of the royal descent line, and *bakungú,* representatives of nonroyal
descent groups.

[7] *wár/a bó/he had them meet*: the verb *iría* literally refers to the action
of carrying, putting, bringing. *kíbu/council*: a large public meeting in
which the members of various descent groups participate under the leadership of the chief to make political or jural decisions. The term *námá*
used later on in the text concerns a secret discussion that may be held during such a public meeting before any major decisions are announced.

[8] *mbu/saying*: invariable word used throughout the text to introduce
a song, a statement, or a dialogue (in direct or indirect or mixed direct-
indirect discourse). According to the context, *mbu* is not translated or is
rendered as "that . . ." or "saying. . . ." *I will kill him/her*: Nyanga is

interdiction, he threw himself hurriedly into the houses of the wives, then launched the sperm where his wives were. Among his wives there was a beloved-one and a despised-one. The despised-one had (her house) built next to the garbage heap and his other wives were in the clearing, in the middle of the village.[9] After a fixed number of days had elapsed, those [his] seven wives carried pregnancies, and (all) at the same time.[10]

Close to the village of Shemwindo there was a river in which there was a pool, and in this pool there was a water serpent, master of the unfathomable.[11] In his dwelling place, in the pool, Mukiti heard the news that downstream from him there was a chief who had a sister called Iyangura; she was always glistening (like dew) like sunrays because of beauty.[12] After Master Mukiti had heard the news of the beauty of that young woman Iyangura, he went in pursuance of her in order to

---

ambiguous here; it is not clear from the forms used whether the chief plans to kill the mother or the child; to the audience, however, which is fully acquainted with many similar stories, it is clear that the chief is threatening the child.

9 The distinction between the beloved wife and the despised wife is currently made in many Nyanga tales; it is part of the tensions that exist in the polygamous household. The distinction is not made verbally by the husband, but exists de facto and is also made in conversations among the co-wives and by outsiders. Here, the distinction is presented as a formal arrangement whereby the despised wife would live away from the others, near the garbage heap, near the uncleared boundary line of the village and the forest. This is not so in fact. The image of building a hut on the garbage heap is connected with a pun: hírare, garbage heap, and nyírare, general form for co-wife.

10 ná/and: this word basically means "and, with," but according to its many possible positions in the sentence, it can add rich shades of meaning to the general statement, such as to evoke the unexpected, the abnormal, and so on. The surprise lies here in the fact that all the wives are pregnant simultaneously and after so short a period of marriage.

11 Mukíti: this fabulous water serpent is said to live in deep pools, and is therefore called here miné-máriba, master of the pools with which the Nyanga identify mystery. Many tales deal with Mukiti, who is represented as a fairly mild creature (not a terror like the forest spirit Mpacá or the dragon Kiṛmu), sometimes married to a human wife he has lured into the water. He is said to be the chief of the water.

12 kwáríkángá/in his dwelling place: locative expression based on the verb iríka, to be seated, to be located. It often occurs in the text where we have translated it as "in his dwelling place, in their homestead."

43

court her.[13] Mukiti reached Tubondo; Shemwindo accommodated him in a guesthouse.[14] When they were already in twilight, after having eaten dinner and (food), Mukiti said to Shemwindo: "You, my maternal uncle, I have arrived here where you are because of (this one) your sister Iyangura."[15] Shemwindo, having understood, gave Mukiti a black goat as a token of hospitality and, moreover, said to Mukiti that he would answer him tomorrow.[16] Mukiti said: "Yes, my dear

---

[13] *Muna-Mukiti/Master Mukiti*: the expression *muna/bana* generally means "of the species, group, subject of." The names of most descent groups are preceded by it. In tales it is often used to introduce the hero and seems to be close in meaning to Master, Maître. *kikumi/young woman*: nubile girl, maiden, a concept that refers to the category of women who have passed the *kitásá* age level and are ready for marriage. In general, it stresses the role and position of women as marriage partners; men, e.g., refer to all married female members of their descent group as *kikumí*. *kámukóhe/in order to court her*: *ikóhe* actually stands for the discreet winking that is part of the secret courtship of the Nyanga.

[14] *mwicumbi/in a guesthouse*: any house in which visitors are accommodated for the night can be called *icumbi*. Only important persons, e.g., elders of descent groups or political officeholders, have specially built, oval-shaped guesthouses. Accommodating visitors in a house and giving them food are considered to be the fundamental signs of hospitality, friendship, and generosity. Only after a full welcome has been expressed are the issues that led to the visit raised.

[15] *irengera/eat dinner*: technical term for the main evening meal eaten at about 6 P.M. The Nyanga also have a morning meal (*usimbiro*) and a late supper (*utóte*) which is consumed in strict privacy by husband and wife. The term (*biyo*), food, is superfluous. It is interesting that Mukiti calls Shemwindo maternal uncle. There is no interpretation given in the text for this form of address. We can, however, conceive of a situation whereby Mukiti goes to marry his *musárá*, matrilateral cross-cousin, identifying the girl's brother with her father (common in some kinship nomenclatures of eastern Congo peoples). The Nyanga have ambivalent attitudes toward cross-cousin marriages: generally speaking, marriages between children of full siblings of opposite sex are not tolerated; in the classificatory sense, the more common form of cross-cousin marriage is between a man and his patrilateral cross-cousin (the opposite of what happens here). As so often happens, we have here, in Mukiti's words, a strange blend of direct and indirect discourse. Literally, Mukiti says: "You, his maternal uncle, it is the reason why he has arrived here where you are."

[16] *washee . . . nceo/he gave as a token of hospitality*: *ishea*, with or without *nceo*, is a technical word, used for any gift of hospitality to a relative, to a jocular relative, or to a blood friend. It is different from sharing food with a stranger or an unimportant person. Stress is placed on

father, I am satisfied."[17] When the night had become daylight, in the morning, Mukiti made himself like the anus of a snail in his dressing up; he was clothed with raphia bunches on the arms and on the legs, and with a belt (made) of bongo antelope, and he also carried an *isia*-crest on the head.[18] In their homestead, Shemwindo and his sister Iyangura also overstrained themselves in dressing up.[19] The moment Mukiti and Shemwindo saw each other, Mukiti said to his father-in-law. "I am astonished—since I arrived here, I have not yet encountered my sister."[20] Hearing that, Shemwindo assembled all his people, the counselors, and the nobles; he went with them into secret

---

the fact that the goat is black; black goats are rare. In the traditional system of matrimonial exchanges among the Nyanga, the goat was given to the future son-in-law as a form of consent. The action is somewhat shortened here, since the prospective parents-in-law generally reserve their definite answer for some time.

17 *titá shé-karúo/my dear father*: lit., my father, master or possessor of the ladle. This is an honorific term much used by the Nyanga under the form of *nyakarúo* to refer to their wife or mother. The emphasis is on the ladle (*irúo*) that women use to stir the banana paste, and to the *mirúo*, ceremonial meal that accompanies the rituals celebrated at the birth of a child.

18 *búri kanyero kánkó/like the anus of a snail*: symbol of neatness, cleanliness. The idea of beauty is further enhanced by the belt made of bongo antelope, the symbol of beauty and greatness. The idea of festivity is rendered by the bunches of raphia fibers and the *isia*-crest which the Nyanga wear in many of their dances. The *isia*-crest consists either of part of an elephant tail or of whiskers of leopards and genets fixed into a little brass disc.

19 *bímónya/overstrained themselves*: lit., *imóna* means to undergo an initiation (circumcision or initiation into an association) with the implication of the pains, strains, and difficulties it entails. The reflexive causative form of *imóna* used here stresses that they exposed themselves to such hardships.

20 *ishibé/his father-in-law*: this terminology conforms with the fact mentioned earlier that the girl's brother takes the position of the unmentioned girl's father. *mubítu'ani/my sister*: as stated, Mukiti is marrying his matrilateral cross-cousin, who is known descriptively as *musárá*. As among other eastern Congo populations, a female cross-cousin is also known as sister in the system of terminology. In fact, the Nyanga severely criticize the few individuals who marry their cross-cousins by saying: You married your sister. There is strong emphasis here on various close kinship relationships, whereby Mukiti tries to prove by all means that he has kinship rights in the girl.

45

council.[21] Shemwindo said to his people: "(Our) sororal nephew has arrived in this (village) looking for my sister; and you then must answer him." The counselors and nobles, hearing that, agreed, saying: "It is befitting that you first present Iyangura to Mukiti." They passed with Iyangura before Mukiti. Mukiti, seeing the way in which Iyangura was bursting with mature beauty, asked himself in (his) heart: "Now she is not the one (I expected to see); she is like a *ntsembe-tree*."[22] Iyangura, indeed, was dressed in two pieces of bark cloth imbued with red powder and *mbea*-oil.[23] Seeing each other, Mukiti and Iyangura darted against each other's chests; (they) greeted each other. Having greeted each other, Iyangura said to Mukiti: "Do you really love me, [you] Mukiti?" Mukiti told her: "Don't raise (your) voice anymore, [you] my wife; see how I am dancing, my back (shivering) like the raphia-tree larva, and my cheeks contain my laughing."[24] After Mukiti and Iyangura had

---

[21] *námá/secret council*: a decision-making process in which Mukiti cannot participate. Again, it is not necessary for all to participate, but, by stressing total participation, the importance and unusual character of the affair are once more underlined.

[22] *búkókóbócáángé/was bursting with mature beauty*: the expression is difficult to translate; we have given it a reasonable interpretation. The expression is commonly used, particularly by men, to refer to the beauty of women. The verb *ikókóboka* literally signifies the bursting of nuts detaching themselves from the tree, but it connotes, at the same time, the idea of glitter, refulgence, very much like the French *éclat*. *Now she is not the one . . .* : current way of expressing great astonishment; the meaning conveyed is that the girl is much more beautiful than he had anticipated. She is therefore compared to the *ntsémbe-tree*, a tall, straight, very smooth tree that cannot be cut in the fields lest lightning strike the house where its wood is burned.

[23] Women traditionally have two pieces of bark cloth hanging from their belts, one in the front and one in the back. Underneath, they wear a small piece of cloth (*mushúkú*) which covers the genitalia. Red ointment made from camwood or from red clay and castor oil is widely used.

[24] *bókane múmakuba/darted against each other's chests*: this way of greeting is normal between related individuals. The narrator emphatically insists on the irresistible attraction between Mukiti and Iyangura, as if he wanted to excuse her marriage and her absence from the village where the hero is to be born. In order to prove his feelings, Mukiti makes what the Nyanga consider to be a forceful demonstration of love by dancing before Iyangura, the movements of his body reflecting the joyful undulations of the larvae found in a fallen raphia tree.

seen each other in this manner, the counselors and nobles of
Shemwindo answered Mukiti, saying: "We are satisfied, [you]
Mukiti, because of your word; now you will go to win valuables;
whether you win many, whether you win few, from now on you
win them for us."²⁵ After Mukiti had been spoken to in that
way, he returned home with soothed heart.²⁶ Returning home,
they fixed him seven days for bringing the valuables.²⁷

After Mukiti was home, he assembled his people (and) told
them that he was just back from courting, that he had been
assigned nine thousand, and a white goat, and a reddish one,
and a black one, and one for sacrifice, and one for the calabash,
and one for the mother, and one for the young men.²⁸ The

---

25 The specific amount of matrimonial goods to be given is not prescribed;
this is normal because it is a cross-cousin marriage. The noticeable indiffer-
ence and skepticism of the speakers are striking here. Their attitude owes
partly to the fact that they know Mukiti to be a strong man; there is also
the implication that from now on Mukiti is indebted to them.

26 *nti émutima wámámusįka/with soothed heart*: lit., it is that the heart
climbs down in him; the verb *isįka* (to climb down, e.g., from a tree) is
currently used to indicate relief of tension; "the heart is high" (*kwiyo*)
means tension, anxiety. It is normal for Mukiti to be unsure about the outcome of his request for three reasons. First, marriages with matrilateral
cross-cousins are unusual; second, Iyangura is of noble descent, and girls
of her rank among the Nyanga can only be married to spirits; third, Mukiti
had not secretly linked himself to his female cross-cousin by giving her a
certain kind of present, the meaning of which is unclear to her and the
acceptance of which signifies her agreement. Let us, finally, point out that
it is unusual for a man to go to ask for his cross-cousin (or sister, as she
is called); there is verbal symbolism involved in the request made not for
the girl but for a little calabash.

27 *bámuraa/they fixed him*: the verb *įrana* literally means to say good-bye
and to leave an oral will. The number of days fixed is purely symbolic.

28 *bihumbi mwendá/nine thousand*: i.e., nine thousand matrimonial
goods (*béhe*) or an amount of nine thousand measures of *butéá*-money
(*byábutéá*), all simply to say that an enormous amount of goods is requested.
The different types of goats specified bear on actual matrimonial practices;
each has a well-defined destination. The white goat is to be shared by the
young men of the girl's descent group; the reddish one goes to the girl's
mother's descent group; the black one goes to the girl's mother; the goat
for sacrifice is to be distributed by the head of the girl's descent group
among all fifteen male and female members; the goat for the calabash (syn.
with the other one for the young men) is to be shared by all the male
members of the girl's descent group who supply her with chickens. The
enumeration of goats is not complete; among those mentioned, however,

counselors and the nobles, hearing that, clapped their hands, saying to their lord that they were satisfied, that they could not fail to find that payment of goods (enough), because this maiden was not to be lost.[29] After the seven days were fulfilled, in the morning, Mukiti took the marriage payments to go, and his people remained behind him; they went to Shemwindo's to give him the payments. On leaving his village, he went to spend the night in the village of the Baniyana.[30] The Baniyana gave him a ram as a token of hospitality. The Banamukiti and Mukiti himself slept in that village, being like a blister because of repletion.[31] In the morning, Mukiti woke up; he went to throw himself into the village of the Banamitandi; the Banamitandi gave Mukiti a goat as a token of hospitality; he spent the night there.[32] In the morning, he set out from one of the ways out (of the village) together with his people, (and)

---

some are part of *ndjiko* (the core group of marriage payments), and others fit into the category of reciprocal gifts exchanged during the course of married life. The usual procedure for arranging a marriage and the various, gradual steps by which a legal marriage is insured are much more complicated than suggested here.

29 *bákóngóta múmịne/clapped their hands*: this is one of the ways in which people mark their agreement in important discussions. It can also be done by humming (*nịnga*). *nyeré-kurwábó/their lord*: compound word, which literally means master-lord in a village (*ubúngú*) and is currently used to refer to a chief, to the head of a descent group; women also use it in addressing their husbands in order to flatter them.

30 *múmukomá-kóma/in the morning*: i.e., next morning. When the heroes in the epic set out on a trip or an exploration, they always do so in the early morning. *his people remained behind him*: this does not mean that the chief leads the line and that all the others follow but that the journey is made in his name, on his behalf; he is the greatest of them all. Again, it is unusual for the groom himself to take the payments to his wife's family unless he has no close relatives living. *Baniyana*: lit., the kinship group of the hundreds, of those who are very numerous; here, "the hundreds" refer to the bats. As mentioned later in the text, the bats are generally represented as the blacksmiths who "forge" (strengthen) the heroes.

31 *kihárábúté/ram*: this is a sign of exceptional hospitality; mutton is highly rated for its fat; moreover, sheep have a sacred character, whereas goats are used in profane contexts. *Bana-Mukịtị*: all people who are following him and who are under his authority.

32 *Bana-Mitandị*: lit., the kinship group of the spider webs, which here stands for the spiders themselves. In tales, spiders appear as helpful creatures, makers of bridges that save the heroes.

went to arrive at long last in the village of his fathers-in-law, in Tubondo, at Shemwindo's.[33] When they arrived in Tubondo, Shemwindo showed them a guesthouse to sleep in and also gave them a billy goat as a present of hospitality. In the late evening, Iyangura heated water for her husband; they went together to wash themselves.[34] Having finished washing themselves, they anointed themselves with red powder; they climbed into bed; Iyangura put a leg across her husband.[35] In the morning, there was a holiday.[36] Shemwindo assembled all his people; they sat together in a group. When all the Banashemwindo were grouped together, Mukiti came out with the marriage payments (and) placed them before his fathers-in-law. His fathers-in-law were very satisfied with them. They told him: "Well, you are a man, one who has his nails cut."[37] After they had

33 *wísica kwikúra/he set out from one of the ways out*: lit., he put his own burden down at the way out of the village. A traditional Nyanga village had two *ikúra*. The village was fenced and had two entrances (one "upstream" and one "downstream") where connecting paths to other villages began; *ikúra* was the cleared space in front of the two gateways, but outside the fence, i.e., outside the village. *bishibé/fathers-in-law*: all brothers and male agnatic parallel cousins of one's real father-in-law are terminologically identified with one's father-in-law.

34 *they went together to wash themselves*: it is customary for a woman to wash her lover's or husband's feet before going to bed.

35 It was also customary for a woman to anoint her husband or lover with red ointment and to rub some of it on the bed itself, so long as they did not have children. *wákinduca ná moké nwîndi/put a leg across her husband*: one of the many euphemistic expressions used in speaking about sexual intercourse. It must be noted that sexual intercourse is permitted only after the girl has been conducted to her husband's village, and it is most unusual for a man to have sexual intercourse with his wife in her parents' village.

36 *mushibo/holiday*: a day of rest when nobody goes to work in the fields or forest. On the occasion of important initiations, sacrifices, deaths, or marriages of important individuals, such days of rest are publicly announced by the village headman or high political officials; a village or an entire chiefdom may be affected by such a prescribed holiday. Supernatural sanctions are said to await those who do not observe the prescriptions.

37 *Banashemwindo*: all the people placed under chief Shemwindo's authority. *wábúme ukeráá byára/a man, one who has his nails cut*: the son-in-law is twice praised for his strength, for his strong personality. The term *wábúme*, a man, is used by the Nyanga for an adult male who has gone through many experiences, has much knowledge, and has achieved full social and ritual status in his society. To have one's nails cut means

completely laid hold of the marriage payments, the Banashemwindo told Mukiti to return to his village; they would conduct his wife to him.[38] Hearing this, Mukiti said: "Absolutely
all is well; what would be bad would be to be deceived." He
returned to his (village). When he was already in his village,
Mukiti had his people prepare much food because he was
having guests come. When Shemwindo, who had remained in
his village, realized that Mukiti had been gone a day, in the
morning, he set out to follow him; they went to conduct Iyangura.[39] While going, the attendants carried Iyangura, without
(allowing her) foot to set on the ground, in mud, or in water.[40]
When the attendants arrived with the (incoming) bride at
Mukiti's, Mukiti showed them to a guesthouse; they sat down
in it. They seized a rooster "to clean the teeth."[41] In this guesthouse they had Iyangura sit down on an *utebe*-stool.[42] When
she was already seated, she took out the remainder of the
banana paste from which she had had breakfast in her mother's
house in their village.[43] She and her husband Mukiti ate it.

---

the same as saying that one cannot be stopped by anything, that one is
able to overcome doubt and fear. In contradistinction, the expression
evokes the image of the long-nailed, fear-inspiring Mpaca, small, old
spirit of the forest.

[38] *ihéruka*: the technical term for conducting a wife to her husband's
village. The marriage sequences and proceedings are considerably simpli-
fied in this text.

[39] The preparation of food is one of the principal ceremonies on all
important occasions (birth, marriage, initiation, sacrifices, and so on)
except funerary rites.

[40] *ébahérúcii/the attendants*: a wife is conducted to her husband's village by a number of related women (paternal aunt, grandmother, brothers' wives, junior sisters). The men do not carry the bride, as suggested here,
but they help her to cross a river or to go through mud.

[41] The bride is not usually taken to a guesthouse, but to the house of her
husband's mother. *A rooster "to clean the teeth"*: beautiful expression not
technical among the Nyanga clearly suggesting the poetic skill of the
narrator. Once again it should be noted that a son-in-law does not normally
give chickens to his wife's people; he receives chickens from them.

[42] *utebe-stool*: Iyangura sitting on such a stool suggests the exceptional
ceremonial circumstance. Normally women sit on a piece of wood or on
a skin; the *utebe*-stool is sacred; women sit on it only when their hair is
shaved at the end of the mourning period for a husband or son.

[43] *múmwábó kurwábó/in her mother's house in their village*: typical
construction with locative prefixes, connectives, and pronouns. The English translation renders precisely the ideas conveyed by this construction.

When her husband had finished eating from that piece of paste, they had still more banana paste with taro leaves prepared for them. When the paste and the leaves were ready in the house, they told Mukiti to sit down on an *utebe*-stool; and they placed the paste between both (of them). When they were grouped like that, they told Iyangura to grasp a piece of paste in her right hand and make her husband eat it together with a portion of meat.[44] Iyangura took a piece of paste (from the dish); she had her husband eat it; and her husband took a piece of paste, and he too had his wife eat it.[45] After (both) husband and wife had finished eating the paste, the counselors of Mukiti gave Shemwindo a strong young steer as a gift of hospitality.[46]

After they had finished eating this young steer, they answered Mukiti, saying: "Don't make our child here, whom you have just married, into a woman in ragged, soiled clothing; don't make her into a servant to perform labor."[47] After they had said this, in the early morning right after awakening, they went, having been given seven bunches of *butea*-money as a departure gift by Mukiti.[48] When the bridal attendants ar-

---

44 Emphasis is placed here on the ritual importance attached to the right, in general, and to the right hand, in particular, among the Nyanga.

45 Reference is made here to the final marriage rite whereby the husband and wife ceremonially feed each other. This, however, is done only when the bride is sexually pure; the rite described here is directly in contradiction with the sexual relations between Iyangura and Mukiti mentioned earlier. *nyényi/with a portion of meat*: lit., any ingredient (vegetables, sauce, fish, meat) added to the banana paste. Banana paste is the single most basic item in the Nyanga diet; great value is placed on meat (dried or fresh) which is absolutely necessary for a successful ceremonial meal.

46 *kimása cénkambú/a strong young steer*: the Nyanga living in the rain forest have no cattle; they are surrounded by the cattle-owning inhabitants of the savannah highlands. The Nyanga also traditionally trace their origin to the pastoral Bunyoro (Uganda). The term *kimása* is used to designate a young male buffalo.

47 Advice of this type is currently given at the end of the marriage ceremony. The girl is then called *mwán'itú* (our child) by the members of her group in order to stress their collective sense of duty and responsibility. *nya-turíco, nya-mirémbe/a woman in ragged, soiled clothing*: lit., a mother of holes, a mother of hanging things; the form *nyá-* (mother of) has many specialized usages to show that a female individual has a special association with a given object, right, disease, child, activity, and so on.

48 *mianda/bunches*: a heap, a lot, not a special measure of money. The same term is used, e.g., for a bundle of firewood or a heap of leaves. The

51

rived in Tubondo, they were very happy, along with their chief Shemwindo. Where Mukiti ‚and his people and his wife Iyangura remained, he made a proclamation saying: "[You] all my people, if one day you see a man going downstream, then you (will) tear out his spinal column, you Banamaka, Banabirurumba, Banankomo, Banatubusa, and Banampongo; however, this path here which follows the flow of the river, (it) is the great path on which all people pass."[49] After he had passed this interdiction regarding these two paths, and while in [this] his village there lived his Shemwami called Kasiyembe, Mukiti told his big headman Kasiyembe: "You, go to dwell with my wife Iyangura at the borders of the pool; and I Mukiti shall from now on always reside here where all the dry leaves collect in flowing down, where all the fallen tree trunks are obstructed in the middle of the pool."[50]

Where Shemwindo lived in Tubondo, together with his wives and all his people, they were very famous [there]; his

---

choice of words is always very precise and technical; gift-giving when the guests are leaving is called ịkósóra.

[49] Mukiti addresses various species of fishes and crabs which are presented as kinship groups under his control. *You (will) tear out his spinal column*: you will beat him up. The spinal column is called "the bone of the back." The proclamation made by Mukiti results from a kind of premonition; it is of fundamental importance to the further intrigue of the epic. Mukiti already knows that the hero Mwindo will come through the water in search of his aunt Iyangura; he therefore places a taboo on the river; the path that runs along the water, however, is said to be a public road on which all are allowed to pass. This interdiction by Mukiti will provide the hero Mwindo with an initial set of battles to fight and to win.

[50] It is understood, although not explicitly mentioned in the text, that Mukiti is a sacred chief and Iyangura is his *mụmbo*, or ritual wife, whose son is to be his successor. It explains why Iyangura lives separately from Mukiti in a hamlet of her own, under the supervision and protection of an officeholder called Shemwami (father of the chief). Reference is thus made to an extremely complex set of customs and practices relating to the position of the ritual wife. The personal name Kasiyembe is rare in Nyanga society. It is derived from a small reed pipe, which generally accompanies praise songs for the chiefs. *mutámbo/headman*: common generic term referring to the senior member of a descent group or to the head of a hamlet or village; Kasiyembe is the headman of the hamlet in which the chief's ritual wife lives. *And I Mukiti shall . . . pool*: a very beautiful and succinct description of how the Nyanga conceive of the pool as a dwelling place of the water spirit Mukiti.

fame went here and there throughout the entire country.[51] When (many) days had passed that his wives had remained pregnant, one day six of his wives pulled through; they gave birth merely to female children.[52] One among them, the preferred-one, remained dragging herself along because of her pregnancy. When the preferred-one realized that her companions had already given birth, and that she remained with (her) pregnancy, she kept on complaining: "How terrible this is! It is only I who am persecuted by this pregnancy. What then shall I do? My companions, together with whom I carried the pregnancy at the same time, have already pulled through, and it is I who remain with it. What will come out of this pregnancy?"[53] After she had finished making these sad reflections, reawakening (from her thoughts) [where she was], at the door then there was already a bunch of firewood; she did not know from where it had come; lo! it was [her] child, the one that was inside the womb, who had just brought it.[54] After some time had passed, looking around in the house, there was already a jar of water; she did not know whence it had come; all by itself it had brought itself into the house. After some time had passed, raw *isusa*-vegetables also arrived there at the house. When the preferred-one saw it, she was much astonished; lo! it was the child in her womb who was performing all those wonderful things.[55]

---

51 *nkúrú/fame*: not to be confused with *nkúru* (turtle); this fame can be good or bad. The concept of fame, glory, reputation, often mentioned in the text, is to be distinguished from other recurrent concepts, such as *karamo* (Lat., *salus*), health, long life, safety; *maá* (Lat., *vis*), physical strength, force; *buingo* (Lat., *fortuna*), destiny.

52 *bịkokora/pulled through*: lit., *ịkokora* means to pull a thing out in order to make it longer; to undo the knots; the image conveyed is that the women "unknotted" themselves. The Nyanga explanation of this metaphor is that, in giving birth to girls, the women conformed with their husband's prescriptions.

53 *narandwá na/I am persecuted by*: the verb *ịranda* means to sew, to baste; thus the woman exclaims that she is "sewn" by the pregnancy, or that the pregnancy sticks to her.

54 The simple meaning of this passage: the woman suddenly wakes up from the sad dreams she has been having because of the birth delay; her eyes wander around the hut until they light on the object placed near the entrance by her unborn child.

55 To make the meal complete, the unborn child brings to its mother

When the inhabitants of the village saw that the preferred-one continued to drag on with (her) pregnancy in her house, they got used to sneering at her: "When then will this one also give birth?" Where the child was dwelling in the womb of its mother, it meditated to itself in the womb, saying that it could not come out from the underpart of the body of its mother, so that they might not make fun of it saying that it was the child of a woman; neither did it want to come out from the mouth of its mother, so that they might not make fun of it saying that it had been vomited like a bat.[56] When the pregnancy had already begun to be bitter, old midwives, wives of the counselors, arrived there; they arrived there when the preferred-one was already being troubled with (the pains of the) pregnancy.[57] Where the child was dwelling in the womb, it climbed up in the belly, it descended the limb, and it went (and) came out through the medius. The old midwives, seeing him wailing on the ground, were astonished, saying: "It's terrible; is the child now replacing its mother?"[58] When they saw him on the ground, they pointed at him asking: "What (kind of) child (is it)?" Some among the old midwives answered: "It's a male child." Some of the old midwives said that they should shout in the village place that a male child was born. Some refused, saying that no one should shout that it was a boy who had just been born, because when Shemwindo heard that a boy had been born, he would kill him. Where the counselors were sitting together with Shemwindo, they shouted, asking: "What child is born there?" The old midwives who

---

some vital supplies (water, firewood, vegetables), the daily collection of which usually causes much hardship for women. *tushįngįshį/wonderful things*: in this category the Nyanga group the bad omens (*bihúnda*), the good omens (*myangiriro*), and the extraordinary happenings (*bįshįsharo*) such as these, which cannot be known in advance through various ominous signs.

[56] It is a widespread belief that bats give birth to their young through the mouth by vomiting them.

[57] *barįkį/midwives*: not a specialized category of women; the term refers to older women who stand in a certain kinship relationship to the young mother and who are well informed about the various procedures, prescriptions, and teachings connected with childbirth.

[58] *wahingá/replacing*: the verb *ihinga* designates the exchange of one object for another.

54

were sitting in the house kept silent, without giving an answer. After the birth of the child, the midwives gave him the name Mwindo, because he was the (first) male child who followed only female children in [their] order of birth.[59]

In that house where the child had been born (that day), there was a cricket on the wall.[60] Where Shemwindo was staying, after he had asked what child was born and the midwives were unwilling to give him an answer, the cricket left the house where the child had been born and went to say to Shemwindo: "You, chief, a male child was born there (from where I came); his name is Mwindo; that is why those who are in that hut there have not answered you." When Shemwindo heard that his preferred-one had given birth to a boy, he took up [to go with it] his spear; he rubbed it on a whetstone; he sharpened it; he went with it where the child had been born (that day). The moment he prepared to throw it into the birth hut, the child shouted from where it was; it said: "May this spear end up (each time it is being thrown) at the bottom of the house pole; may it never end up where these old midwives are seated here; may it neither arrive at the place where my mother is."[61] Shemwindo threw the spear into the house six times, each time reaching nothing but [at] the pole. When the old midwives saw that extraordinary event they stormed out of the house; they fled away, saying (to one another) that they should not go to die there. When Shemwindo

---

[59] It is customary for midwives to inform the men in the men's house of the birth of a child and to reveal its sex by laughing in a special way. It is not normal for midwives to name the child immediately after its birth; the child usually receives a name from its grandfather on the third day after its birth. One of the midwives goes to "buy" the name from the men, who are united in the men's house, with some measures of *butéá*-money and an empty dish. The name Mwindo is given to a boy who is born in a family where there are only girls or to a girl who follows a number of boys. Several informants saw a relationship between the name Mwindo and the verb *iindo* (to fell trees or to eradicate). Mwindo is also the name of a spirit of the Nyanga pantheon.

[60] *kitúndúkútú/cricket*: in tales, he is thought to bring bad omens and to divulge secrets.

[61] *irungú/birth hut*: not a specially built hut, but any hut where an as yet unnamed child resides. *ndúí/house pole*: middle pole of the hut which sustains the roof; it is said to be the dwelling place of the tutelary spirit of the house; children must never sit near it.

had become exhausted from running back and forth with his spear and had completely failed to kill Mwindo, he spoke to his counselors, saying that they should dig a grave in order to throw Mwindo into it, because he did not want to see a male child. When the counselors had heard the order of the lord of their village, they did not disagree with him; they dug the grave.[62] When (the grave) was finished, they went to fetch the child Mwindo; they carried him (handling him); so they went to bury him in the grave.[63] Mwindo howled within the grave, saying: "Oh, my father, this is (the death) that you will die, (but) first you will suffer many sorrows."[64] While Shemwindo was hearing the sound of the Little Castaway, he scolded his people, telling (them) to cover the grave right away.[65] His people went to fetch fallen plantain stems; they placed them above him and above the plantains they heaped much soil.[66] Lo! at his birth, at that very moment, Mwindo was born with a *conga*-scepter, holding it in his right hand.[67] He was also

---

[62] *kabúrị/grave*: rare use of a Swahili word.

[63] *bámubétábeta/they carried him (handling him)*: the verb means to lull to sleep in the arms, but here the narrator simply suggests the way in which Mwindo is being carried and insists that Mwindo is really a small child, whatever his amazing feats are going to be. *ikịsa*: specialized term for ceremonial burial.

[64] *rwákwi . . ./this is (the death)* . . . : the word death is not mentioned, of course, and that makes the way in which the threat is uttered remarkable; but the verbal prefix used leaves no doubt in the Nyanga mind that reference to death, misfortune, is intended. The verb *ikwá* has many shades of meaning in the text, ranging from to die in the physical sense to suffering, diminution of status, excessive emotional experience, and weakening or loss of life force.

[65] *ékikoé/the sound*: only the distinctive sound or voice. *kátáwá/the Little Castaway*: the epithet is not used again in the epic; the term is currently applied to the children of a despised wife, implying neglect and rejection by the father.

[66] *mitámbá/fallen plantain stems*: technical term applied to any kind of cut or fallen banana tree.

[67] This passage in which the attributes of the hero at birth are described is the only one in the entire epic mentioned out of context by the narrator. *conga-scepter*: a flyswatter made from a buffalo tail or from the hairy tail of certain species of antelopes. The Nyanga attach great ceremonial and magic importance to these tails, which are carried, e.g., in the *kiowa* possession dances. The *conga*-scepter is the single most important attribute of Mwindo: throughout the epic it helps him to fly through the air, to kill, to destroy, to advise; it is the material symbol of the hero's force (physical and mental).

born with an adze, holding it in his left hand.[68] He was also born with a little bag of the spirit of Kahombo, wearing it slung across his back on the left side; in that little bag there was a long rope (within it).[69] Mwindo was born laughing and also speaking.[70]

When the day had ended, those who were sitting outdoors, seeing that where Mwindo had been thrown away [earlier in the day] there was light as though the sun were shining there, went to tell the men (about it) and the (latter) also arrived (there); they saw the place; they could not (bear to) stay a moment "which is long as what?" because the great heat, which was like fire, burned them.[71] Each time they did (as follows): as [this] one passed by, he cast his eyes there and proceeded on.[72] When they already were in the first vigil, when all the people were already asleep, Mwindo got out of the grave; he went to sneak into the house of his mother.[73] As Mwindo was wailing in the house of his mother, (and) when where he was

---

[68] mbasį/adze: used by children to cut shrubs and small trees; also used to sculpture dishes and pestles, for harvesting honey, and so on. Serves as an emblem of the bitųmbų, individuals who have the traditional right to organize a cycle of circumcisions and to perform masked dances while carrying the adze.

[69] kakú/little bag: made from raphia fibers and used by men as a shoulder bag for carrying food, small tools, tobacco. It is also part of the cult objects hung in the shrine of the female spirit Kahombo. Kahombo is a spirit of good fortune and the bag stands here as a symbol of the good fortune with which the hero is born. murį/a rope: lit., a liana; here it is a kind of magic line by means of which the hero will later communicate with his paternal aunt.

[70] It is unusual for the hero's speaking and laughing capabilities to be accented. If the hero were an animal, the two gifts would deserve special mention. The hero is human, and it is revealed later in the text that he likes to talk and boast excessively, two habits the Nyanga criticize constantly. Mwindo's epithet is Kábútwa-kénda (the Little-one-just-born-he-walked). For the narrator, and for the auditors, there is clearly something humorous about stressing two activities (laughing, talking) that, if practiced excessively, are subject to severe criticism.

[71] kashángį kárehyánį/a moment "which is long as what?": current expression to say a very short period of time, a moment that has no length.

[72] wásúsa éměso/he cast his eyes: the verb normally used is isunda; isúsa, which is employed here, means to plant a knife in the meat.

[73] mahombekerera/first vigil: this is a precise moment in the division of day and night as conceived by the Nyanga; it is the time when the men have left the meetinghouse, when all the house doors are closed, but when not everybody has gone to sleep.

sitting Shemwindo began to hear the way in which the child was wailing in the house of the preferred-one, he was very much astonished, saying: "This time what was never seen is seen (for the first time); again a child cries in that house. Has my wife just given birth to another child?"[74] Shemwindo died of indecision (whether or not) to stand up, because of fear. Owing to his virile impetus, Shemwindo stood up; he went into the house of his wife, the house of the preferred-one, slithering like a snake, without letting his steps be noisy. He arrived at the hut; he peeked (through the open door), casting an eye into the house; he saw the child sleeping on the floor; he entered the hut; he questioned his wife, saying: "Where does this child come from again; did you leave another one in the womb to whom you have given birth again?" His wife replied to him: "This is Mwindo inside here."[75] Where Mwindo was sitting on the ground, he kept silent. Shemwindo, witnessing this marvelous event, his mouth itched (to speak) (but) he left the house without having retorted another word.[76] Where he went, he went to wake up the counselors. Arriving there, he told them: "What is there (behind me), is what is there; it is astounding."[77] He told them also: "Tomorrow, when the sky will have become day, then you will go to cut a piece from the trunk of a tree; you will carve in it a husk for a drum; you will then put the hide of a *mukaka*-antelope in the river to soften."[78] When the sky had become day, all the people assembled together [calling one another]; they went to see

---

[74] Difficult construction; the opposition is centered in *muri įna* (in the house of his mother) and *kwárikángá* (in the house where the boy's father was sitting).

[75] *kantsóka/like a snake*: the prefix *ka* has the fairly rare meaning here of "in the manner of, like."

[76] *kanangano/marvelous event*: lit., something that tells a tale.

[77] Expressions similar to "what is there is what is there" are used frequently in daily speech to refer to extraordinary events.

[78] *muhoró/husk*: the term stands for the hollowed, wooden frame of a drum before the membrane has been attached to it. The wooden frame and the completed drum itself are objects to which many prescriptions are linked. The Nyanga distinguish according to size and sound three types of drums (*mukintsá, kioma,* and *kandúndú*) which are normally kept by the elder of a kinship group in the men's meetinghouse or in a shrine. *mukaka-antelope*: the membranes of drums are made from elephant ears and from the hides of several types of antelope, including the waterbuck referred to here.

Mwindo in the house of his mother. Mwindo was devoured by the many longing eyes. After they had looked at him, the counselors went to the forest to cut a piece of wood for the husk of the drum.[79] They arrived in the forest; they cut it (the piece of wood); they returned with it to the village. Arriving in the village, they carved the wood; they hollowed it out so that it became a husk. When the husk was finished, they went again to fetch Mwindo; they carried him (handling him); they stuck him into the husk of the drum. Mwindo said: "This time, my father has no mercy; what a small baby is willingly maltreated!"[80] The Banashemwindo went to get the hide for the drum; they glued it on top of the drum; they covered it (the drum) with it.[81] When Shemwindo had seen how his son had been laid in the drum, he declared to all his people that he wanted two expert divers, swimmers, to go [the next day] and throw this drum into the pool where nothing moves.[82] After the divers, swimmers, had been found, they picked up the drum; all the people abandoned the village; they went to throw Mwindo. When they arrived at the pool where nothing moves, the swimmers with the drum entered the pool, swimming in the river. When they arrived in the middle of the pool, they asked in a loud voice: "Shall we drop him here?" All those who were sitting on the edge of the river answered "Yes," all saying together: "It is there, so that you will not be the cause of his return."[83] They released the drum in the middle of the pool;

---

79 *báhita/they went: ihita* is a technical term that simultaneously means two things: to go down the hill (traditionally all Nyanga villages are located toward the tops of the hills) and to leave the village in order to do some kind of work (cultivation, trapping, fishing) in the forest. *mundura/ forest*: the part of the forest close to the village.

80 *busará/forest*: the general term for forest, as opposed to village (*mbúka*); the forest is then differentiated into various categories according to type of vegetation, proximity or distance from the village, types of activities pursued in it. *kabóntsó-bóntso/small baby*: a few days or weeks old. This is, of course, a humorous note, but throughout the epic the hero continues to insist on his youth and smallness.

81 The verbs *ikanga* and *ibamba* are technical for fixing the membrane of the drum with pegs and laces.

82 *bindami/divers*: the fishing technique of diving with nets is known in some areas of Nyanga country.

83 Note that the swimmers go to throw the drum into a pool, which is said to be a place of danger and the abode of Mukiti.

it sank into the depths.[84] The waves made rings above the place where the drum had entered. After the swimmers had thrown him into the pool, they returned to the shore. Shemwindo was very pleased with them: "You have performed (good) work!" He gave each swimmer a maiden; thus those two got married because of (receiving) a gift for their labor.[85] That day, when Mwindo was thrown away, earth and heaven joined together because of the heavy rain; it rained for seven days; hailing left the earth no more; that rain brought much famine in Tubondo.[86]

After they had thrown Mwindo away, they returned to Tubondo. When they arrived in the village, Shemwindo threatened his wife Nyamwindo, saying: "Don't shed tears weeping for your son; if you weep, I shall make you follow up where your son has been thrown away." That very day, Nyamwindo turned into the despised-one.[87] Unable to weep, Nyamwindo went on merely sobbing—not a little tear of weeping!

Where Mwindo dwelt in the pool where he had been thrown

---

84 *ékumunda/into the depths*: lit., inside the pool, i.e., it was submerged.

85 *uhémbo/gift*: not just any gift, but a kind of prize, of award, given for special achievements; e.g., in this category of gifts fall the presents given to an outstanding dancer or to people who perform clearing work in one's banana grove. There are many occasions on which chiefs give women as "presents" to officeholders, to followers, or to persons who perform special jobs for them.

86 *ŷéca ná mitabero irínda ikenga/it rained for seven days*: lit., there passed seven days it rains continually (habitually). *mutabero/day*: literally means a period of work, an order of work. At this early stage of the epic, several basic elements that set the heroic model are already present. Mwindo is born against the will of the chief (not of a virgin, but of the chief's favorite wife). He is born in an abnormal way (longer period of gestation and through mother's medius by his own will). From birth on he has extraordinary gifts (walking, laughing, talking) and magical powers (particularly *conga*-scepter) at his disposal which will permit him to cope successfully with his enemies. He is self-conscious and self-assertive. Not being wanted, he is thrown away: his fate affects the cosmic order (rain, hail, famine). His force and his will to overcome his enemies are still weak at this stage of the epic, but gradually increase to reach the level of absolute superiority.

87 *Nyamwindo*: Mwindo's mother; teknonymic name. *nya-kashómbé/despised-one*: the wife is not formally declared to be disgraced, but it is a *de facto* condition, which is declared a disgrace by the woman concerned.

away, when he was in the water on the sand, he moaned inside the drum; he stuck his head to the drum; he listened attentively; he said: "I, to go downstream the river, and this without having warned my father and all his people who have thrown me away so that they hear the sound of my voice—well then, I am not Mwindo."[88] Where the drum was in the water on the sand, it arose all alone to the surface of the water. When the drum was at the surface of the pool—in its middle—it remained there; it did not go down the river; neither did it go up (the river).

From Tubondo, from the village where the people dwelt, came a row of maidens; they went to draw water from the river at the wading place.[89] Arriving at the river, as soon as they cast their eyes toward the middle of the pool, they saw the drum on the surface of the water, which was turning around there; they said inquiringly to one another: "Companions, we have dazzling apparitions; lo! the drum that was thrown with Mwindo—there it is!" Where Mwindo dwelt inside the drum in the pool, he said: "If I abstain from singing while these maidens are still here drawing water from the river, then I shall not have anybody who will bring the news to the village where my father is in Tubondo."[90] While the maidens were in the act of drawing water and still had their attention fixed

---

88 *wáhúrúkírire/he listened attentively*: the verb specifically applies to the way in which the children by different wives of the same man eavesdrop upon the conversations of the other women for their mother.

89 *hítúkúriro/wading place*: the wading place is not, in fact, meant here, but rather a spot a little upstream from the wading place where women draw water; between both spots is a bathing place. In the preceding passage, and in many others throughout the text, the Nyanga obsession for place designation is striking. The religious effort to be very precise in assigning spatial relationships is one of the most singularly typical traits of Nyanga thinking, but, of course, it makes translations cumbersome.

90 *bana-kítú/companions*: lit., members of our . . . (chiefdom, kinship group); people who interact with one another. The precision and the richness of the terms used are once more revealed here, e.g., "we have dazzling apparitions (*ihúmánana*, to be witness of something extraordinary, to have the apparition of a spirit or of the spirit of a paternal aunt in a dream); "said inquiringly to one another" (*bábúsá-nya*, the effect is achieved here by the suffix-*nya*). In none of the hundreds of tales that I collected in all corners of Nyanga country did I encounter such richness, diversity, and precision of language, such poetic quality and style.

there toward the drum, Mwindo, where he dwelt in the drum
in the pool, threw sweet words into his mouth; he sang:[91]

> Scribe, move on![92]
> I am saying farewell to Shemwindo!
> I am saying farewell to Shemwindo!
> I shall die, oh! Bira![93]
> My little father threw me into the drum!
> I shall die, Mwindo!
> The counselors abandoned Shemwindo;
> The counselors will become dried leaves.[94]
> The counselors of Shemwindo,
> The counselors of Shemwindo,
> The counselors have failed (in their) counseling!
> My little father, little Shemwindo,
> My little father threw me into the drum
> I shall not die, whereas (that) little-one will survive![95]

---

91 *énderi̧/sweet words*: lit., sweet grains; the terms can also be used for
an oral will left by a dying father or for a prophetic statement. In the
song that follows, Mwindo forecasts that he will find his paternal aunt
and that he will overcome his father and his father's counselors.

92 *Karáni̧/scribe*: a Swahili word. This exclamation made by the narrator must be considered in the light of the general circumstances under
which he sang his epic. We were sitting with him and patiently writing
down the words that he sang and chanted. The encouragement is directed
toward the assistant singers and the percussionists as much as toward
myself. At the very start of a song or dance, there is in a moment of dis-
organization, of hesitation, a searching for exact rhythms and words. During such moments, even in important initiatory situations, all kinds of
improvised sentences may be sung.

93 *Bi̧ra*: under this term the Nyanga classify all those who are not of
their culture, particularly the uncircumcised Hunde. There is raillery
and challenge in this verse. Mwindo, in a somewhat covert way, says: "Do
you, weaklings, think that I shall die now?" The tones used in the songs
are not always regular ones; they are influenced by the music and singing.
Thus Bi̧ra is indicated here with two low tones, whereas normally it is
pronounced Bi̧rá, with a rising and a low tone.

94 *Katitá/my little father*: the ka- prefix used here may have a diminutive
or pejorative meaning. It is also to be noted, however, that Mwindo, who
has a baby's stature, tends to view all others in terms of his own size.
ntsêkwá/I shall die: difficult to interpret. It may be understood in three
ways: "I shall die"; "shall I die"; or, if one accepts an eventual omission
of *mbu*, "thinking that I shall die." The last interpretation makes the text
more comprehensible: "My little father threw me into the drum! (thinking
that) I shall die."

95 Difficult verse, which can be rightly understood only if we accept two

The little-one is joining Iyangura,
The little-one is joining Iyangura,
Iyangura, the sister of Shemwindo.[96]

When the girls heard the way in which Mwindo was singing in the drum in the pool, they climbed up to the village, running and rushing, after they had left the water jars at the river, behind (them), in disarray.[97] When they arrived within the inhabited area, the men, seeing them appear at the outskirts running and rushing, took their spears and went, believing that they were being chased by a wild beast.[98] Seeing the spears, the maidens beseeched their fathers: "Hold it! We are going to bring the news to you of how the drum that you threw into the pool has stayed; it is singing: 'The counselors of Shemwindo, the counselors have failed in (their) counseling; the counselors will become dried leaves.'" When he heard that, Shemwindo told the girls that they were lying: "What! the drum that we had thrown away [yesterday] into the pool arose again!" The maidens assented (to it): "Mwindo is still alive." They had seen him with (their own) eyes, and he (really) was still alive. When Shemwindo heard that, he assembled (again) all his people; the village remained empty; everybody deserted (the village) for the river carrying spears, arrows, and fire (torches).[99]

---

different subjects: I shall not die (*ntákwi*) and he (my father) that little-one survive! (*kárami; ka-* bearing on *katitá*).

96 *Kábingúrá/the little-one is joining*: the prefix *ka-* bears on Mwindo himself. He has already called himself a little baby (*kabóntsóbóntso*) and he continues to refer to himself with this diminutive prefix (*ka-*).

97 *kumbúka/to the village*: the term *mbúka*, village has many interesting usages, which are revealed later in the text. Joined to the locative prefix *ha-* (*hámbúka*), it stands in opposition to *múnumba* and means outside, outdoors, as against inside, in the house, indoors. Joined to the locative prefix *ku-* it may designate two different things according to the context of oppositions in which it is used. If opposed to *kubusará* (the forest), it means "the village, the immediate surroundings of the village"; if opposed to *kwirúngá* (the craters of the volcanoes said to be the domain of the spirits), it means "the world inhabited by mankind."

98 *kihuká/wild beast*: the term can either indicate any kind of animal not raised in the village or specifically refer to some animals thought to be very dangerous, like the leopard and gorilla.

99 *tóto/hold it*: an onomatopoeia meaning don't!; for mercy's sake! The young maidens seem to be somewhat on Mwindo's side, and, later on, they

Where Mwindo dwelt in the river, after he had seen the way in which the maidens had cleared (the river) for the village, he also stopped (his) singing for a while; he said that he would sing again when the people arrived, because these girls had just witnessed his astonishing deed. All the people of the village, children and youngsters, old people and young men, women, when they arrived at the river, seeing the drum in the middle of the pool, grouped together looking attentively at the drum. When Mwindo noticed them waiting in a group on the shore (of the river), he threw sweet words into (his) mouth; he sang:[100]

> I am saying farewell to Shemwindo;
> I shall die, oh Bira!
> The counselors abandoned Shemwindo.
> Scribe, move on!
> The counselors will turn into dried leaves.
> What will die and what will be safe
> Are going to encounter Iyangura.[101]

When Mwindo had finished singing like that, saying farewell to his father and to all the Banashemwindo, the drum sank into the pool; the waves made rings at the surface. Where Shemwindo and his people were standing on the shore, they were very perplexed; they nodded their heads, saying: "How terrible it is! Will some day then be born what is never being

---

are found among his followers. *éngoma twaréré twatáá ŷo/the drum that we had thrown away yesterday*: typical way of expressing a recent past, literally means: the drum, we have slept we have thrown it away. *Carrying spears*: although the people know that the girls speak about Mwindo, they nevertheless make preparations, as if going to a big fight or as if setting out on a longer hunting expedition.

100 *bámatécá/waiting in a group*: *itéca* literally means to have somebody prepare food (which implies that one is waiting to get it). The narrator describes these people as if they were waiting there while food was being cooked for them.

101 *Kákwi na Kárami/what will die and what will be safe*: Mwindo is speaking about himself, of course, giving himself the epithets of Life (*Káramo*) and Death (*Kokú*). The translation of *ka-* as a neuter form "*What* will . . ." is justified when the usage of this prefix is examined in an expression like *káriho* (what lives, what is alive). When a woman has a very difficult childbirth, the midwives say: "There will not come out what is alive (*káriho*)."

born?"[102] After they had witnessed this extraordinary event, they returned to the village Tubondo.

Where Mwindo headed inside the water, he went upstream; he went to the river's source, at Kinkunduri's, to begin it.[103] When he arrived at Kinkunduri's, he lodged there; he said that he was joining Iyangura, his paternal aunt, there, whither she had gone; the news had been given him by Kahungu.[104] He began the trip; he joined his aunt Iyangura downstream; he sang:

Mungai, get out of my way!
For Ikukuhi shall I go out of the way?
You are impotent against Mwindo,
Mwindo is the Little-one just-born-he-walked.
I am going to meet Iyangura.
For Kabusa, shall I go out of the way?
You are helpless against Mwindo,
For Mwindo is the Little-one-just-born-he-walked.
Canta, get out of my way!
Canta, you are impotent against Mwindo.
I am going to encounter Iyangura, my aunt.
For Mutaka shall I go out of the way?

---

102 *cásúmá/terrible*: the verb *isúma* is used whenever there are formidable physical, moral, or intellectual difficulties present.

103 *he went upstream*: the passage could imply two things: either that Mwindo had been thrown into the river where Mukiti did not live, so he was now traveling upstream to the source of another river where Mukiti had his dwelling place; or that the river into which Mwindo had been thrown consisted of two levels: an upper one, through which the hero could freely move, and a lower, or even subterranean one, which was the realm of Mukiti and his allies. It was in this lower level that Mwindo would encounter many difficulties. An interesting ritual concept is also linked with this passage. For the Nyanga, all bad things go downstream with the river. The frequent ablution ceremonies are held successively at different, but adjacent, spots along the river; the second ablution is always made a little farther upstream from the first, and so on. When the seventh and last stage of ablutions is completed, purity is achieved. In the pages that follow the hero encounters greater and greater obstacles during the river travel. In Nyanga thinking, this can happen logically only when he goes downstream (implying greater and greater accumulation of dirt and of inimical forces). *Kinkunduri*: the name for a species of crab found near river sources.

104 *Kahúngú*: a hawk, which, like the crowned eagle, often figures in tales as a friendly messenger.

65

You are helpless against Mwindo!
I am going to meet Iyangura, my aunt.
For Kitoru shall I get out of my way?
You see, I am going to encounter Iyangura, my aunt.
I stated that:
For Mushenge shall I get out of my way?
You are impotent against Mwindo!
See, I am going to encounter Iyangura, my aunt,
Iyangura, sister of Shemwindo.
For Nyarui, shall I get out of my way?
Whereas Mwindo is the Little-one-just-born-he-has-walked.
I am going to encounter Iyangura, my aunt,
Sister of Shemwindo.
For Cayo shall I get out of my way?
You see, I am going to encounter Iyangura, my aunt,
Sister of Shemwindo.
Look! You are impotent against Mwindo,
Mwindo the Little-one-just-born-he-walked.
He who will go up against me, it is he who will die on the way.[105]

Each time Mwindo arrived in a place where an aquatic animal
was, he said that it should get out of the way for him, that they
were powerless against him, that he was going to his aunt
Iyangura. When Mwindo arrived at Cayo's, he spent the night
there; in the morning he went right after awakening; he sang:

> For Ntsuka shall I go out of the way?
> You see that I am going to encounter Iyangura.
> You see that you are powerless against Mwindo.

---

[105] Several species of fishes and crabs, such as Mungai, Ikukuhi, Kabusa,
Canta, Mutaka, Kitoru, Mushenge, Nyarui, Cayo, are mentioned in this
song. They are all personifications of ugliness and hatred and considered
to be allies of Mukiti. The names of these fishes remind the Nyanga of
certain verbal forms that connote the idea of evil. *utúkocé/you are im-
potent/you are helpless*: negative of verb *ikoca*, to be able, to have the
power, to have the capacity, to realize something. Mwindo often utters
this expression to convey the idea that he alone is the hero. *Kábútwa-
kénda/the Little-one-just-born-he-walked*: lit., little thing that was born, it
walked. This is Mwindo's single most important epithet; the epithet is
also found in tales as a name for extraordinary individuals. *Narimbura
mbu/I stated that*: the narrator puts himself in the position of Mwindo;
there are other instances in the text of this identification between Mwindo
and the narrator. *ngi wakwiri muntse/it is he who will die on the way*:
i.e., he will die lonely and abandoned.

Mwindo is the Little-one-just-born-he-walked.
For Kirurumba shall I go out of the way?
You see that I am going to encounter Aunt Iyangura.
You see that you are powerless against Mwindo,
For Mwindo is the Little-one-just-born-he-walked.
For Mushomwa shall I go out of the way?
You see I am going to encounter Aunt Iyangura.
You see that you are powerless against Mwindo.
For Mwindo is the Little-one-just-born-he-has-walked.

Musoka, the junior sister of Mukiti, had gone to live upstream from Mukiti:[106]

For Musoka shall I go out of the way?
You are powerless against Mwindo
Mwindo is the Little-one-just-born-he-has-walked.

When Musoka saw Mwindo arriving at her place, she sent an envoy to Mukiti to say that there was a person there where she was, at Musoka's, who was in the act of joining Iyangura. The envoy ran quickly to where Mukiti was; he arrived there (and) gave the news: "There is a person back there; he is in the act of joining Iyangura." Mukiti replied to that envoy that he should tell Musoka that that man should not pass beyond her place; "If not, why would I have placed her there?" That envoy arrived at Musoka's; he announced the news of how he had been spoken to by Mukiti. Musoka kept on forbidding Mwindo like that, without knowing that he was a child of Mukiti's wife, Iyangura. Musoka replied to Mwindo, saying: "Mukiti refuses to let you pass; so it is your manhood that will permit you to pass; I here, Musoka, I am placing barriers here; you will not find a trail to pass on." Mwindo answered her, softening his voice: "I, Mwindo, never am I forbidden (to pass on) a trail; I will thrust through there where you are blocking." Mwindo hearing this pulled himself together; he left the water above (him); he dug inside the sand; and he went to appear in between Musoka and Mukiti. After Mwindo had passed Musoka,

---

106 Further enumeration of fishes and crabs, the personified allies of Mukiti, whose names evoke the idea of evil and hatred, e.g., *ntsúká*/vb. *isúka*, to frown in anger; *mushómwá*/vb. *ishómbwa*, to hate. Musóka, represented here as the junior sister of Mukiti, is a female water spirit for which the Nyanga have a special cult.

having broken through the dam of Musoka, he praised himself: "Here I am, the Little-one-just-born-he-walked; one never points a finger at me." When Musoka saw him anew downstream, she touched (her) chin, saying: "How then has this tough one here gotten through? If he had passed above (me) I would have seen his shadow; if he had passed below (me), I would have heard the sound of his feet."[107] Musoka complained a lot saying that she would be scolded by Mukiti because she (had) let somebody pass.

After Mwindo had passed Musoka, he began a journey to go to Mukiti's; he sang:

> In Mukiti's, in Mariba's dwelling place![108]
> For Mukiti shall I get out of my way?
> You see I am going to encounter Iyangura,
> Iyangura, sister of Shemwindo.
> Mukiti, you are powerless against Mwindo.
> Mwindo is the Little-one-just-born-he-walked.

When Mukiti in his dwelling place heard (this), he moved, asking who had just mentioned his wife. He shook heaven and earth; the whole pool moved. Mwindo on his side said: "This time we shall (get to) know each other today, we with Mukiti; (for) I Mwindo never fear an insolent child, so long as I have not measured myself against him."[109] When Mwindo heard that, he said: "This time, the husband of (my) aunt is lying; it is I Mwindo who am being forbidden the road to (my) aunt!" Mwindo pulled himself together; he went to appear at the knot where Mukiti was coiled up. When Mukiti saw him, he said: "This time it is not the one (whom I expected to see); he surpasses (expectation)!" He asked: "Who are you?" Mwindo referred to himself saying that he was Mwindo, the Little-one-just-born-he-walked, child of Iyangura. Mukiti said to Mwindo: "How then?" Mwindo answered him saying that he was going to encounter his paternal aunt Iyangura. Hearing that, Mukiti

---

107 *one never points a finger at me*: i.e., nobody ever argues with me, nobody ever taunts me. *She touched her chin*: to express astonishment.

108 *Mariba*: lit., pool; Mukiti receives as an epithet the name of the place where he is thought to dwell.

109 *kitaba/an insolent child*: lit., a fat, indolent boy, spoiled and without energy.

said to Mwindo: "You are lying; here never anybody passes, who would have crossed over these logs and dried leaves; so, then, you never go to sleep thinking! You alone are (the man) who in spite of all will (be able to) pass here where I am!" While Mukiti and Mwindo were still talking to each other like that, maidens went from Iyangura's place to draw water; at Mukiti's place, there it was that the water hole was. As soon as the maidens witnessed the way in which Mwindo constantly mentioned Iyangura saying (she was his) aunt, they ran to Iyangura; they arrived there (and) said to Iyangura: "Over there, where your husband Mukiti is, there is a little man saying that Mukiti should release him, that he is Mwindo, that he is going to encounter Iyangura, his paternal aunt." When Iyangura heard that news, she said: "Lo! that is my child, let me first go to where he is." Iyangura climbed up the slope; she went to appear at the water hole; she looked to the river that she first might see the man who was mentioning that she was Iyangura. As soon as Mwindo in his place saw his paternal aunt coming to see him, he sang:

> I am suffering much, Mwindo.
> I will die, Mwindo.

While his aunt Iyangura was then descending (the slope), he went on singing looking in the direction from which his aunt was coming.

> Aunt Iyangura,
> Mukiti has forbidden me the road.
> I am going to meet Aunt Iyangura,
> I am going to encounter Iyangura,
> Sister of Shemwindo.
> For Mukiti shall I go out of the way?
> I am joining Iyangura,
> Sister of Shemwindo.
> For Mukiti, my father, shall I go out of the way?
> You are powerless against Mwindo,
> Katitiiri and Mpumba
> And Rintea and Sheburenda![110]

110 The current kinship term used by a woman for her brother's son or daughter is *mwána*, my child. Mwindo speaks about Mukiti as *titá*, my father; because Mukiti is his paternal aunt's husband, Mwindo pays re-

> My father, I shall die [today], Mwindo!
> Aunt Iyangura howled, she said,
> Aunt Iyangura "of the body."[111]

Iyangura said: "If the sororal nephew of the Banamitandi is in this drum, let it arrive here so that I can see it before me." When the aunt cited the Banamitandi in this way, the drum refused to move in the direction of Iyangura. Inside the drum, Mwindo complained that this time his aunt missed (the mark). His aunt spoke again: "If you drum, (if) you are the sororal nephew of The-one-who-hears-secrets, come here; draw near me." When his aunt had mentioned in that way Those-who-hear-secrets, the drum still refused to draw near her. His aunt said anew: "If you really are the nephew of the Baniyana, come here before me." When Mwindo heard that, he went singing, in [his] leaving the pool:

I am going to my Aunt Iyangura,
Iyangura, sister of Shemwindo.
Kabarebare and Ntabare-mountain,
Where the husband of my senior sister sets *byoo*-traps.[112]
And a girl who is nice is a lady,
And a nice young man is a *kakoma*-pole.[113]
We are telling the story
That the Babuya have told [long ago].[114]

---

spect to his aunt by using an honorific term for her husband. A paternal aunt's husband is normally identified with a maternal uncle. *Katitiiri* . . . : four symbolic personages, whose names (derived from insects) are specially selected by Mwindo to express his scorn for the pettiness of Mukiti's allies.

111 *Sinkárí Yangura wamùmubi/Aunt Iyangura "of the body"*: a double meaning lies in this expression. It indicates that Iyangura is a uterine sister of Mwindo's father; it is also a sign of tenderness.

112 *byoo-traps*: a trapping device currently in great use which is placed in the neighborhood of rivers and brooks. The names of mountains stand as designation for estates.

113 *marámí/lady*: Nyangaized French word *madame*. *kakoma-pole*: poles that form the framework of the house walls; they symbolize straightness. In these and many of the following verses, the narrator intersperses several reflections of his own in Mwindo's song. The narrator's joyful imagination is at work in these improvised passages.

114 *We are telling the story* . . . : *uano* is the term used for tales in general; the narrator says that what he is telling here is from (or part of [*mùano*]) a story first told by people of the Babuya descent group, a group represented in the village where the narrator lived.

We are telling the story.
Kasengeri is dancing (wagging his) tail;
And you, see! (this) tail of *nderema*-fibers.[115]
Nkurongo-bird has gone to court *mususu*-bird;
Muhasha-bird has contracted asthma.[116]
If I am at a loss for words in the great song,
If it dies out, may it not die out for me there.[117]
I cannot flirt with I-have-no-name;[118]
They are accustomed to speak to Mukiti (with) bells.
The tunes that we are singing,
The uninitiated-ones cannot know them.
I cannot be given *mburu*-monkey and still eat a lot,
I would remain satisfied with my flat belly.[119]
I have seen a rooster cock-a-doodle-dooing;
I also saw *muntori*-bird pointing him out.[120]
The little guardian of the rice (field)
Is never confused about
When sky has become day.
I see that meditations kill;
They killed the couple, otter and his mother.
If little pot travels too much,

---

115 *Kasengeri*: the name of an animal sometimes used to designate a good dancer. *Is dancing (wagging his) tail*: the Nyanga expression *múconga* (on the tail, part of the tail) implies that when he dances, the most visible part is the tail. The narrator, who dances while singing this song, wears around the upper arm an armlet made of fibers cut from dried banana leaves. He praises himself as a good dancer and asks the onlookers to observe the movements of his arms adorned with the fiber armlets.

116 The narrator evokes certain tales about the *bulikoko*-bird, a symbol of good singing and of elegance, as opposed to *muhasha* who does not sing well (suffers from asthma, they say; gasps for breath all the time).

117 *carwimbo/the great song*: omission of the high tone on *ca-* seems to mean that the song is personified. The various improvisations made here result from the fact that the narrator had lost the thread of Mwindo's song and of the story as a whole.

118 *ntsira-rina/I-have-no-name*: term with which women who have had many miscarriages are designated.

119 *Narika nakéndéré bura/I would remain satisfied with my flat belly*: lit., I sat down, I was plaiting for the belly; "plait for the belly" is a stereotyped expression for "to admire." The meaning, then, of these two verses is that the narrator would like to be as perfect as the *mburu*-monkey, who is admired for his flat belly and is said to eat very little.

120 *birangira/cock-a-doodle-dooing*: an onomatopoeia. The two verses refer to a tale in which a rooster and a sparrow are the main actors.

It means little pot looks for a crack.[121]
He who (one day) ate *ntsuka*-fish does not sojourn long.
It is as though he had eaten the heart of the plunger.[122]
If Nyabunge coils (like) the whirlpools,
Then she loses her way home.
I learned that a catastrophe happened:
(One suffering from) frambesia and a leper on a bed.
If you hear the uproar of an argument,
It means the old woman has gotten more than the young mother.
I always sit down thinking about myself,
As (in the game) "throat and top."
I have cultivated bananas for the dragon
(So heavy) that a cluster had no one to carry it.
The *muhangu*-animal that tries to make the first banana fruits drop.
If the mother of the girl dies because of the young man,
It means an *atumbu*-insect falls from the *ntongi*-tree.[123]

When Mwindo was still in the act of going down [with] the river, the moment he joined his aunt he went to arrive before her where she was. His aunt seized the drum; her people gave her a knife; she slashed the drum; removing the hide, she saw the multiple rays of the rising sun and the moon. That is the beauty of the child Mwindo. Mwindo got out of the drum, still holding his *conga*-scepter and his axe, together with his little bag in which the rope was. When Kahungu saw Mwindo meeting with his aunt, he went to bring the news to the *mutambo*-elder who had been given to Iyangura to keep watch over her continually.[124] He arrived there, he gave him the news: "You, you (who) are here, it is not (merely) a little man who appears over there; he is with many stories and feats; you are dead."

---

[121] References to three different tales.

[122] A proverb; *ntsuka-fish* is a delicacy. If this fish is given to a guest, he will be sure to come to visit again.

[123] Neither coherence nor consistency should be sought in this song. Three things are brought out: the narrator has somewhat lost the thread of his story; he is hungry; enjoying himself, he digresses by throwing out to his audience a number of personal praises, personal reflections, collections of tales and proverbs. Nyanga songs are very often nothing more than a loose piecing-together of totally unrelated verses. What counts here is the singing, the dancing, the rhythm, and the music, not the verbalizations; the aim is not to convey ideas, but to enjoy sound and rhythm.

[124] *kéntsé/the rising sun*: as a star the sun is known as *mwĭshi*, a term that also designates the heat carried by the sun. *kéntsé*: the light, the radiance of the sun; it is also a spirit and may be used as a girl's name.

Hearing this news, Kasiyembe said: "[You] envoy, you go!
When you will have arrived at Mwindo's, tell him he should
not even try to pass this side; (otherwise) I shall tear out his
spinal column; I here am setting up traps, pits and pointed
sticks and razors in the ground, so that I shall know where he
will step." Seeing that, Katee went to appear where Mwindo
was (and) told him: "You, Mwindo, your mates are holding
secret council against you; they are even preparing pit traps
against you, and pointed sticks and razors.[125] I (am) Katee, don't
you always see me on the ground, in the depth of the earth?"
Mwindo answered him: "Yes, I always see you; it is on the
ground that you live." After having given Mwindo the news
of that danger there in order to warn him, Katee also told him:
"I am going to have a road go by, so that it emerges from the
place where you are, and I want to make it come out inside
the house of your aunt, at the base of the house pole." Mwindo
said "Yes" to him. Mukei began to dig in the ground, inside
it. Mwindo told his aunt Iyangura: "You, Aunt, proceed ahead;
you be already on your way home; I shall meet you there; and
that Kasiyembe threatening me over there, I shall first meet up
with him; if he really has force, I shall deal with him (today)."
He also said to his aunt: "Tell him, the one who is threatening
me there, that he should prepare himself." Master Spider also
emerged from within the pits, (he was) building bridges; he
made them come out above the pits; the pits became merely
bridges; he said to himself that it was there that Mwindo was
going to play. "As far as I, Master Spider, am concerned,
Mwindo cannot completely perish, since we are there." After
his aunt had thus been told by Mwindo to proceed going, she
did not tergiversate; she went home. Back there where Mwindo
had remained, he took the road (made by) Katee; he came out
in the house of his aunt, at Iyangura's, thanks to his *kahombo*.[126]
When Kasiyembe saw him, he said: "Mwindo is already over
here; now, from where has he emerged?" The people of his

---

125 *mishíngá/stories and feats*: lit., a story in which the marvelous element and extraordinary deeds are underscored. *Kahungu*, the hawk, and
Katee, the hedgehog, act here as messengers, in favor of Mukiti's allies
and of Mwindo, respectively.

126 *muhéngéré/road*: a well-cleared trail. *ndákí/road*: a word derived
from Lingala and generally used to designate a road built by Europeans.
utúnge/as far as I . . . am concerned: a verbal form that means as much

village said that they did not know from where he had emerged.

When Iyangura saw that her son Mwindo had already arrived, she said to him: "My son, don't eat food yet; come first
to this side, so that we may dance (to the rhythm of) the drum.
After Mwindo had heard the words of his aunt, he left the
house (and) appeared where his aunt was outdoors; he told his
aunt that there he was, that he was going to dance without
having eaten food, that he was going to faint with this drum.[127]
His aunt replied to him: "Not at all! Dance all the same, [you]
my son; and as for me, what shall I do then, since the one
whom I was given to take care of me is saying that you must
dance? What then shall we do? Dance all the same!" Hearing
the word of his aunt, Mwindo said: "Oh! Right you are; let
me first dance; hunger never kills a man." Mwindo sang; he
howled, he said:

> Kasiyembe, you are powerless against Mwindo,
> For Mwindo is the Little-one-just-born-he-walked.
> Kasiyembe said: "Let us dance together."
> Shirungu, give us a morceau!
> If we die, we will die for you.
> Kasengeri is dancing with his *conga*-scepter,
> *Conga*-scepter of *nderema*-fibers.[128]
> I am saying farewell to Mpumba,
> My Mpumba with many raphia bunches.

Mwindo went round about in the middle of the pits; he
marched (with the body) bent over the pits, without even being
injured by the razors; he passed and passed everywhere where
Kasiyembe had placed traps for him, without injuring himself.

---

as, insofar as, equal to, as far as it concerns, in person. The Spider intends
to say: as long as I am a spider, if I am truly a spider, in my capacity of
being a spider. *kahombo*: the name of a tutelary spirit; the word is used
here in the abstract to designate good fortune.

[127] The invitation for him to dance made by his aunt should not be
considered as perfidy on her part. She knows that Kasiyembe has set traps
for Mwindo and she wants Mwindo to give proof of his invulnerability.
That he was going to faint: it is rare for Mwindo not to praise himself.
Here, he is still boasting: he knows in advance that he will be saved and
merely wants to give an impression of great drama.

[128] This song is again a mixture of Mwindo's and the narrator's words.
Mwindo provokes Kasiyembe. The narrator addresses himself to one of
the percussionists, Shirungu; he stresses the difficulty of his task, but
promises to accomplish it to please his audience.

After Mwindo had passed and passed where traps had been set up for him, he danced; he agitated his *conga*-scepter to and fro, singing:

> It is Katee who is crackling of dried leaves,
> And it is Kantori who is Shebireo.[129]

He also pointed out the Banamitandi, saying:

> You have seen that I am a follower of the Banamitandi.
> May Kahungu go to see now.
> May I see over there Shemumbo's village.[130]
> I am seeing that (among) the chimpanzees of the *ficus*-tree,
> The one who is repleted comes down.[131]

Iyangura told her son to eat some food, saying that since the time he arrived he had not spit his saliva while eating food.[132] Iyangura gave her son a bovine as a token of hospitality; he/she felled it. Eating it were those who were on the side, the maidens, who ate from it (for several days); he did not put [from] it in the mouth trying to eat from it. After Mwindo had eaten the hospitality gift of the bovine, which his aunt had offered to him, together with the maidens, Kasiyembe, the man of hatred, persisted in trying to kill him, saying:[133] "Is this the boy against

---

[129] The first verse is in praise of Katee, the hedgehog, who helped him and whose habit it is to draw dried leaves into its burrow. The second verse recalls a tale about the sparrow Kantori.

[130] *naréshiá/I am a follower*: i.e., someone who gives service and allegiance, receiving protection in return. *Shemumbo's village*: Shemumbo is the father (or giver) of a chief's ritual wife whose son is successor to the throne. The words have a double meaning: Mwindo refers to his father's village as the place of origin of his aunt Iyangura, who is now Mukiti's ritual wife; he also sees himself as the prospective chief of the land and looks upon his father merely as the provider of a ritual wife.

[131] Reflection made by the narrator in reference to a tale.

[132] *itúra oté/spit his saliva*: i.e., has not rinsed his mouth with water before eating.

[133] It is to be understood that Mwindo does not eat the food. He receives the hospitality gift, but gives permission to the maidens to consume it. *After Mwindo had eaten the hospitality gift*: not to be understood literally; the verb *irisa/to eat* often means nothing more than to receive. *hima n'ébikumi/together with the maidens*: there is some ambiguity here as to whether he and the maidens received the gift (the interpretation we prefer) or whether the gift he received from his aunt consisted of a cow and a group of maidens.

whom I shall be impotent, whereas I heard that he came from
the inside of a drum?"[134] Kasiyembe implored Nkuba, the
lightning-hurler, saying: "You, Nkuba, you will have to come
down; may you cut Mwindo into two pieces, in the house here
where he is together with all these maidens who are with him
here." When Mwindo heard the way in which Kasiyembe
threatened him, over and over again, he told the maidens sitting
with him in the house to sit down on one side with him because
Kasiyembe wanted to bring lightning down on him. Then
Mwindo said threateningly to Master Nkuba: "You, Nkuba,
since you come down, you must come down on one side of the
house; don't come down on the side where Mwindo is." Master
Nkuba, on hearing the voice of Kasiyembe, descended onto the
house where Mwindo was; Mwindo pointed him out, saying:
"You too will die the same (death); you are climbing on a hard
tree." Master Nkuba came down seven times; each time he
descended onto one side of the house in which Mwindo was, he
did not come close to the place where he was; the fire burned
on one side; that side became merely ashes. Where Iyangura,
aunt of Mwindo, was sitting, tears rolled from her eyes and
reached her legs, she saying that lo! her son was dying and that
she had not even seen him well. Mwindo then came out of the
house together with the maidens; he presented himself (before)
the crowd of people; he declared about himself that there he
was, the Little-one-just-born-he-walked. He said to his aunt to
come close to where he was so that he could speak to her; his
aunt came close to him; Mwindo spoke to her: "No more crying;
it is you, my aunt, who are the reason Kasiyembe made this evil
test come over me; in the day of tomorrow, if you will see me
no more, it means that I am not worthy of Mwindo."[135] He told
his aunt that within the twinkling of an eye, the mop of hair

---

134 *muŷú/the boy*: used in a pejorative sense; a male who is not yet an
adult.

135 *Nkúbá* is the divinity of lightning who is always described as being in
a destructive mood, ready to put his powers of devastation at the disposal of
any solicitor, good or evil. Nkúbá tries to aid several enemies of Mwindo,
but is always unsuccessful; later, he will become a friend and ally of
Mwindo. *mirábyo/the lightning-hurler*: lit., efflorescence of plants or
flames of lightning.

of Kasiyembe would already be burning.[136] Where Kasiyembe
was, (people) were all of a sudden struck (by the fact that) in
the mop of hair of Kasiyembe the fire was already flaring up;
the tongues (of flame) rose into the air; all the lice and all the
vermin that were nestled on his head, all were entirely consumed. When they saw the mop of hair of Kasiyembe burning,
the people of Kasiyembe thought about fetching water in the
jars in order to extinguish the fire on the head of Kasiyembe.
When they arrived at the jars, in arriving there, there was no
water left; all (the water) had dried up in the jars, there was
not a drop (of water) left in them. They went straight to the
herbaceous stalks of the plantains; they arrived there when they
were (already) dried up, without a drop (of water) in them.
They said: "What then! Spit some saliva on (his) head!" Saliva
was lacking among all the people; their mouths were wanting
of saliva.[137] When they experienced this, they said: "This
Kasiyembe is about to die. Go and look for help for him at his
Master's; it is at Mukiti's that there is a pool." They went
there. Arriving there, they found Mukiti with butterflies and
flies flitting about him; for him, too, the water had dried up;
the whole pool had dried up, without even a drop (in it). When
his aunt saw that, she went to beg before her son: "Widen
your heart, you my son 'of the body,' you only child. By any
chance did you come here where I am in order to attack us?
Set your heart down; undo my husband together with his
mutambo-elder, this one Kasiyembe; heal them without har-
boring further resentment against them."[138] After the aunt had
finished humbly imploring her son, Mwindo had his heart go
down; he woke up Kasiyembe, waving his *conga*-scepter above
him; he sang:

---

136 Kasiyembe is described as a kind of fool, as an evil element (symbol-
ized by the thick mop of hair).

137 The richness of verbal expression is well illustrated in this short
passage. To say that jars, banana trees, and mouths were lacking liquid,
the narrator uses four verbal phrases: not to remain (*nti kúsįrá*), not in
them (*angá . . . Mubyó*), to fail (to catch animals) (*ihína*), and to miss
(*irúka*).

138 *kokórá émutima/widen your heart*: lit., unknot, stretch your heart;
has the same meaning as *sįcá émutima/set your heart down*. In Nyanga
thinking the heart "is knotted" or "is high" when one is angry or in deep
emotional shock.

He who went to sleep wakes up.
You are impotent against Mwindo,
Mwindo is the Little-one-just-born-he-walked.

"Wake up thanks to my *conga* here of *nderema*-fibers."

He who went to sleep wakes up.
Look, I am playing with (my) *conga*-scepter.

Suddenly, Kasiyembe was saved. And the jars, water re .urned again in them; and the herbaceous stalks of all the plantains, in them again was water; and there where Mukiti was, the water came back again for him; the river was full again. When they saw that feat, they were much astonished, saying: "Lo! Mwindo, he too, is a great man."[139] Kasiyembe gave Mwindo a salute, saying: "Hail! hail! oh! Mwindo." And Mwindo answered, "Yes." After he had accomplished that deed, Mwindo said to his aunt that tomorrow he would be going to Tubondo to fight with his father, because his father had thrown him away twice; now he would in his turn go to stand up against him. The aunt told him: "Oh! my father, you will be impotent at your father's, in Tubondo; you, (just) yesterday's child, born just a while ago, is it you who will be capable of Tubondo, village with seven meeting places?[140] Iyangura! I had you taken out from within the drum; as far as I am concerned, I say 'No,' strongly; never again try to go alone; the lonely path is never nice." When Mwindo heard the way in which his aunt was speaking, he refused; he wiped out his aunt('s words) (by) humming to himself. The aunt told him: "You, (my) young man, to give birth to a son is to rest. Do not go to fight with

---

139 *wábǔme/a great man*: i.e., a full-fledged adult male, and not a boy as Kasiyembe called him. The song is a recurrent magic formula, that Mwindo uses to regenerate his enemies. The narrator, who is adorned with fiber armlets and is dancing with a *conga*-scepter (like the one the hero Mwindo is supposed to have), again identifies himself and his own dancing with Mwindo's actions.

140 *karamo karamǒ ka/hail! hail*: this is the current Nyanga greeting; *karamo* means health, salvation, life (good and long); *aé/yes* is the current answer after the greeting of *karamo*. *é titá/oh! my father*: father, mother, and paternal aunt currently call their own son or nephew "father" when they want to please him or to give him advice. *ubútwǎyo tété-tétéyo/born just a while ago*: rare usage of *tététété* normally meaning "fast."

your father; if you go, at any rate, then I also shall go with you
to see how your father will be cutting you into pieces." She went
to tell the maidens to pack up her household objects, so as to
go with Mwindo, because the lonely path is not nice; it never
fails to find something that could kill a man. When the sky
had become daylight, they had breakfast before the journey of
returning back to Tubondo. Mwindo went together with his
aunt, together with his servants who were chanting the refrain.
Mwindo sang:

> *Ntiriri-liana* has become *mubanga*-rope,
> And *musara*-liana has become a *mukendo*-bag.[141]
> Scribe, march!
> I am going over there to Tubondo;
> I shall fight over there in Tubondo,
> Even though Tubondo has seven entries.
> We are saying, oh Bira!
> Aunt, give me advice
> To fight with the people downstream;
> They carry spears and shields.
> In Ihimbi where dwelt Birori,
> I shall die (today), Mushumo.
> On Ntsuri-hill where dwelt Ruronga,
> (In) Munongo where dwelt Shecara,
> Bitumbi-hill of Shemene Ndura,
> And the old ones fight because of a wind.
> On Mbare-hill where dwelt Karai,
> He was the one who gives much tribute of words.
> Mbare-hill is together with Irimwe-hill, his kinsman,
> Tunkundu-hill is together with Nteko-hill, his kinsman.
> May I mention Mabura Banyore,
> Homeland of my mothers,
> Kabotyo Munyangoro
> Nyabuke Kamwikoti.[142]

---

[141] *mushŭkĭra/young man*: stress is on "growing"; currently used to
designate an adolescent. *ntiriri-liana has become . . .*, *mucara-liana has
become . . .*: these two lianas are not normally used to fabricate a carrying
rope or a shoulder bag; Mwindo intends to say that the order and balance
of events and actions are upset.

[142] The narrator again inserts personal recollections in Mwindo's song.
He speaks about Ihimbi, the area from where he comes, and about the
characters whom he met there or whose fame was well established, e.g.,
Birari, the diviner, and Karai, the daredevil. In the names mentioned here

Big legs ravaged Mpurwa,
And the baboon ruined Kamuri.[143]
Sky became day, I was (still) speaking
Like the sound (of) Mukuki.[144]
The sky in this village takes a long time to become day:
It is the single man who is cooking hard-to-cook food.[145]
Mikere-river is together with Mboru-river, his kinsman,
And Batoi-river is together with Tua-river, his kinsman.
Who will take me to Bukuca, to Ngara?
Mbuhi is of both Mutatea and Mwindo,
Kirambo is of Mamboreo.[146]
May the people of Ntande not regret (the lack of) meat,
(For) they have had a woman who fishes (with a net).
Mpinga (is) land
Whereas Nkasa is the natal village of Burongo
And of Mwindo.
May the Batembo not regret (the lack of) meat.
They hold Mutumba and Kunju.[147]
And Birere-hill of Rukobakoba;
I cannot fish with the Baroba.
From Europe there come (all kinds of things)!
The sun is setting downstream

---

there are many *quid pro quo*'s, e.g., Kabotyo Munyangoro, Nyabuke Kam-wikoti: we consider these to be the double names of two individuals, a male and a female; in fact, a valid interpretation could also be the following: Kabotyo of the Nyangoro group, she who is famed (*nya-*) for the beads around the neck. *shé-mutúro wábinwa/who gives much tribute of words*: this is not to praise, nor is it to criticize the individual who speaks too much, but refers to one who gives tribute in words, one who is helpful because of his skill as judge and speaker.

[143] *Cámwindí/big legs*: praise name for an elephant. Mpurwa and Ka-muri are names of estates.

[144] *Mukuki*: one of the Nyanga closed associations.

[145] This is a frequently heard proverb that evokes the sad fate of the single man.

[146] The narrator refers to certain rivers that are the limits of the landed estates controlled by descent groups to which he is personally linked. In mentioning the mountain Mbuhi, he designates one of the limits between the Nyanga and the Funa (a subgroup of the Hunde tribe); part of this mountain is in Nyanga control, part belongs to the Funa.

[147] *a woman who fishes (with a net)*: women normally fish with baskets and participate in communal fishing with poison, *buróngo/land*: Nyanga-ized Swahili word for soil, land. In two consecutive verses the word is used both as the generic term for land and as the name of a person. *Batembo*: one of the descent groups found in Nyanga country.

From the Batika-Rukari.
Maere, little girl of Rukunja,
Maere, what did you eat when you came?
I have not eaten anything extraordinary;
I have eaten a goat for sharing purposes,
And I also ate *mususa*-vegetables (picked in) the village.
They were full of sand and slime.
To a trap that is not well set
Katiti-pigeon (only) leaves its tail.
The *nkurongo*-birds of this village are mean;
The *nkurongo*-birds, as soon as they have seen people,
Flutter (their) tails.
In Kumbukumbu of the Batobo
Where dwelt Nkuru and Rukari.[148]

Mwindo sang:

Scribe, march!
I am going with the aunt.
The Little-one has slept all prepared for the journey.
Oh! my father, the Little-one set out right after awakening.
(I warn you) we are already underway, we,
To Bat of the Baniyana.[149]

---

[148] *Burăȳa/Europe*: Nyangaized Swahili word. *mpéné kishăngire/a goat for sharing purposes*: i.e., a goat or other animal that is not the object of taboos or prescriptions concerning who can eat from it and under what circumstances it can be eaten (chickens are never in the category of *kishăngire* because there are strict prescriptions for in-laws concerning their distribution). The narrator is complaining that he did not get a special hospitality gift, i.e., that he was compelled to eat with the others. *mususa-vegetables*: a vegetable that is a major ingredient for Nyanga dishes. Some are grown behind the houses, like the one referred to here; others are grown in the banana groves. The latter are much more appreciated; the former are used only when one is in a hurry or short of supplies. The narrator complains again about the kind of food he has received. As noted, most of the verses of this song have nothing to do with the story, but are merely the narrator's personal reflections about people, landed estates, stories. He also expresses his frustration at the lack of consideration with which he is being treated.

[149] *twară twendănge băte (I warn you) we are already underway, we*: lit., we are eating we are going; the expression *twară* and the verb to go are often used to say that one is already on his way, that one is going without further delay. The image conveyed here is that whereas people normally sit down quietly to eat, at this point there is no question of sitting; one is moving and can only hurriedly take a bit of food from a friend or relative while passing through the village.

During this journey that Mwindo was making in spite of all with his aunt, evening went to find him at his maternal uncles, the Baniyana. He slept there after they had killed a goat of hospitality for him. After he, together with his paternal aunt and the servants of the aunt, had eaten that goat, Mwindo said to his maternal uncles: "I am going to fight Shemwindo in Tubondo; forge me, you [who are] blacksmiths of large light spears, you my uncles.[150] The Baniyana said that they were going to forge him. They dressed him in shoes made entirely of iron and pants of iron; they also forged him an iron shirt and a hat of iron. They told him: "Since you are going to fight your father, may the spears that they will unceasingly hurl at you go striking on this iron (covering) that is on (your) body." After the uncles had finished forging him, they said that they could remain no more; they would be going with him so that they might see the way in which they would knead him. In the morning, Mwindo began the journey together with his uncles and his aunt Iyangura, and the servants of his aunt. Mwindo went singing, he howled, he said:

> I shall fight over there at Shemwindo's.
> The cattle that Shemwindo possesses,
> May they join Mwindo.
> Oh! scribe, march!

When they were on the point of arriving there, when they already had the village in sight, Mwindo's aunt said to Mwindo: "Oh! my father, let's get out of here, look how there is dizziness over there in your father's village; Tubondo over there is a village of seven ways out; there are many people over there; they will destroy us." Mwindo answered his aunt: "I, Mwindo, I never am afraid of a big child with whom I have not yet fought; I want to try this Shemwindo out first; he is too much spoiled by pride."[151] Mwindo went on, singing:

---

[150] *forge me*: the hero asks that his maternal uncles *forge him*, i.e., make him strong and resistant. The image of the hero being forged occurs in other tales. The bats are always represented as blacksmiths because, as the Nyanga say, of the kinds of sounds and excrements they produce.

[151] *pantaró/pants*; *shịmịshị/shirt*: Nyangaized French words *pantalon* and *chemise*, respectively. *nkobịra/hat*: Nyangaized Kingwana word *kofia* (*kofera*, hat). *look how there is dizziness over there* . . . : the dizziness is felt by the onlookers when they are in the glen and look up the hill at the huts built on the steep crest.

We are going over there to Tubondo
Where dwelt Shemwindo.

When they arrived in the glen, he said: "Let us spend the
night in this village." His aunt howled, she said: "Where will
we sleep, here there is no house? Lo! Kiruka-nyambura has arrived, bearer of rain that never ceases."[152] The aunt shouted,
she said: "Oh! my father, where shall we sleep? The rain has
just rumbled, (the) young woman is destitute."[153] Mwindo
looked around, he said that he wanted (to have) houses: (and)
the houses built themselves. Mwindo said that his uncles
(should take) that row there, and his aunt that other row; and
Mwindo's house planted itself in the middle of them. His aunt
shouted saying: "Yes, my father Mwindo, hail for (these) [our]
houses. Lo! Shemwindo has brought forth a hero: Kahombo,
my father, I shall give you (some) paste. Let us go with our
prestigious man; may our prestigious man escape thunder and
lightning![154] Shemwindo brought forth a hero who is never
afraid, and Mwindo himself is a hero."[155] When they were there

---

152 *Where dwelt Shemwindo*: in his vision of things to happen, Mwindo
sees his father's village already destroyed and his father fleeing. *Kiruka-
nyambura*: lit., Kiruka, she who drags along rain; the Nyanga believe that
rain is caused by an old woman who lives in the sky.

153 *munyeré/the young woman*: a word of the Hunde vocabulary (*mun-
yére*): the high tone has been placed on the last syllable to enhance the
ironic effect of her exclamation.

154 *mutangá/row*: technical term for a row of huts. *muraj/hero*: the
term emphasizes the idea of strength and aggressiveness; e.g., bees may be
called *baraj*; the soldiers introduced by the Europeans also went under
that name. *Kahombo*: the name of the spirit of good fortune; Iyangura
uses the term here to praise Mwindo as a benefactor. *I shall give you some
paste*: when a young woman says this to her father, she means that she will
bear children, her father's grandchildren on whose behalf he will eat
banana paste during the ablution ceremonies. *karáni witu/our prestigious
man*: lit., our clerk; it is a Nyangaized Kingwana word. In the rural com-
munity the position of clerk (i.e., a man with some degree of education)
had become synonymous with status and prestige.

155 *Shemwindo brought forth a hero . . . and Mwindo himself is a hero*:
a double meaning is contained in these words. On the one hand Iyangura
praises both Shemwindo and Mwindo (she always manifests respect and
a kind of awe for her brother, and is therefore torn between her love for
Mwindo and her attachment to Shemwindo). On the other hand, Iyangura
seems to state that Mwindo does not merely owe his herioc qualities to
being the son of Shemwindo.

in the glen, the houses having built themselves, Mwindo's aunt said to him: "Oh! my father Mwindo, let us get away; you are powerless against this mass of people who are in Tubondo." Mwindo said that first he would try. Iyangura, Mwindo's aunt, said to him: "Oh! my father Mwindo, what shall we eat then? Look! the great number of your uncles here, and I too, Iyangura, have a line of people, and you, Mwindo, you have drummers and singers with you; what will this whole group eat?" Mwindo, hearing what his aunt had just told him, agreed, saying: "You are not lying, [you] my aunt; I see that the whole group that is with us is already hungry." He lifted his eyes to the sky; he said to himself that he first wanted to have all the food that was over there in Tubondo come; so (the food) having joined him, he would go to fight with them. Mwindo sang while transporting the food that was with his father. His aunt shouted, she said: "Oh! my father, what shall we eat (today)?" Mwindo howled, he sang:

> The pastes that are in Tubondo,
> May the pastes join Mwindo,
> Mwindo, the Little-one-just-born-he-walked.
> The animals that are in Tubondo,
> May the animals join Mwindo.
> The meats that Shemwindo stores,
> May the meats join Mwindo Mboru,
> Mwindo, the Little-one-just-born-he-walked.
> The wood that Shemwindo keeps,
> Oh! father, may it join Mwindo Mboru,
> For Mwindo is the Little-one-just-born-he-walked.
> And the fire that Shemwindo possesses,
> May the fire also join Mwindo.
> And the water that Shemwindo possesses,
> May the water also join Mwindo Mboru.
> The jars that are at Shemwindo's
> May the jars join Mwindo,
> Mwindo, the Little-one-just-born-he-walked.
> The clothes that are at Shemwindo's,
> May the clothes join Mwindo,
> Mwindo is going to fight!
> The wooden dishes that are in Tubondo,
> May the wooden dishes also join Mwindo,
> Oh father! the Little-one-just-born-he-has-walked

Hopes to be victorious.
The beds that Shemwindo possesses,
May the beds join Mwindo.
And the wicker plates that Shemwindo possesses,
May the wicker plates also join Mwindo.
And the salt that Shemwindo possesses,
May the salt also join Mwindo,
The Little-one-just-born-he-walked.[156]

It was in this way that Mwindo was speaking!

And the chickens that Shemwindo possesses,
May the chickens also join Mwindo.
The cheerleaders are in unison;
They thus having achieved unison long ago.
The cheerleaders are in unison;
They have achieved harmony in the middle of the village.
That which-will-die and that which-will-be-saved,
May it join Iyangura here,
Iyangura, sister of Shemwindo.
The goats that are at Shemwindo's,
May the goats join Mwindo.
The cattle that are in Tubondo,
May the cattle join Mwindo.
The cattle bellowed, saying,
"Oh father! let us join Mwindo."
The dogs that are in Tubondo,
May the dogs join Mwindo.
The dogs barked, saying,
"Oh father! let us join Mwindo."
We are seated, stretching out our voices
Like the diggers of pits (for trapping).
The banana groves that are in Tubondo,
May the banana groves join Mwindo.
And the tobacco also that is at Shemwindo's,
May the tobacco also join Mwindo.
The *mukusa*-asp swallowed froth;
Anger is in the heart.
And the pipes that Shemwindo possesses,

---

[156] This song gives a short inventory of some of the most significant items in the diet and the technology of the Nyanga. The idea of ownership is rendered by the verbs *kuba na* (to be with) and *ibika* (to keep, to guard, to have in trust, to stock, to lay down).

May the pipes also join Mwindo.
The spears that are at Shemwindo's,
May the spears join Mwindo.
The adzes that are at Shemwindo's,
May the adzes join Mwindo.
The billhooks that are at Shemwindo's,
Oh father! may the billhooks join Mwindo;
May there be none left to go gardening.
The pruning knives that are at Shemwindo's,
May the pruning knives join Mwindo,
Little pruning knife, little scraper of *mbubi*-lianas.
May the little pruning knife join Mwindo.
The little dog bells that Shemwindo possesses,
May the little dog bells join Mwindo;
May there be nobody left to go hunting.
The bags that Shemwindo possesses,
May the bags also join Mwindo.
The razors that Shemwindo possesses,
May the razors also join Mwindo;
May there be nobody left who is shaved.
The *butea*-rings that Shemwindo possesses,
Oh father! the *butea*-rings,
May they be ready to join Mwindo;
May there be nobody left who wears (them).
The necklaces that Shemwindo possesses,
May the necklaces also join Mwindo;
May there be nobody left who wears (them).
The needles that Shemwindo possesses,
May the needles also join Mwindo;
May there be nobody left to do hook work.
The fire drill that Shemwindo possesses,
May the fire drill also join Mwindo;
May there be nobody left who makes fire.
The hoes that Shemwindo possesses,
Oh father! the hoes,
May they join Mwindo;
May there be nobody left who hoes.
The pots that Shemwindo possesses,
May the pots also join Mwindo;
May there be nobody left who cooks.
The baskets that Shemwindo possesses,
May the baskets join Mwindo;
May there be nobody left who goes to work.

The *mumanga*-piercer that Shemwindo possesses,
May the *mumanga*-piercers join Mwindo;
May there be nobody who bores shafts.
Let us recite from the story
That the Babuya are used to reciting.
The *bisara*-billhooks that Shemwindo possesses,
May the *bisara*-billhooks join Mwindo;
May there be nobody who prunes banana trees.
And the bellows that Shemwindo possesses,
May the bellows also join Mwindo;
May there be nobody left who smiths.
And the hammers that are at Shemwindo's,
May the hammers also join Mwindo;
May there be nobody who smiths.
And the blacksmiths whom Shemwindo has,
May the blacksmiths also join Mwindo;
May there be nobody who smiths.
The *nkendo*-knives that are in Tubondo,
The *nkendo*-knives that Shemwindo possesses,
May the *nkendo*-knives join Mwindo;
May there be nobody who plaits.
The raphia palm trees that are at Shemwindo's,
May the raphia palm trees join Mwindo;
May there be nobody who plaits
Or who traps.
And the drums that are in Tubondo,
Oh father! the drums,
May they join Mwindo;
May there be nobody who dances.[157]

Mwindo and his uncles and his aunt and the servants who
had arrived with them, the singers and the drummers, when
(the latter) opened their eyes—all the things that were in Tubondo at Shemwindo's (had) joined them there where they were.
When the aunt of Mwindo saw all those things, she said to her
son Mwindo: "Oh father! You will suffer because of those things

---

[157] This song continues the inventory of Nyanga material culture. In the
beginning, the inventory is interrupted by the narrator's praise for the
singers and percussionists who accompany him (*The cheerleaders are in
unison* . . .). *We are seated*: another reflection by the narrator about the
length of the story and his fear that it may become monotonous. *The
mukusa-asp*: reference to a story.

(belonging to) other people which you are gathering together."
Those who were with Mwindo in the vale were sick with the
indisposition of being gorged with food; they were not cold
any more; they refound (their) heat; they said: "Lo! Mwindo
is a man who does not lie when he says that he is the Little-one-
just-born-he-walked; he always has something to rely upon.[158]
The one who will try to climb on him will be the first to die
on the great road; he is not a man to provoke." When Mwindo
had seen that the things of his father had come to join him, he
said that his father (now) remained over there merely as a destitute person. He said to his aunt that he wanted his uncles to
go ahead and fight first, and that he, Mwindo, would remain
with his aunt for a while here in the vale so that he might first
see the way in which his uncles handled their force. After he
had thus sent his uncles out to go to fight, his uncles departed
to fight, and he remained with his aunt in the vale. Where his
uncles passed, they fought on land and in the air, but the
people of Tubondo said: "You will not solve the case today."[159]

After a while, Mwindo's uncles were completely wiped out;
they died; the people of Tubondo wiped them out. One of
Mwindo's uncles escaped in the middle of the war, being already seriously injured; he fled to Mwindo to report the news
to him. He arrived there and said: "There where we have gone,
the people of Tubondo have overcome us, all the people—your
uncles—are dried up." When Mwindo's aunt saw this messenger
—the blood had covered his whole body—and also heard the
news of how the people had completely dried up, she exclaimed:
"Oh, father Mwindo, I have told you that when I said that you
are helpless against the people of Shemwindo over there; you

---

[158] *kárịkịré kínyihiré/he always has something to rely upon:* lit., he is
sitting he thinks about himself, i.e., he is sure of his force.

[159] *to die on the great road:* i.e., to die in solitude and abandonment.
kihuhúru/a destitute person: lit., a man heavily intoxicated with beer.
bútịngengá . . . bátịnge/the way in which his uncles handled: interesting
syntactic construction found *passim* in the epic; translated, the duplication
of the verb with different prefixes and markers means: how they take/
handle (it) . . . when they take/handle (it). *ékwantsi n'ékwịyo/on land and
in the air:* everywhere; it is not to be understood as if the uncles were
flying. *mutûkeri ro/you will not solve the case:* lit., you will not cut it;
ro bears on the word *ubántsá,* case, palaver.

said, 'Not at all'; first pick up this *nkebe*-tooth here, this first achievement; look how they have been wiped out."[160] Mwindo said to his aunt: "I too, I shall go to find out first the reason why my uncles are all wiped out, and if Shemwindo does not come up face to face with me, then I am not Mwindo." His aunt said to him: "Oh, father Mwindo, don't! You will be the reason for which the whole group that has arrived with us (will) be wiped out. If you vex the people over there in Tubondo, then we are all on the verge of dying." Mwindo did not listen to the mouth of his aunt; he said that he was going to fight: "You, aunt, remain with my axe here and my little bag in which there is a rope; and I, Mwindo, am leaving with my *conga* here." Mwindo went. Where he headed, he went to climb up to Tubondo. As soon as the people of that village saw Mwindo arriving at the village entrance, they pointed him out; they said to Shemwindo: "See that little man alone there who makes his appearance at the village entrance through which the war came." Shemwindo answered his people: "What will a little man do all by himself? Even if he comes, we shall cut his throat so that he will die." His people answered him: "There from where *bisibisi*-insects emerge, one day red ants will issue; this one little man can make us run in this village without our being able to do anything against him." Shemwindo answered his people: "Let this little fool go swaggering toward the garbage heap." Mwindo emerged at the village entrance while singing; he agitated his *conga* round about. When Mwindo arrived in Tubondo, he got into the middle of the village; he said to the people of that village that he wanted to dance (to the rhythm of) a drum. The people of that village answered him: "You are helpless against our drums here, you (are a) little fool." Mwindo answered them that this was an insult, that he had not even had time to rest.[161] The people of that village told him that there was no drum there. To that Mwindo said that the drums would be coming. Mwindo went on speaking

---

[160] *mubándá/seriously injured*: used for an injured animal as well as for a human being. *bákusįka/are dried up*: *isįka* is said of water that is absorbed into the soil. *nkebe-tooth*: i.e., the first fruits of your efforts; this is said ironically.

[161] *he had not even had time to rest*: Mwindo expresses his surprise that they are so fast in challenging and slandering him.

in that way with the people of that village, his father being in his compound. Mwindo sang:

> He is climbing up here in Tubondo,
> He is going to fight with Shemwindo.

While he was singing, he went on enunciating (distinctly): "May what will die and what will be saved join Iyangura." He raised his voice to the sky, he sang:

> What will never die but will be saved,
> May it, oh father, join Iyangura,
> Iyangura, sister of Shemwindo,
> Mother mine of the cradling string.[162]
> Oh! father, what will die and will be saved,
> May it join its aunt,
> Sister of Shemwindo!
> My junior and my senior sisters,
> Be ready to join me.
> What will never die but will be saved,
> May it join Iyangura,
> Aunt, sister of Shemwindo.
> My senior brother, come,
> What will die and will be saved,
> May it join Aunt Iyangura.
> May you, oh my mothers, come!
> What will not die but be saved,
> May it join Aunt Iyangura.
> I die, oh Bira!
> What has been said will be said again.
> Let me fight here in Tubondo,
> Even if Tubondo has seven entrances.
> The counselors have hesitated (to counsel) Shemwindo.
> What will die and be saved,
> May it join Aunt Iyangura.
> The counselors retreated (before) Shemwindo.
> What will die and be saved,
> May it join Aunt Iyangura.

---

162 *nyámwako/mother . . . of the cradling-string*: this is the highest honorific name a person can give to his mother or aunt. Nyanga women carry their babies tied on their backs in a network of flat-woven raphia bands; these bands have an exceptional religious and emotional value and are said to be part of the child's personality.

Nkuba, my friend, may you be victorious.[163]
Hatred is in the heart.
When I shall have a bridge built for myself,
He who crosses it will cut himself.
I implored Aunt Iyangura,
Aunt Iyangura, may you be blessed.[164]

Mwindo shouted, saying:

Hatred is in the heart.
My friend, Nkuba, may you be victorious.
I shall fight here in Tubondo,
Even if Tubondo has seven entrances.
Here in Tubondo seven lightning flashes!
I shall fight here in Tubondo.
I want seven lightning flashes right now!
Mwindo reviewed (the causes of) his griefs;
The counselors retreated (before) Shemwindo.
The counselors did not know how to counsel.
It's you who will turn into dried leaves,
—In the river—
My father threw me into the drum.
I shall fight here in Tubondo;
May Tubondo turn into dried leaves,
Merely.
The counselors retreated (before) Shemwindo;
The counselors did not know how to counsel;
May the counselors turn into dried leaves.
My friend, Nkuba, may you be victorious.
Hatred is in the heart.
I implored Aunt Iyangura,
What will die and be saved,
May it join Iyangura,
Aunt, sister of Shemwindo.
My little fiery father,

---

163 *Botó ná bababá báni/My junior and my senior sisters: motó*, junior, can bear both on male or female siblings or parallel cousins; *babá* can bear only on senior female siblings or parallel cousins. We know that Mwindo had several sisters, all born before him of different wives of his father; it is implied that he also had junior brothers. *ubúráne* is a verb that has bearing on a secular trial in which no spirits are involved; it means to win a trial, to be acquitted.

164 *ukasananga/may you be blessed: ikasana* means to win the favor of the spirits.

> My little father threw me into the grave.
> My father believed that I would die;
> My little father threw me into the grave.
> My little father believed that I would die.
> If you believe that girls are (worthy) beings
> It is (because) oh father, they bring in goods.[165]

In his heart he was saying that girls were people worthier than he, that they transcended him; "You will find out (about it) today."

> Girls are (worthy) beings
> Oh, father, it is (because) they bring in goods.[166]
> Tubondo, seven lightning flashes!

Mwindo raised his eyes into heaven (and) said:

> My friend, Nkuba,
> Here in Tubondo seven lightning flashes!

While Mwindo was looking up into the sky, he (also) stretched his *conga* toward there. From the sky at Nkuba's, things came; there appeared seven lightning flashes; they descended on Tubondo in the village. Tubondo turned into dust, and the dust rose up; all who lived there turned into mere dust. Where Shemwindo was sitting in (his) compound, he exclaimed: "There is no time for lingering here." Having spoken like that, he went down behind the house; he went without looking back. Where he fled, he went to arrive where there was a *kikoka*-plant. He tore it out; he entered at its root's base. After he had become victorious in Tubondo, Mwindo praised himself in the middle of the village; he said: "This time the one who climbs on me, the one who digs into me while fighting with me, will be wearing himself out in vain." He spoke like this when the corpses of his uncles who were the first to die had

---

165 In this song, Mwindo predicts the coming destruction of his father's village; he asks for the help of the spirit of lightning and summarizes his grievances against his father and his father's counselors. He states that his father, because of his greed, had only wanted daughters, since they are the providers of marriage payments.

166 *bákéngi behe/they bring in goods*: *iké* means to rain; *iké behe* is a stereotyped expression to designate the process of providing and receiving marriage payments.

already begun to decay. Mwindo went down to where his aunt had remained in the glen in order that they would rise up to the peak. He arrived at his aunt's; the aunt asked him: "Good news there from where you are coming?"[167] Mwindo answered her that Tubondo was on fire. He also told them: "Now let's go up to Tubondo which is high up; let's get away from here in the glen."[168] When the aunt began preparing her belongings, Mwindo forbade her; he said to her: "Leave the things; they themselves will join us over there in Tubondo." Having spoken like that, he went, and his aunt followed him together with the group of servants who had come with them. They climbed up to Tubondo; they arrived there. When they were already in Tubondo, the things that they had left in the glen joined them. Mwindo said that he could not chase his father so long as he had not resuscitated his uncles. He woke them up beating them (with his) *conga* and singing:

> He who went to sleep awakes,
> My uncle, my mother, wake up.
> I have been testing the Baniyana.
> My uncle, my mother, forge me![169]
> Shemwindo, you are powerless against Mwindo,
> Mwindo is the Little-one-just-born-he-walked.
> My uncle, my mother, forge me.
> You are a blacksmith of light spears.

Mwindo finished waking up all his maternal uncles; they resuscitated. Where Shemwindo had fled, he went harming himself running into everything; he went to arrive at Musia's,

---

167 *kikoka-plant*: a kind of fern that grows in the forest and is found in the clearing around the villages. The Nyanga use the plant for brewing beer and in various magical contexts. In tales, heroes and other characters are said to hide in this plant or, more often, to go underground by entering it. *mahyó/good news*: a Hunde word for greeting.

168 *kwákangámá/which is high up*: *ịkangama*, to be taller, in a comparison between two people.

169 *nashiángá/I have been testing*: this seems a logical interpretation, since his maternal uncles had earlier challenged Mwindo saying that they would accompany him to see him beaten by Shemwindo. The verb used here is either *ishia*, to test, to put to proof, or *ishia*, to give allegiance to a chief or other person. The latter interpretation also makes sense, since Mwindo is a sororal nephew of the Baniyana and can consider himself to be their subject.

93

the place where no one ever clusters around the fire.[170] In
Tubondo, where Mwindo settled with his aunt, with his uncles,
and with his servants, singers, and drummers, he told them:
"Let's join Shemwindo whither he headed to Muisa's; let us
go in search of him." His aunt handed over to him his bag in
which there was the rope; she also handed over to him his axe,
whereas he still clasped his *conga*, he its owner. Mwindo said
to his aunt: "You, my aunt, remain here in this village in
Tubondo with these uncles here and the group of singers and
drummers, along with whom we came; because you are used
to eating terrestrial foods, you are not capable of all the ad-
ventures and the dangers that I am used to experiencing wher-
ever I pass."[171] Mwindo said to his aunt: "You, my aunt, you
stay here in the village of your birth, in Tubondo; here is the
rope; remain with one end, holding it in your hand, whereas
I shall follow my father where he fled to Muisa's; if (one day)
you feel that this rope has become still, if it does not move
anymore, then pay no more attention to where I have gone;
lo! the fire has dwindled; I am dead then." After he had spoken
like that, Master Sparrow alit where he was, he told him:
"Come here for me to show you the path that your father took
and where he entered at the base of the root of the *kikoka*-
plant; indeed, when your father fled, I, Sparrow, was on top
of the roof; your father fled while I was seeing him stumbling."
After Sparrow had given him the news, Mwindo in [his] leaving
said farewell to his aunt; he held one end of the rope and the
aunt remained holding (the other) end of the rope. Mwindo
rushed hurriedly toward the village exit. When he arrived at
the *kikoka*-plant, where his father had entered, he too pulled

---

170 *nti íyé wịcábiránge/harming himself running into everything*: ¡cába
literally means to cut (firewood); the reflexive form of the verb is often
used to describe the way in which an injured animal bumps against bushes
and trees. *Muisa*: one of the Nyanga divinities, who is said to live in a cold,
desolate, subterranean place where fire is unknown.

171 Before engaging in his subterranean peregrinations. Mwindo is compelled to leave his aunt and all his other companions behind, because they
do not have his supernatural gifts ("they eat terrestial foods"). He does,
however, remain in contact with his aunt by means of a rope. *ébiburá/
dangers*: lit., the fire sparks of the blacksmith's forge; the blacksmith is
said to be immune to them.

out the *kikoka*-plant; he entered at its base; he passed through; he went to appear at the well. Arriving there, he met Kahindo, daughter of Muisa.[172] Kahindo embraced him, saying: "This is my welcome, Mwindo." Mwindo in reply said "Yes." Kahindo was sick with yaws; the yaws started at her tooth and went up to the perineum; they descended the legs (and) went up to the toes of the sole of the feet.[173] When Mwindo tried to go through, Kahindo forbade, saying, "No, no." She said to him: "Where are you going?" Mwindo answered her that he was going to Muisa's to look for his father because it was here in this village of Muisa that he was. She told him again: "Stop first here where I am. Over there in Muisa's village one never goes through; is it you who will (succeed) in getting through there like that, with all (your) pride?" Kahindo said to Mwindo: "Now you are going to Muisa's. When you will have arrived there, having entered the meeting place, if you see a very big man and tall too, curled up in the ashes near the hearth, it is he who is Muisa; and if he greets you, if he says: 'Blessing (be) with you, my father,' you too will answer, 'Yes, my father'; and when he will have left you a stool, then you will refuse it; you will tell him: 'No, my father; will the head of a man's father become a stool?' When he will have handed over to you a little gourd of banana beer for you to drink, you will refuse, answering: 'No, my father, even though a person is one's child, is that a reason why he should drink the urine of his father?' After Muisa will have recognized you in that way, he will say to you: 'Blessing, blessing, Mwindo'; and you will answer him: 'And to you blessing, blessing also, father.' When he will have given you paste to eat, you will answer him: 'Even though a person is

---

172 *Kahindo*: the Hunde name for Kahombo, the female spirit of good fortune among the Nyanga. Both are also personal names given to males as well as to females who stand in a particular ritual relationship to this spirit.

173 *wámukókére/embraced him*: this form of greeting is normal between mother and child, but not, as here, between persons who are strangers to each other. *karibŭ nko/ this is my welcome*: *karibu* is a Swahili term for "come in." *binyóra/yaws*: children usually have them now; the disease is more rare in adults. To criticize somebody because of ingratitude, the Nyanga say: "I cured your yaws."

one's child, is that a reason why he should eat the excrements of his father?' "[174]

After Mwindo had heard Kahindo speaking these useful words to him, he said to himself that he could not leave without washing the yaws of Kahindo. Mwindo began washing the yaws of Kahindo; he smoothed them, taking away all the scabs of the yaws. After Mwindo had washed the yaws of Kahindo in that way, after he had also healed them entirely, Mwindo passed ahead of her; he went and climbed up to Muisa's; he arrived there and headed for the meeting place. Muisa, seeing him, greeted him with "Blessing." Mwindo answered, "Yes, my father." Muisa recollected: "Let them give a chair to Mwindo to sit on it."[175] Mwindo answered him: "Not at all, my father, even though a man is a guest, is that a reason for him to sit down on the head of his father?" Muisa also said that he had left a gourd of beer here: "Let me pour you a bit." Mwindo said: "No, my father, even though a man is a guest, is that a reason for him to drink the urine of his father?"[176] Muisa said: "Blessing, blessing, my father." Muisa again said: "Let them prepare some paste for you, oh Mwindo!" Mwindo answered him: "No, my father, even though a man is a guest, is that a reason for him to eat the excrements of his father?" Hearing that, Muisa said to him: "Blessing, blessing, Mwindo." Seeing Mwindo escape those ordeals, Muisa said to Mwindo: "Go and take a rest in the house there of your sister Kahindo."[177]

---

[174] tŏto/no, no: onomatopoeia used to forbid children to do something; kŏko/no would be a more general term. Both expressions are accompanied by a gesture of prohibition. From the use of tŏto, it is once again clear that Mwindo looks like a child. Similar ordeals for testing shrewdness are currently found in Nyanga tales. makangura/blessings: the verb ikangura designates the action of pulling at one's limbs and fingers in a Nyanga gesture of blessing or of well-wishing.

[175] wisubukia/recollected: the literal translation; the implication is that Muisa, stunned by his meeting with Mwindo, almost forgot to expose him to trickery, but reflected and then suddenly regained his self-control.

[176] In the answers given by Mwindo, which were recommended by Muisa's daughter, Mwindo changes mwana, child, to mweni, guest. The connotations of the terms are not far apart for mweni designates a known guest who is related.

[177] your sister Kahindo: the implication is not that Mwindo is related to her but rather that both are of about the same age.

Mwindo went inside. When he arrived in Kahindo's house, he
looked around in it; he saw Kahindo inside the house; Kahindo
had made herself like the anus of a snail in dressing up and in
rubbing herself with red powder and castor oil. Mwindo, seeing
her, was about to step back because of seeing sunbeams inside
the house. Kahindo, seeing him, said to him: "Come in, oh
Mwindo!"[178] Mwindo said: "May the one who remains behind
hurt himself, oh my sister!" When she saw that Mwindo had
entered into the house, she said to herself: "Lo!, Mwindo has
hunger." She got up, she went to make some paste, "a little
like that," of ashes.[179] After she had stirred it, she brought it to
Mwindo in her sacred hut.[180] When Muisa saw Kahindo bringing (the paste) to Mwindo, he dashed quickly toward the house
of his daughter; he went to spy where Mwindo was. He said to
Mwindo: "Oh, my father Mwindo, you are eating this food;
tomorrow, as soon as you are up and about, you will start cultivating a new banana grove for me; may you first cut leaves, then
plant the banana trees, then fell the trees; may you then cut
the newly grown weeds, then prune the banana trees, then prop
them up, then bring ripe bananas. It's after you will have performed all those works that I shall know to give you your
father."[181] After Muisa had spoken like that to Mwindo, he

---

178 *had made herself like the anus of a snail*: i.e., was very clean. *karibu/
come in*: derived from Swahili. It is not a Nyanga custom to use such
expressions when one wants to enter a house. If someone asks to come
in, the person inside the house simply says *aé/yes*.

179 *wásitaré/may [he] hurt himself*: Mwindo's answer can only be understood in terms of the confusion the narrator had deliberately created between the Swahili word *astarehe* (which the Nyanga pronounce as
sitarehe) and the Nyanga verb *isitara,* to injure oneself or to knock against.
In Swahili custom, the visitor answers *astarehe* (be at rest!) when the
person inside the house has permitted him to come in. *túrehě mpe/a
little like that*: this expression is accompanied by a gesture. *A paste made
of ashes*: this is the mythical food of Muisa, who lives in cold ashes.

180 *iremeso/sacred hut*: an oval-shaped hut dedicated by the Nyanga as
a shrine to the spirit Kahombo. Nyanga men, who are ritually married
to the spirit Kahombo, spend part of their time in it in the domestic
cycle of living alternately with different wives. They also receive their
guests in the hut.

181 Muisa rapidly enumerates the basic steps of banana-growing, using
an extremely precise technical vocabulary. *úseki na tó/then prop them up*:
tó (them, used in connection with *esâmpókó,* banana trees) is grammatically

also said to him: "When you leave for cultivating, I shall give you a man to observe the way in which you are performing the cultivation." After he had spoken like that, he left the doorway; he returned to his meeting place. Where Mwindo was sitting in the house, he started eating the paste. When the sky had become daylight, in the morning, Mwindo equipped himself with his billhook; Mwindo went to cultivate. Muisa picked out one man (who) accompanied Mwindo going to the fields. When they arrived in the forest, the man whom Muisa had picked out showed Mwindo a mountain with mango trees on it. Mwindo, seeing that mountain, placed the billhooks on the ground; all by themselves, they laid out the fresh trails.[182] Having finished the trail, they cut the grasses. Having cut the grasses, the banana trees planted themselves; the banana trees having planted themselves, Mwindo sent a bunch of axes down on them; the axes by themselves finished felling the trees. Finishing there, he sent a bunch of billhooks down on it; those billhooks went across the banana grove cutting the newly grown weeds.[183] Where the companion of Mwindo was sitting, he returned to Muisa. When he arrived there, he brought Muisa the news, saying: "This time he there is not (merely) a cultivator; he is fast, a cultivator of marvelous things; he has not touched one iron tool; the iron tools themselves are cultivating—and felling trees and cutting weeds." Having given the news, he returned again where Mwindo was on the fresh banana field. Where Mwindo was, the billhooks having finished cutting their weeds, they now cut gaffs; the gaffs themselves propped up the banana trees. The gaffs having finished sustaining the trees, the banana stems were ripe. The companion ran to bring the news to Muisa. He arrived there and said to Muisa: "It is not

incorrect. The correct form *só* is always avoided by the Nyanga, because it is also the term for "your father." The patterns of euphemistic speech compel the avoidance of the ambiguous usage of this word. *he went to spy*: it is considered bad for a father to spy on his unmarried daughter.

182 *mango trees*: i.e., trees hard to fell. *mikandé/fresh trails*: when planting a new banana grove, the Nyanga first clear two narrow trails that stand perpendicular to each other, then they cut the brush in such a way as to form the third side of a triangle with the cut grasses.

183 The various sequences of agricultural activities are correctly described: the Nyanga fell the trees *after* planting the stipes; they do not burn.

a man who is there; he has cultivated today; the banana trees already have stems and the bananas already (are) ripe."[184] He also said to Muisa that Mwindo was already on his way (with) that stem of bananas. Hearing this, Muisa said: "Lo! this boy here will (manage to) get through again there in the forest; I went to sleep after having deceived him in the evening, (but) he got himself loose; he has escaped that danger; and today I have again tested him, (but) here he is about to escape again." Having thus been astonished (because of) Mwindo, Muisa sent his *karemba*-belt of cowries over there; he said to it: "You, my *karemba*, you are going to Mwindo; when you will have seen him, you will have to bend him, then you will have to smash his mouth against the ground." *Karemba*, having heard the way in which it had been instructed by its master, went to the banana grove. When it saw Mwindo in the banana grove cutting up the banana stems on which there were ripe bananas, it went to where he was; it fell upon him where he was; it made Mwindo scream; it crushed him; it planted his mouth against the ground—froth came out; he lacked the way of getting his breath out; urine and excrements agreed (to get out); they lacked the one who could remove them. Having seen its master missing all means of getting out, Mwindo's *conga* recalled (its duty); it wagged itself above the head of Mwindo; Mwindo succeeded in sneezing; he raised his eyes upward; he opened his eyes; he raised them; he gazed about a little. After Mwindo had been wedged by Muisa's *karemba*, the rope became still, it did not move any more. Where his aunt had remained in Tubondo, where she had held one end of the rope, she threw herself down saying that lo! her son was dead. She uttered a cry, low and high, imploring the divinities, she said: "It is the one who will escape there who is (my) child."[185] Where Mwindo was, when he lifted up (his) eyes, he sang:

---

184 This, like the preceding passage, is exceptionally precise in the use of technical terms and in the correct description of labor sequences, for example, *n'esâmbú ŷé mbuŷa na/and the bananas already are ripe*: *mbú* is the generic term for edible bananas, *mbuŷa* the generic term for any ripe banana.

185 The narrator first describes fully in colorful language what happens to Mwindo: how he is beaten by Muisa's belt and saved by his *conga*-scepter. He then turns to the effects that Mwindo's seeming death had upon

Muisa slaughtered Mwindo,
I shall die, oh Bira!
Muisa, you are helpless against Mwindo,
Against Mwindo, the Little-one-just-born-he-has-walked.

Mwindo, while singing, remembered his aunt: "You there in Tubondo, I had already felt that my rope did not move, that it had become still because Muisa had already wedged me; he had wrapped me up like a bunch of bananas; but don't suffer from anxiety any more, there where you are, because my hope has just warned you (that) I am saved. It is my *conga* that set me up again." Having reported the news to his aunt in recollecting her, Mwindo now sent his *conga* to Muisa in the village, saying: "You, my *conga*, when you will have arrived where Muisa is in the village, you will have to smash him with force; you must plant his mouth to the ground; his tongue must penetrate inside the earth; so long as I shall not be back, so long as I shall not have come there into the village, you should not have released him again." The *conga* went whirling around; when it arrived at Muisa's meeting place, it smashed him; it planted his mouth to the ground; the tongue dug into the earth; urine and excrements lacked *mpunga*-leaves, and the one who would take them away was also missing; breath found no way of coming out.[186] Where Mwindo remained in the banana grove, he prepared a load of green bananas together with ripe bananas. He returned to the village. When he

---

his aunt. *She threw herself down*: a normal manifestation of sorrow. *émuréngé émwįhį n'émore/a cry, low and high*: lit., a cry, nearby and far, or a cry, short and long. This expression is currently used to say that one does his best, exhausts all means. *It is the one who will escape there who is (my) child*: in her imploration to the divinities, the aunt means to say that in whatever shape Mwindo may return to her after this beating, she will care for him.

186 *įsįrį/anxiety*: lit., bad omens. The passage implies that Iyangura and Mwindo are not only linked by a liana, but that there is some kind of mystical, telepathic bond between them for Mwindo is said to inform his aunt about his salvation by merely thinking about her (*wásubukia, mwimumbukia*). The paternal aunt who acts as an advisor is the protagonist in Nyanga dreams. Tales frequently suggest that persons lost in the forest hear the voice of their paternal aunt (represented as a reed flute, *mpingú*) giving advice and warnings. *mpunga-leaves*: the Nyanga version of toilet paper.

cast his eyes at the meeting place, he saw Muisa—foam had come out of his mouth and nostrils. Kahindo, Muisa's daughter, seeing Mwindo, hurried to the place where he was; she told him: "You are arriving, whereas my father here has already cooled off." Mwindo answered Kahindo that he had come here looking for his father: "Now give me my father here, so that I may go home with him." Kahindo answered him: "Begin first by healing my father, so that I know how to unveil your father, so that I may give him to you." Mwindo sang while awakening Muisa:

> He who went to sleep wakes up.
> Muisa, you are powerless against Mwindo,
> Because Mwindo (is) the Little-one-just-born-he-walked.
> Kahombo, whom Muisa brought forth,
> He-who-is-accustomed-to-mocking-himself.
> Muisa, you are helpless against Mwindo.
> A bit of food, thanks, puts an end to a song.[187]

Mwindo went on singing like that while beating Muisa incessantly on the head with his *conga* in order to wake him up. When Musia had awakened, when he was safe, he said: "You, Mwindo, lo! you also are a man." Muisa also said to Mwindo: "You, child, go as soon as you are awake to extract for me my honey which is in that tree there." Mwindo complained: "This time I am dead once more."[188] After Mwindo had been shown that honey by Muisa so as to set out in the early morning to extract (it), sky became night. Kahindo stirred paste for Mwindo; Mwindo ate it. Having eaten the paste, they went to partake in sleep. When the sky had become day, in the morning, Mwindo provided himself with his axe; he went ahead into the forest to extract the honey; he also took fire. When he arrived at the base of the tree, he climbed (up into) the tree; he went to arrive at the fascicle where the honey was; he called: "Is

---

[187] *ịsịsa/cool off*: like food; euphemistic for to die. *A bit of food, thanks, puts an end to a song*: the narrator is invited to go to eat and thanks his host.

[188] *wáhend'ịkundo/ go as soon as you are awake to extract honey*: the verb *ịhénda* followed by verbs like to eat, to go, and so on, designates an activity undertaken in the early morning, shortly after awakening. *nakwịré/I am dead*: complaint currently uttered by women to express suffering, hardship.

this the place?" They answered him: "There it is; 'Lo! he will be able to handle it.' " Mwindo poked up the fire for it. He struck his axe at the tree; he sang:

I am extracting honey in Muisa's (country);
Kabumbu-woodpecker is hanging in the high emptiness.
Women-who-are-lingering-on-the-other-side-of-the river, listen (to)
The way in which the little female forger of words is speaking.[189]
My friend Nkuba, may you be victorious.
Hatred is in the heart.
My little father threw me into the drum into the river;
My father believed that I would fade away.

Where Muisa remained in the village, he said: "Lo! this man will finally extract this honey!" Muisa sent his *karemba*-belt; it went and smashed Mwindo on the tree; it planted his mouth into the trunk of the tree; his breath could not get out; urine and excrements trickled down from him.

Where his aunt Iyangura was, the rope reminded her, she said that lo! her son was dead. This rope had again become still. Where Mwindo (had) left his *conga* down on the ground, the *conga* realized that lo! its master was dead; it climbed up where he was; it went to beat and beat on the head of Mwindo. Mwindo sneezed; he lifted his eyes and a bit of breath came out. Mwindo said: "Lo! while I was perched, lo! I was on the verge of death." When he had opened his eyes, he implored his friend Nkuba; he sang:

My friend Nkuba, be victorious.
Hatred is in the heart.

In climbing down (from the tree), he implored Nkuba, he gazed into the sky: "My friend Nkuba, I am suffering." When

---

[189] *they went to partake in sleep*: the context (she prepared food for him) and the form *bénda* (they went) seem to imply that Mwindo slept with Kahindo, although it would have been normal and less ambiguous to add euphemistic expressions for the idea of having intercourse. *wákúmányie kashá/poked up the fire*: the verbal phrase describes literally Mwindo putting pieces of dried wood and leaves together, burning them in order to smoke out the bees. *Kabumbu-woodpecker is hanging in the high emptiness*: Mwindo compares himself to the toughness of the woodpecker who makes holes in the trees. *nya-kési kábinwa/the little female forger of words*: women who are talkative, but speak skillfully, receive this epithet.

Nkuba heard the cry of his friend Mwindo, he came down onto
the tree; he cleaved it into pieces. His friend Mwindo went
down, (but) he did not have a single wound. When he was
down with the basket of honey, he went up to Muisa's with
the honey. He arrived there; he placed the honey basket down
for him saying that there was the honey, but that he wanted
him to give him his father. Muisa hearing this sent a boy to
look for the place where he had hidden Shemwindo. The boy
arrived there whereas Shemwindo was no longer there; lo! it
was Muisa who had warned Shemwindo that he should flee
to Ntumba's. Having looked for the place where Shemwindo
had hidden himself, and having seen that there was no one
there, the boy returned to Muisa and Mwindo; he arrived
there; he told them: "You, you are sitting here (while) Shemwindo has fled; he is not in the place where he was (before)."
Kahungu came; he gave Mwindo the news: "Your companion
Muisa lies; it is he who has warned your father to flee to
Ntumba's, saying that you are too tough."[190] After Kahungu
had told Mwindo the news in that manner, he flew away into
the sky. Where Mwindo and Muisa remained, Mwindo told
him the truth bluntly. "Give me my father on the shot. Make
him come out from where you have hidden him so that I may
go with him; oh! you are like that, (are you) you scoundrel?
You (had) said that when I would have cultivated a field for
you, when I would have extracted honey for you, you would
then give me my father. I want you to take him out right now;
don't let the saliva dry up without having taken him out."
When Muisa heard how Mwindo was criticizing him, he
twitched his eyes; he said: "This time, this boy makes my belly
swell here in my own village."[191]

---

190 Although the verbal forms used here leave some uncertainty, it seems
quite sure that in this and the preceding passages neither Mwindo nor
Muisa really die; the verb *injnke* means to faint, and *ikurd*, as well as meaning to die, covers a broad range of sufferings. The verb *ihúhúka*, to draw
the last breath, which is not used here, would clearly have signified that
they were really dead. It may be assumed that they were in a kind of deep
sleep, a torpor, unconscious because of the beatings they had received.
Ntumba is a personification of the aardvark, a rare and sacred animal for
the Nyanga.

191 *this boy makes my belly swell*: i.e., is a serious nuisance. The expression is related to the drinking of poison during ordeals.

Having seen that Muisa did not bring his father out, Mwindo beat Muisa on top of his head with his *conga*; Muisa, excrements stuck to the buttocks; he fainted away; urine ran all over the ground; froth came out from his nose and eyes (and) covered his face; he tossed his hoofs up into the air; he stiffened like a *mukusa*-viper.[192] Mwindo said: "Stay like that, you dog"; he would heal him when he would be back from where he was going. Mwindo went in pursuit of his father, where he had gone to Ntumba's. Mwindo went on singing:

> I am searching for Shemwindo
> In the place where Shemwindo went.
> Shemwindo fled into Ntumba's dwelling,
> Into Muisa's dwelling.
> I am searching for Ntumba's dwelling,
> For Munundu's dwelling.
> Ntumba, open for me.
> Shemwindo has set a barrier inside Munundu's dwelling;
> Shemwindo is in flight inside Ntumba's dwelling.
> I am searching for my father Shemwindo
> In Ntumba's, in Munundu's dwelling.
> The sun sets down.
> I am searching for Shemwindo;
> Shemwindo is in flight inside Ntumba's dwelling,
> Inside Munundu's.
> My little father threw me into the drum.

Mwindo implored Nkuba, saying:

> My friend Nkuba, may you be victorious.
> Hatred is in the heart.
> My little father, the dearest one,
> I am searching for my father in Ntumba's dwelling,
> In Munundu's.
> My friend Nkuba, may you be victorious,
> Hatred is in the heart.
> I am looking for my little father, the dearest one.
> My little father threw me into the drum,
> My little father, eternal malefactor among people.

---

192 *wáhúhúka/he fainted away*: the verbal form used here and the description (*he tossed his hoofs up. . . , he stiffened*) means that Muisa really dies.

My little father shot me into the river.[193]
Ntumba, open for me,
I am looking for my little father, the dearest one.

While Mwindo was still pacing around Ntumba's cave where
his father was, and Ntumba from the inside (at first) paid no
attention (to him), then Ntumba made a sign to Shemwindo,
saying: "You be ready to go; the little male at the door here is
strong, and you are witnessing the way in which he is threatening at the entrance of the cave."[194] When Shemwindo heard
the way in which his son toughened himself at the entrance of
the cave, he said: "The little boy comes (to us) with severity."
He said to his friend Ntumba that he was fleeing. Shemwindo
went to escape to Sheburungu's. Where Nkuba was in the
sky, when he heard the voice of his friend, he said: "My friend
is already too tired of beseeching me." Nkuba sent down seven
lightnings; they descended into Ntumba's cave; they cleaved it
into a million pieces; the cave turned into mere dust; the dust
flew up. Realizing that his friend Nkuba had cleft the cave,
Mwindo opened the door; he entered the interior of the cave;
he looked and looked for his father here and there inside the
cave; he did not see him. He met Ntumba inside; he told him:
"You, Ntumba, where did you let my father go, where have
you hidden him?" Ntumba kept silent as though he had not
heard. Mwindo spit saliva at him, saying: "Get out, you
scoundrel! Lo! (while) I was laboring at the door asking that
you open for me, you refused. May you die of scrotal elephan-
tiasis." When Ntumba witnessed the way in which Mwindo
continued blaming him because of his father, saying that he
had made him flee, he said to Mwindo: "You see how my
house was just destroyed and all my crops; what shall I do

193 *Munundu*: lit., the lair of an aardvark, but given here as an epithet
for Ntumba, the aardvark. *katitá kashé-karúo/my father, the dearest one*:
lit., my little father, the little possessor of the ladle. This is a common
honorific term for father, but, as is clear from the context and also from
the diminutive, pejorative *ka-* prefix, it is used sarcastically here. *kashé-
mungó/eternal malefactor*: in Nyanga, the morpheme *shé-* (lit., his father)
is employed in widely different contexts to indicate ownership, association,
mastery, and control over. *kándása/shot me*: *irása* is to shoot an arrow.
194 *kákarámá/is strong*: ikarama, to harden an animal hide by drying
it in the sun.

then?" Mwindo said: "You are crazy; don't make me smell
your breath where I am! So! that's what you are like!" Where
Kahungu dwelt in the sky, he came down; he went to bring
the news to Mwindo; he arrived saying: "You know, you
Mwindo, that Ntumba has made your father escape; your father
has fled to Sheburungu's." Kahungu, having brought Mwindo
the news again, flew away into the sky. Where Mwindo remained at Ntumba's—because of anger and weariness—he said
to Ntumba: "You Ntumba, that is the (death) you will die;
may you never again find food in this country of yours." Having
spoken to him in that way, he went to where his father had
gone; he went in search of him. Where his aunt Iyangura dwelt
in Tubondo, she went on pondering sadly saying: "My heart
will be back only when Mwindo will be back from where he
has gone."[195] She looked at the rope that she was holding; she
said: "Lo! Mwindo is still going in search of the place where
his father went." Where Mwindo continued to follow his father,
going in search of him all wrapped up in hatred, he went to
arrive at the entrance of Sheburungu's village. He met little
children there; they greeted him, saying: "Are you awake, oh
Mwindo?"[196] Mwindo answered them: "Yes." After the youngsters had greeted Mwindo, they told him: "You, Mwindo, don't
draw ahead of us; we are hungry; we ask you for food." Mwindo
implored his aunt Iyangura to send him food (telling her) that
the children of Sheburungu were hungry. While asking for
food from his aunt, Mwindo sang. Mwindo howled, he said:

> Oh! father, where Iyangura remained,
> Sister of Shemwindo,
> I claim seven portions (of food).[197]
> You see where Mwindo passed,
> I am suffering from hunger.
> Aunt Iyangura,
> I am claiming meat.

---

[195] *Sheburungu*: commonly one of the epithets given to the creator god
Ongo.

[196] *ébusíbúké bútí nti wákumukanda*/[Mwindo was] *all wrapped up in
hatred*: in the Nyanga text hatred is personified, i.e., hatred literally made
a package of Mwindo.

[197] *bishá*/*portions of food*: lit., the complete, untouched contents of a
plate.

Mwindo had spoken in that way:

> I claim seven portions (of food).
> You see that I woke up and set out on my journey.
> Where my aunt remained,
> Again I claim seven portions (of food).
> Aunt, I have expressed my desire for meat.

Having implored his aunt, saying that he wanted seven pastes with meat to join him in the place where he was with the children of Sheburungu, when Mwindo looked up, the pastes were already there, having come from his aunt Iyangura. After the food had arrived, Mwindo gave it to the youngsters. The children of Sheburungu began eating the paste, while Mwindo was keeping company with them.[198] When the children had finished eating, Mwindo returned the wicker plates to his aunt Iyangura, saying to line them up in order for him to be able to climb up to Sheburungu's, the household utensils having finished returning.[199] Mwindo sent back the wicker plates, singing:

> I send back the wicker and wooden plates.
> Oh! Aunt Iyangura,[200]
> I send back the wicker and wooden plates.

After he had sent back the wicker and wooden plates, he proceeded to climb up to Sheburungu's, and the youngsters followed him.[201] He went up to Sheburungu's, singing:

---

198 *nti watékésá bo/he was keeping company with them*: lit., to be a mere onlooker while others eat. The idea of nonparticipation in a specific activity is expressed by many different Nyanga verbs.

199 It is altogether normal for Mwindo to insist on returning the dishes to his mother before he continues his search for his father. It is a strict custom among the Nyanga to return all empty plates to their places immediately after the meal is finished. Nyanga men eat together, separately from their wives and young children; in the men's hut they share the various meals prepared by their respective wives. As soon as they are finished eating, the empty plates are sent back to their wives' houses for fear that ill-inspired sorcerers may use the remaining food particles against them. A housewife is always uneasy so long as the plates have not been returned.

200 *Mahime/oh!*: the meaning of this expression varies according to its tones and the context in which it occurs. It introduces a question: Is it not true? Don't you agree? It stands at the beginning of an imploration: Pity! Mercy! It is used in arguments to say: you are my witness.

201 It is customary for children playing at the outskirts of the village to follow arriving visitors. Moreover, Mwindo himself has the appearance of a child.

Sheburungu, you,
I am looking for Shemwindo.
Shemwindo gave birth to a hero
In giving birth to the Little-one-just-born-he-walked.
Sheburungu,
I am looking for Shemwindo,
My little father, the dearest one.

Sheburungu shouted and said:

Oh Mwindo, let us play *wiki* together![202]

And Mwindo shouted and said:

Oh! my father Sheburungu,
I am looking for Shemwindo.

And he—

Oh Mwindo, let us play *wiki* together!

And Mwindo shouted, he said:

Oh my father, give me Shemwindo!
My little father threw me into the drum;
My little father threw me into the river.
The youngsters asked me to play *wiki* with them,
The youngsters—I do not play *wiki* with them.

After Mwindo had entreated Sheburungu, asking him to give him back his father, Sheburungu said to him: "I cannot give you your father; I am asking that we first play *wiki* together, so that I may deliver your father to you, so that you may go home with him." After Sheburungu had spoken like that to Mwindo, Mwindo answered him: "Spread them (the *wiki*) out on the ground; I will not flee from you; you know the dangers from which I have escaped."[203] After Sheburungu had heard

---

202 *túresé/let us play wiki*: *ịresa* means to gamble, it refers to any kind of game that involves an element of chance and in which various goods are staked. The game in which enemies most frequently challenge each other in Nyanga tales is that of *wiki* (handfuls of little black seed are taken with the object of guessing the number of seeds held in each hand). In daily life, this game is played only by men, who often wager large amounts of possessions.

203 *byámoswá we/which I have escaped*: *ịoswa* literally means to be left with only the feathers of the bird one is trying to catch.

the way in which he was being answered by Mwindo, he went to fetch a mat; he spread it out on the ground; he also went to get the very old *wiki*-seeds of the *isea*-tree. Sheburungu wagered: "You, Mwindo, if you beat me, you will carry your father off (with you), and here (are) three bunches of *butea*-money; if you beat me, you will carry them off." Mwindo wagered three bunches of *butea*-money. After they had wagered things with each other in that way, Sheburungu was the first to take a handful of *wiki*-seeds; when he picked them up, with the first take-up, he won Mwindo's *butea*-money. Mwindo wagered the goats that remained in Tubondo; Sheburungu took the *wiki*-seeds; he won all the goats from Mwindo. Mwindo wagered everything and his aunt; Sheburungu again took the seeds; he won all the goods and the people and his aunt from Mwindo.[204] Mwindo remained all alone with his *conga*, his partner Sheburungu having finished winning from him all the things and all the people who lived in Tubondo. After Mwindo had been losing all his things and his people, he wagered his *conga*. When Sheburungu tried to take the seeds, he failed. Mwindo took the seeds; he won from Sheburungu the money that he had wagered. Sheburungu wagered again; Mwindo again took the seeds; he won on eight; all that Sheburungu had wagered, Mwindo won it back.[205] Sheburungu wagered all his objects, together with his cattle. Mwindo took the seeds up again; he won again on eight; he won all the things of Sheburungu: people, goats, cattle. Mwindo piled up (things); Sheburungu remained all alone by himself.

Where Kantori and Kahungu remained, they arrived where Mwindo was; they warned him: "You, Mwindo, come quickly; your father wants to flee again." After he had heard that news, Mwindo abondoned the *wiki*-game; he headed very quickly to join his father in the banana grove of Sheburungu. Seeing him, they put their nails into him.[206] Seeing his father,

---

204 In this *wiki* game men would wager all their possessions, including wives and daughters.

205 *mináni/eight*: to be understood as "at the count of eight."

206 *kisambú/banana grove*: the term designates a banana grove in full production with many banana trees and interspersed with many other crops. *bámuhára mó byára/they put their nails into him*: *ihára* literally means to scratch; the stereotyped expression is used in connection with catching

Mwindo inquired of him: "Oh my father, is it you here?" Shemwindo answered: "Here I am." Mwindo again inquired of his father: "Oh Shemwindo, is it really you?" Shemwindo again answered: "Here I am, you, my son." After Mwindo had seized his father like that, he returned with him; he climbed up with him to Sheburungu's. Mwindo said to Sheburungu: "You, Sheburungu, you have been hiding my father away. This one here is my father, is he not?" Mwindo said further to Sheburungu: "You, Sheburungu, I don't want any of your things that I have won; now keep all your things that I have won; here I am going with my father." When he was about to return with his father, Mwindo gave his farewell to Sheburungu and to all his people: "Oh, my father Sheburungu, farewell!" Sheburungu answered: "Yes, you too, Mwindo, go and be strong, along with your father Shemwindo." After Mwindo had said farewell to Sheburungu, he returned singing:

> Listen, Ntumba Munundu,[207]
> He who went (away) comes back.

Mwindo shook the rope, he reminded his aunt; and where his aunt remained, she had bells attached to the rope. Mwindo sang:

> He who went (away) comes back;
> You see I am carrying Shemwindo.[208]

---

thieves or with arresting someone who resists. The verbal form signifies that Mwindo himself does not lay hands on his father; his followers, in fact, had remained back in the village. "They" may be a rare *plurale majestatis* for "he" or may stand for the young children whom Mwindo had met at the entrance of Sheburungu's village.

[207] The dignified attitude of mutual respect with which father and son treat each other is truly impressive: no fighting, no slander. Mwindo's encounter with his father has a cathartic effect on him; from now on Mwindo is in a reconciliatory mood. The attitude attributed to Mwindo is in line with the Nyanga code of values: the ideal man is not subject to verbosity, rancor; he does not manifest excessive emotions. It is only from the moment of his encounter with his father that Mwindo demonstrates his true greatness. *Rúkira waNtúmba/listen, Ntumba*: the connective form *wa-* occurs here as a kind of synonym of *muna-* with the rare meaning of master or of the kind, species of.

[208] *niríte/I am carrying*: here, the meaning is unclear. The verbal form *niríte* can mean that Mwindo really carries his father on his back, or that he is simply in the company of his father, that he has his father with him.

Mwindo rushed headlong to Ntumba's cave; he arrived there when Ntumba had already finished rebuilding (it). Mwindo sang:

> I am longing for Ntumba Munundu's.
> The country is a *mutaka*-fish.[209]
> He who went to sleep wakes up.

Mwindo said to Ntumba: "Why did you hide my father away? Here I am with my father." Mwindo sang:

> Ntumba, you are powerless against Mwindo,
> For Mwindo is the Little-one-just-born-he-has-walked.
> I am on my way home from this point on in Ntumba's house.
> Look, I am carrying Shemwindo,
> My little father, the dearest-one,
> Shemwindo, senior brother of Iyangura.
> It is Shemwindo, the one who gave birth to a hero.
> Aunt Iyangura, I am on my way back.
> Mwindo is the Little-one-just-born-he-walked.
> I am carrying my little father, Shemwindo.
> *Katakwa*-region, lowland intersected with flooding streams.[210]
> You see, I went to give allegiance to the Baniyana.

When Mwindo arrived at Ntumba's, he related the whole story to Ntumba; he said to him: "You, Ntumba, you were wrong to offend me in vain." All the things of Ntumba, the land, and the banana groves, and the people, everything came back. Mwindo and his father Shemwindo spent the night at

---

nirįte is often used in the latter sense, e.g., when one says *nirįte mpéné* or *nirįte kikumi*, I have a goat or I have a nubile daughter.

209 *écŭo mutáká/the country is a mutaka-fish*: the interpretation of *mutáká* is difficult; said with one low and two high tones, the word designates a little fish with red stripes, which is a symbol of beauty. The meaning would then be: the country is beautiful. *mutaka* with three low tones means landed estate. This interpretation is also possible if we accept tonal change owing to the rhythm of the song. In this case, the meaning would be that there is no state or political unit without land, i.e., a group cannot have political autonomy if it is not in full control of the land.

210 *Katakwa*: an area in Nyanga country known for its rich fishing; the rivers there flood very often leaving small pools and channels full of water and fish where the Nyanga set up weirs and traps. This verse, which is thrown in by the narrator, is freely translated in the spirit of what is meant here and what we were able to observe at the moment it was uttered. It could be handled as: *Katakwá* (region), *kumbo* (downstream), *mikómbį* (flooding rivers).

Ntumba's. After Mwindo had saved all the things of Ntumba, Ntumba said to Mwindo: "Go, you senior, I never utter slander against you; I have no dispute with you." When Mwindo left Ntumba's, together with his father, he went singing, reminding his aunt in Tubondo:

> He who has gone away is back.
> Muisa!
> The sky has become day.[211]
> The rooster cock-a-doodle-dooed,[212]
> And the sparrow pointed him out.
> Mwindo will arrive in the house of Muisa,
> In the house of Nyarire;
> I come from Ntumba's,
> From Munundu's.
> Muisa, you are helpless against Mwindo,
> Since Mwindo is the Little-one-just-born-he-has-walked.
> It is you who are wrong in offending me in vain.
> Look! I am carrying Shemwindo.
> Muisa, you are helpless against Mwindo,
> Since Mwindo is the Little-one-just-born-he-walked.
> Look! I am carrying Shemwindo.
> I am returning to Tubondo,
> Where remained my aunt Iyangura,
> Iyangura, sister of Shemwindo,
> Aunt, birth-giver, Iyangura.[213]
> I shall eat on the wicker and wooden plates
> Only when I shall arrive in Tubondo.[214]

---

[211] *wácere/has become day*: the Nyangaized Hunde form *bwakyére*.

[212] *birangira/cock-a-doodle-dooed*: onomatopoeia borrowed from Hunde.

[213] *Nyarire*: contracted form for Nyamurairi, the god of fire who heads all other divinities. Mwindo did not meet with Nyarire, but with one of his servants, Muisa. *ngi muhemúké/who are wrong in offending me*: *ihemuka* literally means not to give to those who ask; *ngi* (it is) underlines the fact that the injustice of their action is now very clear. *kabúto/birth-giver*: an epithet for a paternal aunt or a father; interestingly, this epithet is not given to a mother. It underscores the importance of the patrilineal ideology in which a paternal aunt is a closer relative than a mother. *kabúto* literally means the action (suffix *-o*) of giving birth, or, rather, of perpetuating patrilineal kinship.

[214] The suggestion is clear that Mwindo does not eat during his various peregrinations.

When Mwindo left Ntumba's village with his father Shemwindo, he went headlong into Muisa's house. When Mwindo was already in Muisa's house, Kahindo came to Mwindo saying: "You see my father here, his bones fill a basket; what shall I do then? It is befitting that you heal my father; don't leave him like that; wake him up, may my father wake up, because he is the chief of all the people." After Kahindo had spoken to Mwindo in that way, Mwindo woke up Muisa singing:

> He who went to sleep wakes up,
> My father Muisa,
> He who went to sleep wakes up.
> Look!
> You,
> It is you who have offended me in vain.
> Look!
> I am carrying my father Shemwindo.
> Muisa,
> He who went to sleep wakes up.
> Muisa,
> You are helpless against Mwindo,
> Mwindo is the Little-one-just-born-he-walked.
> Shemwindo brought forth a hero.
> I am going to Aunt Iyangura's village,
> Iyangura, sister of Shemwindo.

While Mwindo was awakening Muisa, he kept on striking him all the time with his *conga*, telling him: "You have offended me in vain; you have tried to be equal to Mwindo, whereas Mwindo is the Little-one-just-born-he-walked, the little one who does not eat terrestrial foods; and the day he was born, he did not drink at the breasts of his mother." When Mwindo had finished waking up Muisa, Muisa woke up, he resuscitated. After Muisa had resuscitated, Mwindo told him that he had been forged by his uncles, the Baniyana. "My body is covered with iron only; and you, Muisa, don't you see me? Is that why you mounted me?" Muisa asked Mwindo: "You, Mwindo, how were you born? Do you have a medicine that enables your going?" Mwindo unfolded for him the thread of the news of how he was born. He told him: "You, Muisa, lo! have you never heard that I came out of the medius of my mother, that I was not born in the same way that other children are born, that I was born speaking and even walking? You, Muisa, have you never heard that I was thrown into a grave, that they had even put banana stems on it, that I resuscitated again, that my father threw me anew into the drum, that he threw me into the river, that I came out of it again? Have you not heard all these marvelous things, you, Muisa? That is why you dared to make a fool of me."

When Mwindo was already at Muisa's, he agitated the rope where his aunt remained in Tubondo; he reminded her. Iyangura said to Mwindo's uncles, the Baniyana, that in the place where Mwindo had gone, he had long ago finished seizing his father, that he was on his way home with him. While returning to Tubondo, Mwindo said farewell to Muisa; he sang:

> You, Muisa,
> You see me already going,
> You, Muisa, taker of others' things.
> Where Aunt Iyangura remains
> In Tubondo,
> He who went away is back.

When Muisa saw Mwindo going, he said to him: "Oh, Mwindo, you my son, it's befitting that you marry my Kahindo here." Mwindo answered him: "I cannot marry here; I shall marry (later) in Tubondo of Shemwindo."

In leaving Muisa's village, Mwindo began the trip; he and his father went home; they went to appear where they had entered at the root of the *kikoka*-fern. When Mwindo and Shemwindo arrived at the entrance of Tubondo, those who were in the village, Iyangura and the uncles of Mwindo, swarmed in the village like bees; they went to greet Mwindo and his father at the entrance; they met them.[215] Seeing Mwindo, Iyangura and the uncles of Mwindo lifted him up into the air; they carried him on their fingertips. When they traversed the village of Tubondo, Mwindo told them to let him down. They put him down in the middle of the village place;

---

215 *umushata mó/you dared to make a fool of me*: *ishata* literally means to play, to make a game of. *bárubuka . . . biri mintsuntsu/they swarmed like bees*: the verb *irubuka* describes the sudden appearance of a swarm of bees or the way in which clear water is troubled when a stone is thrown into it

they went to take a lot of spearheads, and it is on them that Mwindo sat down—they stood for the *utebe*-stool. His maternal uncles put him to the test like that in order to know if perhaps their nephew was still as they (had) forged him. When Mwindo was on the stool in the middle of the village, he gave his aunt the news from where he had come and the way in which he had fought, searching for his father. He sang:

When I descended with the rope,
Aunt,
I met with Kahindo.
Kahindo shouted (and) said:
"Mwindo, let me charge you with (the following) words:
If you see Muisa,
What Muisa will say,
You should refuse it."
Mwindo said:
"I go to the village, the village place
Where Muisa lives,
If I am not victorious
Where Muisa remains."
When I arrived in the village of Muisa,
Muisa shouted and said:
—Muisa brought out a chair—
"Mwindo, sit down here."
Mwindo shouted, complaining,
Saying, "This is your head, Muisa."
Muisa shouted and said:
"Counselors, give me some little beer
So that I may give it to Mwindo."
And Mwindo shouted, complaining:
"A father's urine a child never drinks."
Muisa said: "Let us fight together."
I have kneaded Muisa.
I was already going.[216]

---

[216] *bámukukuma/they lifted him up*: this is commonly done to honor somebody. *shinga/rope*: Swahili word. Earlier the line connecting him with his aunt was called *muri* (liana). *kumbúka kubutara/to the village, the village place*: the first term stands in opposition to the forest, the second one to the houses. *nará nendánge/I was going already*: typical expression meaning that he did not linger, that he hurried, and literally translated, would read: I set out to eat (while) going.

I arrived in Ntumba's cave,
In the cave of Ntumba Munundu.
Ntumba said: "Let's fight together."
I kneaded Ntumba,
I who had kneaded Muisa.
You too, Ntumba, are powerless against Mwindo,
Mwindo, the Little-one-just-born-he-walked.
I kneaded Ntumba so that I got tired.
Already I was hurrying in Sheburungu's house;
When I arrived there at the entrance of Sheburungu's—a god—²¹⁷
The youngsters howled, saying:
"Oh, Mwindo, we are hungry."
I sent pastes over there;
The youngsters ate the pastes.
Already I was on my way to Sheburungu's,
Together with the youngsters.
Sheburungu said: "Let us play *wiki* together."
I said: "You, Sheburungu,
You are powerless against Mwindo, the Little-one-just-born-he-walked.
Who made Muisa and Ntumba fail."
I shouted, complaining,
I, saying: "Give me my father here."
Sheburungu shouted, saying,
"Mwindo, you are helpless (in) the *wiki*-game against Sheburungu,
Which has beaten Heaven and Earth."²¹⁸
We took a handful of *mbai*-seeds.
Mwindo shouted and said:
"Sheburungu, you are helpless against Mwindo.
Give me Shemwindo,

---

²¹⁷ *kwáshé-Burúngú ongo/Sheburungu—a god*: the exact interpretation is difficult. Sheburungu is sometimes used as the epithet of Ongo, the creator god. But, judging from the fact that in the word order here, *ongo* follows *sheburungu*, it would seem that Mwindo is speaking about one of the Nyanga divinities and not about the creator god. For this reason *ongo* has not been written with a capital letter. As used here, *ongo* is somewhat synonymous with *mushumbú*, the generic term for divinity. Acceptable interpretations, then, are either "Sheburungu, one of the gods," or "Sheburungu, great as a god."

²¹⁸ *Bụtụ́ n'Oto/Heaven and Earth*: both are personified here. I have not found these personifications elsewhere in Nyanga tales. The two verbs *irésa* and *irása* used in the passage should not be confused: the first means to gamble (particularly to play the *wiki* game), the second means to shoot an arrow or to win a game.

You see, I have already beaten you."
Kahungu notified Mwindo;
Kahungu showed me Shemwindo.
It is I who seized Shemwindo,
My little father, the dearest one.
We were already on the return trip;
"Shemwindo, let us go home,
Let us go up to Tubondo
Where remained Aunt Iyangura."
What Shemwindo accomplished!
I arrive at the peak in Tubondo.
You see, I am carrying Shemwindo;
I am carrying my little father, the dearest one.

Iyangura gave her son the order: "Since you have arrived
with your father, bring him first into the *iremeso*-hut to let
him rest there."[219] They carried Shemwindo into the *iremeso*-
hut; he settled down in it. In giving hospitality to his father,
Mwindo killed for him the goat that never defecates and never
urinates; they cooked it, along with rice, for his father.[220] He
said to his father: "Here are your goats! It is you who were
wrong in vain; you made yourself awkward to Mwindo, the
Little-one-just-born-he-walked, when you said that you did
not want (any) boys, that you wanted girls; you did a deliberate
wrong in the way you desired.[221] Lo! you did not know the

---

219 *What Shemwindo accomplished!*: a shortened, euphemistic expression
to say: the deed that Shemwindo accomplished is bad. *iremeso-hut*: an
oval-shaped hut, which is also a shrine for the spirit of good fortune and
a place in which guests are accommodated. The implication is that
Shemwindo is no longer treated as a chief, the possessor of the village
Tubondo, but merely as an important guest.

220 *the goat that never defecates and never urinates*: i.e., a very fat goat
mumpunge/rice: a Nyangaized version of the Swahili word for growing
rice, *mpunga*. Dry rice cultivation was introduced among the Nyanga in
recent decades. The narrator speaks about rice, rather than about banana
paste, to emphasize the fact that much effort was taken to prepare a fine
meal for Mwindo. Rice-growing demands much more attention and maintenance than banana-growing. In addition, the Nyanga feel that it takes
more time to prepare a rice porridge than a banana paste.

221 *uhemúkéngá/you were wrong*: said by someone who asks for a service
and does not receive it; Mwindo criticizes his father's lack of generosity
in this way.

strength of the blessing of Mwindo."[222] After Mwindo had given food to his father as a hospitality gift, Iyangura said to him: "You, my son, shall we go on living always in this desolate village, (we) alone, without other people? I, Iyangura, I want you first to save all the people who lived here in this village; when they have resuscitated, it is then only that I shall know to ask our young man, Shemwindo, to tell me some of the news of the ways in which he acted, all the evil that he did against you." Mwindo listened to the order of his aunt to heal those who had died. His uncles, the Baniyana, beat the drum for him while he, Mwindo, was dancing because of the joys of seeing his father. They sang. Aunt shouted and said:

> My father, eternal savior of people.[223]

Mwindo said:

> Oh, father, they tell me to save the people;
> I say: "He who went to sleep wakes up."
> Little Mwindo is the Little-one-just-born-he-walked.
> My little father threw me into the drum.
> Shemwindo, you do not know how to lead people.
> The habits of people are difficult.
> My little father, eternal malefactor among people,
> Made bees fall down on me,
> (Bees) of day and sun;
> I lacked all means (of protection) against them.[224]

While Mwindo was healing those who died in Tubondo, he continued on in the (following) way: when he arrived at the

---

222 *karamo kémukisa/the strength of the blessing*: *karamo* refers to good health, long life, life force, and is used as a greeting. *mukisa* means recovery from illness and is generally considered to be a blesssing of the spirits.

223 *múmurárá úno/in this desolate village*: the image is that of a filthy village where the grasses are allowed to grow wild. *bushwá ésángoa sishé, serimusúnga/because of the joys of seeing his father*: the word order in Nyanga is reversed; lit., because of the joys of his father, (the joys) of seeing him. *shé-karamo/eternal savior*: *she-* implies a special association of ownership, mastery, control; *karamo* is good health, long life, life force.

224 *yákindi ná mwishi/(bees) of day and sun*: stereotyped expression to say "all of a sudden." Mwindo is saying that his father suddenly and unexpectedly exposed him to all kinds of dangers.

bone of a man, he beat it with his *conga* so that the man would then wake up. The resuscitation was as follows:

each one who died in pregnancy resuscitated with her pregnancy;
each one who died in labor resuscitated being in labor;
each one who was preparing paste resuscitated stirring paste;
each one who died defecating resuscitated defecating;
each one who died setting up traps resuscitated trapping;
each one who died copulating resuscitated copulating;
each one who died forging resuscitated forging;
each one who died cultivating resuscitated cultivating;
each one who died while making pots and jars resuscitated shaping;
each one who died carving dishes resuscitated carving;
each one who died quarreling with a partner resuscitated quarreling.

Mwindo stayed in the village for three days resuscitating people; he was dead of weariness. The people and all the houses—each person resuscitated being straight up in his house.[225] Tubondo filled itself again with the people and the goats, the dogs, the cattle, the poultry, the male and the female ewes, the teenage boys and girls, the children and the youngsters, the old males and females; in the middle of all those people (were) the nobles and the counselors and the Pygmies and all the royal initiators; all those also were straight up. All the descent groups that formerly dwelt in Tubondo resuscitated; again they became as they were before, each person who died having things of a certain quantity, resuscitated still having his things.[226] Tubondo again became a big village with

---

225 *mwífúca bó bo/the resuscitation was as follows*: lit., while revivifying them in this way. *bikango/weariness*: weakness caused by extreme physical strain. *kira/each*: Nyangaized Swahili word, *kila* (each). *wihandá na múmwe/being straight up in his house*: lit., planting himself (like a tree) in his (place or house).

226 The enumeration of animals and people who reoccupied the village of Tubondo is succinct and precise. Listed are the various categories of domestic animals traditionally known by the Nyanga: goats, sheep, chickens, dogs. Cattle (*nkambú*), although they are not traditional and were not found in Nyanga country at the time this text was taken down, are mentioned in this section of the epic. There are various reasons accountable for the inclusion of cattle: the narrator's imagination (he had been traveling and working in neighboring areas), the presence of cattle among most tribes surrounding the Nyanga, and the fact that a few Nyanga chiefs were said to have acquired cattle in the 1950's (cattle pastured by members

seven entrances. When the people were resuscitated, Iyangura began to speak in the middle of the crowd of people, saying: "You, Shemwindo, my brother, in the middle of the whole country of yours, have them prepare much beer and cows and goats; let all the people meet here in Tubondo. It is then that we shall be able to examine in detail all the palavers and to redress them in the assembly." After Shemwindo had heard the voice of his sister Iyangura, he uttered a cry, high and low, to all his people, saying that they should bring beer together.[227] After one week had passed, all groups within his state swarmed into Tubondo, together with beer and meats. On the morning of the eighth day, all the people of all the villages of Shemwindo's state pressed together in the assembly. After all the people, the children and the youngsters, the adults and the elders, had thronged about, Mwindo dressed himself and became like the anus of a snail. His aunt Iyangura, she too threw on her

---

of other tribes in the savanna highlands bordering the Nyanga forests). It is also possible that this part of the text may have preserved a tradition known by the ancestors of the Nyanga before they migrated from the East African grasslands into the Congo rain forest. *Batwá/Pygmies*: there are a few small groups in Nyanga country called Pygmies by the Nyanga which call themselves Baremba. Physically, they are a mixed breed, visibly strong in Pygmy influences; culturally, their pattern of life is very close to that of the Pygmy. Such Pygmy groups are affiliated with certain Nyanga chiefs as their hunters and gatherers; they have highly important ritual duties in connection with the enthronement of chiefs; they have many privileges, including the permission to harvest freely certain species of bananas. *bandírabitambo/the royal initiators*: in each Nyanga state there are from four to seven officeholders who collectively are called *bandírabitambo* and who exercise important ritual duties in regard to the institution of chieftaincy. *Sábe tu kásángá búri to/again they [the descent groups] became as they were before*: interesting construction which literally could be translated as: they (the descent groups) began to be (*sábe*) again (*to*) habitually in the past (*kásángá*) as are they (the descent groups [*búrito*]). The grammatically correct form for *búrito* is *búriso, -so* bearing on *ésángandá*; but the former euphemistic considerations are in operation here: *-so* is a "dangerous" form because it could mean "your father," and this term must never be used in an ambiguous context, or it might bear on such words as *santsa* (pubic hair) or *nyo/sanyo* (vulva), which must be avoided in normal speech.

227 *rákira/have them prepare*: lit., to invite people to do some kind of work on one's behalf. *He uttered a cry, high and low*: i.e, he made the best possible appeal; he did his best to call together as many people as possible.

clothes, those famous ones of Mukiti's. His father Shemwindo, he too dressed himself from top to bottom: *tuhuhuma*-bark cloths on which (were) red color and castor oil, *ndorera*-fringes, *masia*-hair ornaments.[228] He too became something beautiful. After the people had grouped themselves in the assembly, servants stretched mats out on the ground, there where Mwindo and his father and his aunt would pass. All the people in that assembly kept silent pi! There was sacred silence.[229] Those three radiant stars, Mwindo and his father and his aunt, appeared from inside the house. They went into the open to the assembly; they marched solemnly. Those who were in the gathering of the assembly gave them the gift of their eyes: there where they appeared, that is where their attention was focused. Some among them surmised, saying: "I wonder, is Shemwindo born with another young man?" Some answered: "Shemwindo is there with the chief of Shekwabahinga, together with his wife." Some said: "No, Shemwindo is there with his sister, Mukiti's wife, and (with) Mukiti himself." The remainder said that Shemwindo was with his sister Iyangura, Mukiti's wife, together with his son Mwindo, the Little-one-just-born-he-walked, the man of many wonders, the one who was formerly martyrized by his father." Shemwindo and Mwindo and Iyangura went in a line, while appearing in the middle of the gathering of the assembly. Mwindo beseeched his friend Nkuba, asking him for three copper chairs. Nkuba made them come down. When they were close to the ground, being close to the ground, they remained suspended in the air about five meters from the ground.[230] Mwindo and his

---

228 *Cébịndị munáná múmukoma-kómá/on the morning of the eighth day*: lit., (the day) of eight days, in the morning. *sakwá Múkiti ésáncangi/ her clothes, those famous ones of Mukiti*: lit., of at Mukiti's *the* clothes: our translation "those famous ones" is justified both by the reversal of the normal word order and by the augment. Reference is either to the beautiful clothes she wore when she was married to Mukiti or to clothes she had received from him. *wámbare ákwantsi n'ékwịyo/he dressed himself from top to bottom*: interesting use of the current words for land/soil/ below/on the ground (*kwantsi*) and for sky/air/above (*kwiyo*). The expression means that he dressed himself incredibly well.

229 *pi!*: onomatopoeia to stress the completeness of the silence.

230 *métero/meters*: Nyangaized French word *mètre*.

father and his aunt climbed up onto the chairs; Iyangura sat down in the middle of both, Shemwindo on the right side and Mwindo on the left side. When all the men had finished grouping themselves together in the assembly and had finished becoming silent, Mwindo stood up from his chair; he raised his eyes into the air, he implored Nkuba, saying: "Oh, my friend Nkuba, prevent the sky from falling!"[231] Having spoken like that, he lowered his eyes toward the ground, down upon the mass of people; he said, he lauded them, saying: "Be strong, you chiefs." They approved of it. He said: "You counselors, be strong." They approved of it. Then he: "You seniors, be strong." They approved. Mwindo praised the council, holding all the things with which he was born: *conga*, axe, the little bag in which the rope was; he also held an ancient stick to praise the council.[232] After Mwindo had finished praising those who were in the council, he made a proclamation: "Among the seven groups that are here in Tubondo, may each group be seated together in a cluster; and the chiefs and the seniors of the other villages, may they also be seated in their (own) cluster." After he had finished speaking like that, the people grouped themselves in an orderly manner, each group in its

---

[231] *uhángenga ébụtụ/prevent the sky from falling*: the verb *ihánge* means to protect something from falling by supporting it (e.g., said about banana trees with many heavy stems, which have to be propped with gaffs). Mwindo may be implying two things: first, he seems to ask the divinity of lightning to prevent rain from falling; second, he seems to boast about his weight (importance) and that of his aunt and his father who are also sitting in copper chairs suspended from the sky.

[232] This passage is typical of the way in which a solemn meeting among the Nyanga begins. The main speaker recites a number of formulas wishing strength and long life to all participants; he then asks for the blessing of specific categories of persons. All participants answer in chorus *aé* (yes), translated here as "they approved." The praise formula used by Mwindo, *músaruké* (be strong), is unusual, the more common formula being *karamo* (force, life, good health) or *músinjé* (be praised). The verbal form *isaruka* seems to be a reversive of *isara* (to vomit), i.e., may you not vomit (may you be cold). *nkóma ÿĕkibúÿá/an ancient stick*: *kibúÿá* is an uncommon word that might be derived from Babúÿa, a descent group to which the narrator was related. Members of the descent group were said to have been the first to make the Mwindo epic known. If this interpretation is correct, the narrator would mean that the stick Mwindo was holding was one of the sacred emblems of the Babúÿa group.

own cluster. Mwindo also ordered that all his seven mothers
be seated in one group but that Nyamwindo, the mother who
gave birth to him, should separate herself somewhat from his
little mothers. After he had spoken like that, his mothers
moved (to form) their own cluster; his mother who gave birth
to him moved a short distance away (yet remaining) near her
co-spouses. Mwindo also ordered: "Now you, my father, it is
your turn. Explain to the chiefs the reason why you have had
a grudge against me; if I have taken a portion larger than
yours, if I have borne ill will against you because of your
goods, if I have snatched them away from you, tell the chiefs
the news so that they may understand." Where Shemwindo
was sitting, he was flabbergasted: sweat arose from his big toe,
climbed up to his testicles, went to arrive at the hair on his
head; in his virile impetus Shemwindo got up. Because of the
great shame in the eyes of Shemwindo, he did not even praise
the chiefs anymore; he spoke while quivering, and a little
spitting cough clung to the centipede of his throat, without
warning: (all this) caused by the great evil of destruction.[233]
Shemwindo said:

All you chiefs who are here, I don't deny all the evil that I have
done against this, my offspring, my son; indeed, I had passed an
interdiction on my wives in the middle of the group of counselors
and nobles, stating that I would kill the one among my wives who
would give birth to a son, together with her child. Among all the
wives, six among them gave birth only to girls, and it was my beloved-
one who gave birth to a boy. After my beloved-one had given birth
to a boy, I despised her; my preferred wife became my despised-one.
From then on, I always looked at the soles of her feet. In the middle
of all this anger, I armed myself with a spear; I threw it into the
birth hut six times; I wanted to kill the child with its mother. When
I saw that the child was not dead, I made an agreement with the
counselors and the nobles; they threw this child away into a grave.
When we woke up in the morning, upon awakening, we saw the child
already wailing again in its mother's house. When I noticed that, I
asked myself in my heart, I said: "If I continue to fail to kill this
child, then it will oust me from my royal chair; now I, here, have

---

[233] The shame and hesitation of Shemwindo is powerfully described in
this passage; in no other Nyanga text can a depiction so richly evocative
of emotions and physical reactions be found.

seen all these amazing things that he is doing, so this child will cause
me a big problem." It's only then that I carried him into the drum
and that I threw him into the river. Where this child went, I believed that I was harming him, whereas I was only making him
strong(er). From there it is that this child's anger stems. When he
came out of the river he marched right up against me; he attacked
me here in Tubondo; it is from that point on that I began to flee,
all my people having been exterminated. Where I fled, I rejoiced,
saying, "I was safe," (thinking) that where I was going, there was
salvation, whereas I was casting myself into the thorns of rambling
around throughout the country counting tree roots, sleeping in a
filthy place, eating bad foods.[234] From that moment on, my son set
out in search of me; he went to take me away in the abyss of evil in
which I was involved; he went to seize me at the country's border.
I was at that time withered like dried bananas. And it is like that that
I arrive here in the village of Tubondo. So may the male progeny be
saved, because it has let me see the way in which the sky becomes daylight and has (given me) the joy of witnessing again the warmth of
the people and of all the things [of] here in Tubondo.

Iyangura spoke to the men who were sitting in the assembly,
reproaching openly their young man here, Shemwindo:[235]

Here I am, aunt of Mwindo, you chiefs, in your presence. Our
young man here, Shemwindo, has married me out to Mukiti; I got
accustomed to it (thanks to) the confidence of my husband.[236] Thanks
to my labor and to getting along with him, my husband placed me
high up, so that he loved me above all the wives he had married. So
then—you chiefs, may I not bore you; let me not carry you far off in
a long line of many words. Suddenly, this child appeared where I
lived; Mukiti was then on the verge of killing him because he did
not know that he was my child; but his intelligence and his malice

---

[234] In an unusually florid style, Shemwindo gives an admirable summary
of the main events of the conflict with his son.

[235] *Shemwindo*: the narrator mistakenly said that Iyangura reproached
Mwindo. The context indicates that she is critical of Shemwindo and not
of Mwindo. *musike wǎbó/their young man*: a term used by women to
refer to their brothers.

[236] *bánu murįkįre/in your presence*: lit., you are seated. *iwé wǎmenyera
na ko/I got accustomed to it*: the verb *įmenyera* is used for women who
become well adapted to their husband's family and village and do not find
excuses for frequently visiting their own families. *n'erįrisįenya* in the next
sentence, translated as "getting along," literally means to make each
other say yes.

saved him.[237] It is from then on that I followed him and followed him to point out to him the way to Shemwindo's, and (also because of my) desire to see him. It's there that Mwindo's fights with his father began, because of the anger (caused by) all the evils that his father perpetrated against him. He subdued this village, Tubondo; his father fled. Where he fled, Mwindo went in search of him, saying that his father should not go to die in the leaves.[238] When he joined him, he seized him; it is that, that Mwindo has made his father return again to this village, Tubondo. So it is that we are in this meeting of the assembly of the chiefs.

She also said:

You, Shemwindo, acted badly, together with your counselors and nobles. If it were a counselor from whom this plan of torment against Mwindo had emanated, then his throat would be cut, here in the council. But you are safe, it being yourself from whom this plan sprang. You have acted badly, you Shemwindo, when you discriminated against the children, saying that some were bad and others good, whereas you did not know what was in the womb of your wife; what you were given by Ongo, you saw it to be bad; the good (thing) turned into the bad one. So, there is nothing good on earth! But nevertheless, we are satisfied, you notables, (because of) the way in which we are up on our feet again here in Tubondo, but this Shemwindo has committed an iniquitous deed. If the people had been exterminated here, it is Shemwindo who would have been guilty of exterminating them. I, Iyangura, I finish, I am at this point.[239]

After Iyangura had finished speaking, Mwindo also stood up; he praised the assembly, he said:

As for me, I, Mwindo, man of many feats, the Little-one-just-born-he-walked, I am not holding a grudge against my father; may my father here not be frightened, believing that I am still angry with him; no, I am not angry with my father. What my father did against me and what I did against my father, all that is already over. Now let us examine what is to come, the evil and the good; the one of us who will again start beginning, it is he who will be in the wrong, and all those seniors here will be the witnesses of it. Now, let us live in harmony in our country, let us care for our people well.

---

237 In contrast to Shemwindo, Iyangura is talkative; she cannot easily or adequately summarize a situation.

238 *die in the leaves*: i.e., die like an animal rambling around in the forest.

239 *Ongo*: name for the creator god. *nendĕ mpe/I am at this point*: lit., I go, I arrive until here (in my story), the formula regularly used to finish a speech.

Shemwindo declared that as far as he was concerned, the
act of giving birth was not repugnant in itself. (He said that)
where he was here, no longer was he chief, that now it was
Mwindo who remained in his succession, that against the one
who would insult Mwindo in this land the seniors would clap
their hands.[240] When Mwindo heard his father's voice, he
answered him: "You, father, just sit down on your royal chair;
I cannot be chief as long as you are alive, (otherwise) I would
die suddenly. Where the counselors and nobles were seated,
they assented to Mwindo; they said to Shemwindo: "Your son
did not speak wrongly; divide the country into two parts; let
your son take a part and you a part, since, if you were to give
away all authority, you would again be immensely jealous of
him, and this jealously could eventually trouble this country
in the long run." Shemwindo said: "No, you counselors and
nobles, I am not on that side; but I want my son to become
chief. From now on I shall always work behind him." The
counselors told him: "You, Shemwindo, divide your country
into two parts, you a part and your son a part, since formerly
you always used to say that you alone were a man surpassing
(all) others; and what you said happened: that is why we witnessed all these palavers; we had no way of disagreeing with
you because you inspired fear. Lo! if the chief cannot be dis-
agreed with, then it is too great foolishness." Shemwindo said:
"Since you, my counselors and my nobles, come to give this
advice, so I am ready to divide the country into two parts:
Mwindo a part and I, Shemwindo, a part, because of the fear
(you inspire); but in my own name I had wanted to leave the
country to Mwindo, and from then on I would always have
been eating food after my son Mwindo, because I have felt
and do feel much shame in the face of my son and of all the
people.[241]

---

240 *the seniors would clap their hands*: as a denunciation of him. *ikóngóta* literally refers to the gestures made to remove dust from something.
241 The Nyanga text accounts for a common habit of splitting existing states into two or more smaller autonomous ones. Currently the sub-diving is never between a ruling chief and his son; at the death of a chief, however, the state may be divided between two or more of his sons by different ritual wives.

After Shemwindo had spoken like that, he conferred the kingship upon his son: he stripped himself of all the things of kingship which he bore: a dress dyed red and two red belts; he also gave him *butea watukushi* to wear on his arms when he would pile up the *bsebse*-meat, and *butea* (to wear) on the legs; he also gave him a *ncambi*-belt; he also gave him a *kataba*-belt; he also gave him a *kembo*-hat; he also gave him the hide of a white goat.[242] Shemwindo dressed Mwindo (in) all those things while Mwindo was standing up, because a chief is always being dressed in (such) things while standing. The counselors went to fetch the chair imbued with *ukaru*-powder and castor oil; they gave it to Shemwindo; Shemwindo made Mwindo sit on it. Shemwindo handed over to Mwindo the scepter of copper on which there were lamels imbued with *ukaru*-powder and castor oil. He (Shemwindo) handed these things over to him when he was already seated on the chair. When he stood up, his father also handed over to him the wrist protector and the bow; he also gave him the quiver in which there were arrows.[243] Shemwindo also handed Pygmies over to his son; he gave him the *bandirabitambo*-initiators: *mwamihesi, mushonga, mubei, mushumbiya, muheri, shemumbo,* counselors, nobles.[244] They dressed him (in) all these things in the

---

[242] Enumeration of various items of traditional paraphernalia of chiefs: the dress is made of bark cloth dyed red with a mixture of castor oil and camwood powder; the bells are of raphia dyed red; *butea watukushi* are little rings made of string obtained from the raphia palm and are used as money as well as for ornaments; *tukushi* signifies that the rings are worn as armlets; *bsebse*-meat is a strange word, the exact meaning of which I could not obtain; *ncambi*-belt is made of wild boar skin and decorated with leopard, monkey, and genet teeth; *kataba*-belt is made of raphia and is decorated with beads, cowries, and wild boar's hair; *kembo*-hat is made of the skins of genet, flying squirrel, and bush baby.

[243] The chair and the ceremonial spear are some of the royal emblems, as are the wrist protector, the bow, the quiver, and the arrows. The wrist protector is made of the skin of a bush baby and filled with moss and other ingredients; the quiver is made of bark stained black; the arrows have no iron heads and are poisoned.

[244] A Nyanga chief is supposed to have some Pygmies (physically miscegenated, but culturally close to Pygmies) to hunt and to perform important ritual duties for him. He also has a number of ritual experts whose titles are mentioned: *mwamihesi*, the chief blacksmith; *mushonga*, the cook; *mubei*, the barber; *mushumbiya*, the drummer; *muheri*, the

guesthouse. After Shemwindo had enthroned his son like that, Mwindo shouted that he now had become famous, that he would not want (to act) as his father had so that only one descent group would remain on earth. "May all the descent groups establish themselves in the country; may boys and girls be born; may there be born deaf and cripples, because a country is never without (some) handicapped-ones."[245] After Shemwindo had dressed his son in the chiefly paraphernalia, he distributed beer and meat for the chiefs who were there; each group took a goat and a cow. They also gave Iyangura one cow for returning to her husband Mukiti. The chiefs and the counselors who were there said: "Let Mwindo remain here in Tubondo and let Shemwindo go to dwell on another mountain." Hearing this, Shemwindo clapped his hands; he was very satisfied. During Mwindo's enthonement, his uncles, the Baniyana, gave him a maiden, and Shamwami also gave him a maiden; Mwindo's father, he too, gave him a maiden called Katobororo and the Pygmies gave him one.[246] During Mwindo's enthronement, he was given only four women; he went on getting himself married while he was crossing the country. In each place where he made a blood pact he carried off a maiden.[247] During Mwindo's enthronement, the convives grew weary; some of them defecated on (their) heels. After Mwindo had been enthroned, the assembly dispersed: all those who

---

sacrificer. A chief also has his advisors (bakungú), nobles (barúsi). Among these nobles there is a she-mumbo, one who provides the chief with the ritual wife whose son will succeed to the throne.

245 wamasíma/he now had become famous: the verb isíma designates the status and power one achieves through initiation into an association or through enthronement rites.

246 At the chief's enthronement, as suggested in this passage, there are two basic types of exchanges taking place. The chief gives the participants food to be consumed during the ceremonies and other valuables (e.g., goats) to take home; he also assigns portions of land to the incumbents of the ritual offices mentioned in n. 244. On the other hand, the chief receives, without matrimonial payments, wives from several categories of people: one from a very close agnatic relative (his father or brother), one from the Pygmies, one from his maternal uncles, one from Shé- (or shá) mwǎmí (lit., the father of the chief) who is in charge of the protection of the chief's ritual wife.

247 A Nyanga marriage is often preceded by a contract of blood brotherhood between the groom and his wife's brother or between the groom's father and the father of the bride.

came from somewhere returned there; Shemwindo also took
possession of his mountain; he left to his son Tubondo.[248]
When Iyangura, aunt of Mwindo, returned to her husband,
she annointed Mwindo in the middle of the group saying:

Oh, Mwindo, hail!
Blessing, here, hail!
If your father throws you into the grave, hail!
Don't harbor resentment, hail!
May you stand up and make your first step, hail!
May you be safe, may you be blessed, hail!
And your father and your mother, hail!
May you bring forth tall children, boys and girls.
Be strong, my father; as for me, there is nothing ominous left, hail![249]

When Mwindo took leave of his father, his father also gave
him a blessing. Mwindo handed over to his aunt two counselors
to accompany her; he also gave her four goats and a return gift
of twenty baskets of rice and five little chicken baskets.

After a fixed number of days had elapsed since he had been
enthroned, Mwindo said that he had a terrible craving to eat
some wild pig meat. He sent his Pygmies out to hunt (for it) in
the forest. Where the Pygmies went in the forest, when they
were already "in the place of coming whence, going where,"
they felt tired, they slept half way.[250] In the morning they set

---

[248] *mutundu/mountain*: the Nyanga possess two generic terms for
mountain, *ntata*, a "father mountain," and *mutundu*, a "child mountain."
The meaning of this distinction is that in the legal and political sphere,
persons in control of a *mutundu* are subordinate to those ruling a *ntata*,
because *mutundu* is considered to be a mountain or, better, a unit of land
resulting from a partition of *ntata*. This passage implies that Shemwindo
is considered to be politically less powerful than his son Mwindo.

[249] Blessings (anointment of the chest, accompanied by supplicatory
prayers) are extremely frequent among the Nyanga, particularly among
kinsmen, on a variety of social occasions. *úsingiriré/May you stand up
and make your first step*: the verb *isingirira* means the first efforts of walking made by a baby; the meaning here is: may you be successful, may you
be in good health. *May you bring forth tall children*: i.e., of the best stature
according to the Nyanga norms.

[250] *mûntúka-kúnî na mwienda-kúnî/in the place of coming whence,
going where*: in this currently used expression, the Nyanga do not think
in terms of place, but of a state of mind. The entire phrase could be rendered as follows: when they were in the state of wandering whence to
come and where to go. The expression is used to indicate a great distance
traveled.

129

out right after awakening. In leaving right after awakening,
they found the trail of wild pigs; they followed them; in going
say "from here to there," they met them; they sent the dogs
after them, seeing that they were fleeing; the dogs hurled themselves after them.[251] Crossing two plateaus, they met a red-
haired pig dragging its scrotum; they hurled a sharp spear
at it. The pig in question said that it was not great—it turned
its hoofs upward; it died.[252] They cut it into pieces on the spot.
There where they were in the very dense forest, when they were
cutting the pig to pieces, Dragon heard their mumbling.[253]
Dragon said: "What now, people here again? I always thought
that I was the only one living here, whereas there are still other
people there." Dragon went after them, snakelike. When he
came close to them, he threw himself onto them; he took away
three Pygmies from there; he swallowed them. One among the
Pygmies was called Nkurongo; he wrestled himself loose; he
fled, and the dogs followed him; they fled with him. Dragon
said to himself: "Let this wild pork remain here, for I will
trap the dogs and the Pygmy, the one who fled. Dragon nestled
down beside the corpse of the pig. Where Nkurongo fled, when
he arrived, say "over there," he looked back saying: "Lo! our
companions have been overtaken by night; they are already

---

251 *they sent the dogs*: the Nyanga hold the hunting dogs on leash until
they have tracked down the hunted animals. *bana-mbibi bírása/the dogs
hurled themselves*: the verb *írása* literally stands for the action of shooting
an arrow.

252 *dragging its scrotum*: i.e., an old, fat pig. *Muna-katuku/the pig in
question*: the form *muna-*, which generally indicates the species or group,
here seems to have the rare meaning of "in question." *The pig in question
said that it was not great*: i.e., the pig had not the force to resist. *ÿákwa/
it died*: it is as if the pig died as the result of its own decision.

253 *Kirímu/Dragon*: Kirimu frequently occurs in Nyanga tales. He is
described as a big animal with black hide, seven heads, teeth like a dog,
huge belly, and tail of an eagle. The monster lives on the ground in dense
forest and is a solitary hunter that occasionally feeds on human beings. In
some tales Kirimu is said to have a human wife whom he captured. The
precise details of the seizure are not given. He never has children of his
own, but occasionally he keeps a human child whom he treats well, fat-
tening him in order to eat him later. In the Nyanga tales Kirimu is regularly killed by a clever man, a hero, or even by a young child who destroys
him with a knife after letting himself be swallowed or who kills him by
throwing hot stones into his mouth or by cutting a rope by which he is
trying to climb a tree.

dead." At the time when he fixed his eyes on him (the Dragon), he saw that he had seven heads and seven horns and seven eyes. He said: "This time it is an enormous lump; Mwindo, who is usually capable against people, this time will be powerless against this one in fighting with him."[254] When that little Pygmy there was already on the crest, he shouted: "I flee, eh!" He kicked up his heels onto his shoulders; he fled and the dogs followed him. He went to appear in the village of Tubondo; when he was nearly bursting with breath, he arrived in Mwindo's house. After he had rested awhile, "for as long as it takes a pot of paste to be cooked," Mwindo asked him: "Peace there, from where you are coming?" He answered him: "There is no peace there, you [my] chief! We went to the forest, four of us; Dragon has swallowed three (of us), and I, Nkurongo, escaped among them, together with the dogs. But it is not Dragon; he is as large as the sky." Hearing that, Mwindo said: "Well, now, this time it's tough; my Pygmies in their very first hunt are already exterminated in the forest." He looked up to the sky, lowered his eyes to the ground; he said: "Oh, my *conga*, be victorious in the day of tomorrow." And that day his father, Shemwindo, was in the village. Mwindo said to his father: "The rooster is going to die of *mukeri*, I shall already be on my way; I shall go right after awakening with this Pygmy only to fight with Dragon."[255] When Shemwindo heard this, he forbade his son: "Oh, my father, no, don't go there; Dragon has always been a destroyer; he has eaten from man's bones; if you again provoke this Dragon, then you cause great (disaster) in this country."[256] Mwindo said to his father: "I do not care, at any rate, I am going from dawn on; you stay behind to tell the counselors that I have gone to fight with Dragon."

---

254 *butúmámba/enormous lump*: lit., a heap of soil, a dike.

255 *The rooster is going to die of mukeri*: Mwindo means to say that he will be on his way long before the rooster crows. The Nyanga hate the matutinal crowing of the rooster; they find it ominous and fear it to be an announcement of death in the village. People curse the rooster by saying "may you die of mukeri"; mukeri is the name of a disease, but it is also used as a synonym for malediction.

256 *cámarángá mukakúa ná kakúa kábea/he has eaten from man's bones*: lit., he has been eating (since long ago and continues to do so) from the bone and bone of men (from many a man's bones).

When it was very early morning, Mwindo took up his *conga*, and the Pygmy preceded him. They thus proceeded in the forest. When they appeared at the place where they had cut the pig into pieces, the Pygmy pointed at Dragon, saying: "There he is." Mwindo said to the Pygmy: "Stop first; let me take a look at him." Mwindo said to the Pygmy: "You, stay here. When Dragon will have swallowed me, it is you who will announce the news in the village." Mwindo took his subduer of a *conga*; he went snakelike after the Dragon. When he saw himself eye-to-eye with him, Mwindo designated him, saying: "You will not judge me; today: you and I." Dragon was seized with surprise; he stood up. When he was about to fly against Mwindo, Mwindo put sweet words into his mouth, he sang:

> Dragon, you are helpless against Mwindo,
> For Mwindo is the Little-one-just-born-he-walked.
> Dragon, you have challenged Mwindo.
> Dragon, you are powerless against Mwindo,
> For Mwindo is the Little-one-just-born-he-walked.
> Shemwindo gave birth to a hero.
> Comrade, you are powerless against Mwindo.

When Dragon attempted to swallow Mwindo, Mwindo exclaimed: "This time he is finished." Mwindo also approached where he was; Mwindo beat him (with) his *conga*. Dragon fell upside down; he died. Mwindo called, shouting to his Pygmy to come to cut up the Dragon. The Pygmy came. When he was about to touch the Dragon with his great knife, Mwindo forbade him, saying: "First, leave him like that; let us call people in the village so that they may go and carry him to the village in order that Shemwindo could see the wonders that I perform." Mwindo implored those who were in the village; Mwindo sent his *conga* to the village to go and bring the people so that they could go and fetch this god of a dragon. He sang:

> Oh, my *conga*, go for me.
> Those who have remained in Tubondo over there,
> Those who have remained in Tubondo over there,
> At Shemwindo's,
> May Shemwindo send people to me.

Where *conga* went, when it arrived in Tubondo, it arrived just in front of Shemwindo. It wagged itself in front of him, and all the people of the village abandoned (their homes);

they went to see the way in which *conga* was wagging itself before Shemwindo. Shemwindo said that *conga* is giving the news: "If Mwindo is not dead, it is Dragon who is dead." Shemwindo sent there a group of people saying:

> Be ready to leave the village![257]
> Go and join Mwindo!
> In the dense forest there are many (things);
> There are snakes that bite.
> Go and join Mwindo,
> Where Mwindo has gone.
> Shemwindo has given birth to a hero.

Having wagged itself in front of Shemwindo, the *conga* flew away, together with the people whom Shemwindo had provided. *Conga* was flying with those people through the air; it went to descend with the people at the place where Mwindo was. When Mwindo saw his *conga* with the people, *conga* came into Mwindo's hands. Mwindo said to the men to lift up Dragon. They made a stretcher; they put Dragon on top of (it). Some among them seized the pig that had been killed by the Pygmy. When the carriers of Dragon had left say "as far as that," the stretcher broke because of Dragon's weight. They made another stretcher; they put Dragon on it again; they lifted him up; they had him arrive at the village. When he (Dragon) appeared in the village, the whole village crowded together: so many young, so many old people![258] They let Dragon down in the middle of the village. When the people saw him, they were very astonished; they whooped, they said: "Now, things will be coming out of the forest!" Some among them said: "At any rate, he who has killed this one cannot fail to kill one of his relatives." When Mwindo heard those people speaking like that, he killed them on the spot; they were three;

---

[257] *Muna-kítú/comrade*: the term is usually employed in reference to a kinsman; it occurs in disputes to designate (somewhat pejoratively, like the French *mon cher*) the opponent. The implication is also that Mwindo treats Kirimu not like a superior force, but like a kind of congener. *Múkai ékwikúra/be ready to leave the village*: lit., look at the way out of the village; have the eyes fixed at the exit.

[258] *n'ébanúnké, n'ébanúnké, n'ébakúngú n'èbakúngú/so many young! so many old people!*: astonishment about their number is expressed here through word repetition, an appropriate gesture, and through the insistence on final vowels.

they died.[259] Mwindo said to his people to cut up Dragon, and
he, Mwindo, sang:

> Dragon is being skinned and cut up on the little raphia palms.[260]
> Shemwindo howled, saying:
> Dragon is being skinned and cut up on the little raphia palms.
> Dragon always devours people;
> Dragon has exterminated people.
> Shemwindo, my father, be afraid of me.

When they opened the belly, there came out a man who leaped
up, being alive; there came out another man; he came out; he
too was alive. When they opened the belly, there came out another one who leaped up, being alive. After Dragon had been
cut up and the three Pygmies had come out alive, Mwindo
gave the order that he personally wanted (the following):
"When you will begin to eat this Dragon, you will eat him with
bones and all; don't throw any of them away." After Dragon
had been cut up, Mwindo distributed to all his people all the
meat with the mass of bones; he told them also that in case he
would see a little bone behind somebody's house, he would
make him pay for (it). When Dragon had been divided up and
divided again into many parts, they seized his eyes; they roasted
them hot on a piece of potsherd. Each time that there appeared
a splatter and it burst open, there came out a man. When all
the eyes of Dragon had been roasted, there appeared one
thousand people. Mwindo said: "These are my people." And
he gave them a mountain.[261]
Where Nkuba resided in the sky it so happened that he had
made a blood pact with Dragon. Where Nkuba was in the sky,

---

259 *bátúra ésândúrú/they whooped*: this expression renders the action of
producing whoops by beating the palm of the hand against the open
mouth, shouting *uuu*. It is viewed as a manifestation of enthusiasm and
astonishment. *wácinja/he killed*: Nyangaized Swahili verb *kucinja* (to kill).
The Nyanga form is *wákera*.

260 *híy'ótubondo/on the little raphia palms*: a pun, because Dragon is
being skinned in the village of Tubondo and is spread out on raphia
leaves (*tubondo*).

261 *báhumo/they opened (the belly)*: *jhúmo* literally means to remove
a dike (stone in some types of fishing) or to make a hole in a pot (so as to
take out something). *he gave them a mountain*: it is customary for a Nyanga chief to bestow upon individuals and groups that place themselves
under his protection a title of perpetual usufruct over parts of his domain.

when he inhaled the odor of his friend Dragon, which was passing with the wind, froth dropped from his nose; tears came out his eyes; he said: "What shall I do with this friend here, Mwindo?" He said that he first wanted to make him suffer in order that he would not begin again. "When I shall have finished making him suffer here where I am, then I shall know to return him to earth to his village." He also said: "If Mwindo had known that he had exchanged blood with Dragon, then he would not have killed his friend the Dragon; in that case, he would not restore him; in that case, he would be lost right here, without having gone back to his country. But he is safe because he did not know that he was my friend."

Mwindo sang:

> Nkuba has just come to take Mwindo;
> Nkuba came to carry Mwindo away
> From the heights of Tubondo,
> When he inhaled the smell (of roasting).
> Mwindo howled, he said:
> Eh! Nkuba, you are helpless against Mwindo;
> Shemwindo brought forth a hero.
> Eh! Nkuba, you are helpless against Mwindo Mboru.

Mwindo said:

> Eh! Nkuba, you are helpless against Mwindo Mboru.
> The cheerleaders were always in unison.
> The tunes that are being sung, the noninitiates cannot understand them.
> Oh, scribe, you,
> You see that I am already going;
> My mother who carried me,
> You see that I am already going.
> The counselors of Shemwindo,
> You see that I am already going.
> Let the counselors of Shemwindo come here.
> *Kubikubi*-star adheres to moon.
> My friend Nkuba, be victorious.
> Nkuba has come to take Mwindo.
> Let us climb up to Nyarire's.

Mwindo said farewell (to the people), one by one.

> My mother who carried me,
> You are seeing that I am already going.
> Nyamwindo howled, complaining.

—And Nkuba at that very moment had just opened (the door)—
"What shall I do with my child?"
Nyamwindo howled, saying:
"I die, I die, along with my child."
Shemwindo howled, saying:
"I die, I die, along with my child."
The little bark loincloth that the Bira debarked,
If it gets used, I set aside the trimming.[262]

After Nkuba had inhaled the smell of his friend Dragon which
came from his friend Mwindo in Tubondo, he descended on
the spot to take Mwindo. He descended; he arrived in Mwindo's
village. Nkuba said to Mwindo: "I come to take you, you my
friend; I want to go and teach you because I am very vexed
with you, you my friend, since you dared to kill Dragon,
whereas Dragon was my friend; so know that you are doing
wrong." Hearing this, Mwindo was not afraid of going away
with his friend; but his people were stricken with anxiety,
thinking that their chief was going forever. Mwindo sang:

Let us go up to Bisherya over there,
For Nkuba has come to take Mwindo.
I am about to climb up to Bisherya over there,
For Nkuba has come to take Mwindo.
Oh, Nkuba, you are powerless against Mwindo,
For Mwindo is the Little-one-just-born-he-has-walked.
Shemwindo gave birth to a hero;
My friend, you are powerless against Mwindo.
Wanderer, go anyway announcing it,
That ntiriri-liana has become mubanga-rope,
And musara-liana has become mukendo-bag.[263]

---

262 This song combines four things: first, Mwindo himself predicts and
describes the coming of Nkuba; second, Mwindo predicts his own salvation; third, the narrator inserts some of his own proverbial reflections;
finally, the narrator describes some of the action pertinent to the departure
of Mwindo: the arrival of Nkuba ("And Nkuba at that very moment had
just opened the door), the complaints of Mwindo's father and mother.
nabika murando/I set aside the trimming: i.e., I keep part of it as a
souvenir.

263 Bisherya: used as a synonym for sky, but it is also one of the places
frequently mentioned in the accounts of the early migration of the Nyanga
from East Africa. The ntiriri-liana . . . : proverb complaining about the
reversal of the normal order of things: the mubanga carrying-rope is not
normally made from lianas, but from raphia, and so is the mukendo
shoulder bag.

What Shemwindo has said
Will be lacking the one who will analyze it.
The sky became day while we were still talking,
Like the association-*mukuki*.[264]
The-ones-who-are-accustomed-to-go-to-sleep, let them go to sleep.
May the one who is always grumbling remain grumbling.
The counselors of Shemwindo,
The counselors threw me into troubles.
Let me speak to Munguto of Wamba,
Where there are chiefs' wives carrying raphia bunches.
I have spoken with my companion odiously;
In case the heart turns away from where it has come: it means it is
     getting accustomed.[265]
Kabarebare and Ntabare,
My father,
Where the husband of my senior sister sets up *byoo*-traps.

Mwindo went on singing like that while Nkuba was climbing
up slowly with him into the air, and the people of Mwindo
had their attention diverted by (what was happening) above.
Nkuba disappeared into the clouds, together with Mwindo;
and they arrived at Nkuba's. When Mwindo arrived at Nkuba's,
Nkuba asked him: "You, my friend Mwindo, you have acted
badly when you dared to kill my friend Dragon, when you
have roasted his eyes so that the odor climbed up to me, so
that I smelled it in the air; if only you had made the odor
descend to earth, then I would not have been angry." Nkuba
still said to Mwindo: "I have rescued you many times from
many dangers, so then you show that you are equal to me."
Mwindo arrived there at Nkuba's; he felt there much cold,
and the icy wind there was strong. No house! They lived there

---

[264] *Búri nkandá mukúkị/like the association mukuki*: The main initiatory object of this association is a sound box (through which the spirit of
the association manifests itself); *nkandá* literally means a package (in
which the sound box is wrapped). The narrator says that throughout the
night they spoke about mysterious things, like the ones revealed by the
sound box in the *mukuki* initiations.

[265] *kátima/odiously*: lit., little heart. *Kútuké mutima nti ịbera/In case
the heart turns away from where it has come*: it means it is getting ac-
customed: free translation that tries to capture the spirit of this very
succinct Nyanga dictum; lit., that the heart leaves a place it is to get used.
When one forgets his place of origin, it is a sign of being well accustomed
to the new place of residence (said about married women).

in mere nomadism, no settling in one spot. Nkuba seized
Mwindo; he climbed up with him to Rain. When Rain saw
Mwindo, he told him: "You, Mwindo, never accept being criticized; the news about your toughness, your heroism, we surely
have heard the news, but over here, there is no room for your
heroism." Rain fell upon Mwindo seven and seven times more;
he had Hail fall upon him, and he soaked him thoroughly.
Mwindo said: "This time I am in trouble in every way." Nkuba
lifted Mwindo up again; he had him ramble across Moon's
domain. When Moon saw Mwindo, he pointed at him: "This
time the news was given us that you were tough, but here in
the sky there is no room for your pride." Moon burned
Mwindo's hair; Mwindo complained: "Oh, father Shemwindo,
bless me, and may my *conga* not get out of my hands." Nkuba
lifted Mwindo up again; he went and climbed up with him
to the domain of Sun. When Sun saw Mwindo, he harassed
him hotly; Mwindo lacked all means (of defense) against Sun;
his throat became dry; thirst strangulated him; he asked for
water. They said to him: "No, there is never any water; now
we advise you to grit your teeth; we advise you to put your
heart on your knee." After Sun had made Mwindo sustain
these pains, Nkuba lifted Mwindo up; he went and made him
arrive in the domain of Star. When Star saw him, he pointed
him out; he told him: "The news about you was given us
that surely you are very tough, but here there is no room for
your heroism." *Kubikubi*-star ordered Rain and Sun (to come).
All—Nkuba, Rain, Sun, Star—all those told Mwindo but one
single thing: "We have respect for you, just that much; otherwise, you would vanish right here. You, Mwindo, you are
ordered to go back; never a day should you kill an animal of
the forest or of the village or even an insect like a centipede
or like a *ntsine*. If one day we would learn the news that you
began again to kill a thing among those that we just forbade,
then you will die, then your people would never see you
again." They pulled his ears seven times and seven more,
saying: "Understand?" And he: "Yes, I have understood."[266]
They also said to Mwindo: "It is Nkuba here who is your

---

[266] This powerful passage relating Mwindo's sufferings in the realm of
Lightning, Rain, Moon, Sun, and Star contains a number of evocative expressions that necessitated a free translation, e.g., *rain fell upon Mwindo*:

guardian; if you have done wrong, it is Nkuba who will give
the news, and that day he will seize you all at once, without any
longer saying farewell to your people.[267]

After Nkuba had made Mwindo ramble everywhere through
the sky, they gave him back (the right) of home, saying he was
allowed to return. On his return, Mwindo had then finished
spending one year in the sky, seeing all the good and all the
bad things that are in the sky. Nkuba raised Mwindo up; he
returned with him home to Tubondo. Mwindo threw sweet
words into his mouth; he sang:

> Mwindo was already arriving
> Where Shemwindo had remained;
> Where Shemwindo had remained
> Mwindo was already arriving
>
> He who went away returns.
> Shemwindo brought forth a hero.
> What will die and what will be safe,
> Oh my senior sister, may it join Mwindo!
> My friend Nkuba, be victorious.
> Let me go to Tubondo,
> To Tubondo, village of my mothers.[268]

---

the verb *ihita* (to descend a mountain) suggests the violence of the falling
rain; *he had hail fall upon him*: the verb *isuruca* (to knock over a banana
tree or to knock a stem down from a banana tree) describes the power of
the action; *Sun harassed him hotly*: the Nyanga text says Sun stretched
him out (like an animal hide set out for drying) on hot, hot things; *thirst
strangulated him*: the verb *ikáma* describes the action of kneading bananas
for beer-brewing. *we advise you to put your heart on your knee*: this expression is used to describe strong, but contained, suffering. When suffering intensely, the Nyanga, in order to restrain from crying, holds his mouth
firmly against the knee or arm as if biting it. *ntsine*: a water strider.
Bámukokota ématé/they pulled his ears: the Nyangaized Swahili verb
kukokota (to pull) is used here instead of the Nyanga *kurwa*, a gesture
certainly inspired by what the narrator himself was able to observe in
European milieus. *never a day should you kill an animal . . .* : the prohibition against hunting and trapping holds for all Nyanga chiefs.

[267] *mucyngi/guardian*: Nyangaized Swahili word; the Nyanga word
would be *murangi*.

[268] *village of my mothers*: Tubondo is, in fact, the village of his father
and his father's agnatic kinsmen. It is not astonishing for Mwindo to say
that it is the village of his mothers: his own mother and the other wives
of his father (who are also called mothers in Nyanga practice) inhabit this
village. Mwindo wants to make it clear that Tubondo is the village where
his own mother—for whom he has a tender love—resides.

May I see my mother.
I descend here in Tubondo,
In father's village, my dearest one.
And if, Mwindo, you kill a game,
It is I who have a right to the tail,
In which (normally) father's elder brother has a right.[269]

The will says: "Mwindo, if you kill an animal, then you die."[270]

Oh Mwindo, never try again!
From now on may you refuse meat.
Nkuba said:
"Never try again."
Shemwindo, you brought forth a hero.
Kiruka-Mbura, advise those leaving
Who makes the trees fall in the forest.[271]
My little father, my dearest one,
My little father threw me into palavers.
Substitute, replace me now! [272]
My father believed that I would faint away;
He threw me into palavers.
Iyobora, open for me now,

---

269 *And if, Mwindo, you kill a game/It is I who have a right to the tail/In which (normally) father's elder brother has a right*: the text is difficult because of succinctness and the reversal of word order. The correct interpretation is that Mwindo brings to his people the message that from now on all tails (of buffalo and elephant and wild boar) are to be given to him rather than to his father's elder brother, even though his father's elder brother is his senior by birth.

270 *ịraị/the will*: before dying, fathers, headmen, chiefs, and other officials orally make their will known. The will bears on succession to office more than on inheritance of goods; it also sets forth various taboos and injunctions. There are strong magicoreligious sanctions against nonobservance of the will.

271 *Kịrụká-Mbụra . . . . Kákịríá/Kiruka-Mbura . . . who makes the trees fall: Kákịríá* (who makes . . . fall) has been translated in conjunction with *Kịrụká*. It is perfectly possible, however, that two different persons are designated here: first, the divinity of lightning (Nkuba) under the epithet *Kịrụká-Mbụra*; second, Mwindo himself under the epithet Kákịríá, "the little one who makes the trees fall in the forest."

272 *Rukombora nkombóre réro/Substitute, replace me now!*: an exclamation inserted by the narrator; he is tired and now desires a replacement. The substantive and verb used are Nyangaized forms of the Swahili verb *kukomboa* (to redeem, to deliver).

Iyobora of Mirabyo.[273]
I have fame here in Tubondo,
(I) Mwindo,
Tubondo (with) seven meeting places,
With seven entrances.
He who will go beyond what Mwindo has said,
He will die (from) seven lightnings—
And one more in addition![274]
The counselors howled, saying
That what has been said will be resaid.
And the common man is incapable of judgment;
Even Shemumbo is incapable of judgment.[275]
Absentminded ones, be never again distracted.
And an old man, he too is incapable of judgment.
It is the great chief who sustains the common man,
And it is the chief's wives who sustain the people.[276]
The words of the *nkebe*-dance are (of) wisdom.[277]
Nyamumbo howled, saying:
"If you arrive at Shemwindo's,
What Shemwindo will say
Will be the announcement of something living.[278]
If Shemwindo says a word,
He will die (from) seven lightnings.

---

273 *Iyobora*: lit., opener; an epithet for the divinity of lightning, another epithet is *Mírábyo* (flashes).

274 *ná nįmá nti ӯawįtómo/and one more in addition*: *wįtómo* stands for the part the person in charge of distributing goods is allowed to set aside for himself before the actual distribution takes place; it is a supplement to which he is entitled because of his special duties. The expression is used here to insist that the individual who transgresses Mwindo's injunctions will certainly die.

275 *Is incapable of judgment*: i.e., has not the authority or the capacity to judge, to render a verdict.

276 *muhangá/great chief*: *stronger than mwami* (chief); refers to a chief who has great fame and who rules over more people than other chiefs.

277 *nkebe-dance*: the short songs used in this common Nyanga dance are mostly proverbs. *mishúma* (more commonly *mishų́mo*)/*words . . . of wisdom*: lit., proverbs, maxims, apothegms.

278 *mwasį wakári-ho . . ./the announcement of something living . . .*: these verses can only be understood in the following way: according to Nyamumbo (Mwindo's mother) the words and decisions of her husband, Shemwindo, are good and adequate; according to Mwindo, his father's deeds are evil; Shemwindo must abstain from making decisions, lest he cause his own destruction.

We shall lack the one who will utter a word,
"We."
Nyamwindo howled saying:
"My son has suffered much.
Slander in this village is outrageous.
Someone's mother-in-law
Allows herself to criticize (that) someone;
And even someone's father-in-law
Allows himself to criticize (that) someone.
A giant of a young man
Laughs at the young woman's.[279]
A Mubuya (today) rainmaker
Formerly did not like to remove dew—
Remover of oil dew.
In Ihimbi, in our country, it is fine;
From it came out an epic.[280]
There lived a divinator.
Stump of the path of the river (trail)
Tears up the clothing of the elegant woman."

When Nkuba was returning with Mwindo, he went on slowly descending with him; he went and let him down in the very middle of the village place of Tubondo. When his father Shemwindo saw his son being brought back by Nkuba, he gave Nkuba a reward of a maiden who was dressed with a bracelet of copper of Nkuba; they also gave him the prescribed white

---

[279] *wamánubá/has suffered*: lit., has suffered from the heat. *Katéré kakúno kásuma/Slander in this village is outrageous*: this and the following four verses are extremely terse statements. Literally they could be translated as follows:
    Slander of this side is tough:
    For a man's mother-in-law
    Slanders (that) man;
    And even a man's father-in-law
    Slanders (that) man.
Cáseá cámwána múkari/Laughs at the young woman's: the implication is that he makes fun of the young woman's words or problems or "thing" (i.e., sex).

[280] *A Mubuya rainmaker*: the narrator refers specifically to a person of the Babuya whom he has known. *In Ihimbi*: the narrator boasts that Ihimbi, the region where he was born and lived, is the cradle of the epic he is relating.

fowl.²⁸¹ It is there that originated the custom of rendering cult to Nkuba; from then on they always dedicated to him a maiden and her copper ring.²⁸² After Nkuba had received (his) gift, he returned to his domain in the sky.

After Mwindo had taken rest, he assembled all his people. They arrived. He told them: "I, Mwindo, the Little-one-just-born-he-walked, performer of many wonderful things, I tell you the news from the place from where I have come in the sky. When I arrived in the sky, I met with Rain and Moon and Sun and Kubikubi-Star and Lightning. These five person-ages forbade me to kill the animals of the forest and of the village, and all the little animals of the forest, of the rivers, and of the village, saying that the day I would dare to touch a thing in order to kill it, that day (the fire) would be extin-guished; then Nkuba would come to take me without my saying farewell to my people, that then the return was lost forever." He also told them: "I have seen in the sky things unseen of which I could not divulge." When they had finished listening to Mwindo's words, those who were there dispersed. Shemwindo's and Nyamwindo's many hairs went say "high as that" as the long hairs of an *mpaca*-ghost; and in Tubondo the drums had not sounded anymore; the rooster had not crowed any more.²⁸³ On the day that Mwindo appeared there, his father's and his mother's long hairs were shaved, and the roosters crowed, and that day (all) the drums were being beaten all around.²⁸⁴

---

281 *a bracelet of copper of Nkuba*: Nyanga women, who are dedicated to the divinity of lightning, wear this bracelet as one of the distinctive em-blems of the cult. *n'énkókó yényangé/and the prescribed white fowl*: "prescribed" in our translation is justified by the augmen *é-*.

282 As in a few other instances, the epic attempts here to account for the origin of particular Nyanga customs. A large number of Nyanga women are dedicated to the divinities of lightning, good fortune, and so on; for many, the implication is that they are married to the spirit and cannot be normally married. These women live in prolonged union with married or unmarried men who have no rights to their children. These children belong to their mother's (i.e., the spirit wife's) descent group.

283 *mpacá/ghost*: specter of the forest; occurs in many Nyanga tales; has much hair, very long nails, and is always fomenting evil plans.

284 *ékwantsi n'ékwiyo/all around*: lit., on earth and in the sky.

When Mwindo was in his village, his fame grew and stretched widely. He passed laws to all his people, saying:

May you grow many foods and many crops.

May you live in good houses; may you moreover live in a beautiful village.

Don't quarrel with one another.

Don't pursue another's spouse.

Don't mock the invalid passing in the village.

And he who seduces another's wife will be killed!

Accept the chief; fear him; may he also fear you.

May you agree with one another, all together; no enmity in the land nor too much hate.

May you bring forth tall and short children; in so doing you will bring them forth for the chief.[285]

After Mwindo had spoken like that, he went from then on to remain always in his village. He had much fame, and his father and his mother, and his wives and his people! His great fame went through his country; it spread into other countries, and other people from other countries came to pay allegiance to him.

Among children there are none bad; whether he be disabled, or whether he not be disabled, he must not be rejected. So then there is nothing bad in what God has given to man.

Heroism be hailed! But excessive callousness either pushes a man into a great crime or brings him a great one, which (normally) he would not have experienced. So, whosoever in a country is not advised will one day carry excrements—and to experience that is terrible.

Mutual agreement brings about kinship solidarity; the one who will save his companion is unknown; it is like the chief and his subordinates. So, the world is but made of mutual aid. So, then, may the chief safeguard (his) subordinates and the subordinates safeguard the chief. Kingship is the stamping (of feet); it is the tremor of people.

Even if a man becomes a hero (so as) to surpass the others, he will not fail one day to encounter someone else who could crush him, who could turn against him what he was looking for.[286]

---

[285] *wátanga/stretched widely*: lit., had many ramifications, like the branches of a tree. *washámbárá/he who seduces*: lit., to talk privately with. . . . *bǎna bare-bare na bihi-bíhí/tall and short children*: i.e., children of all kinds.

[286] These four statements contain the narrator's explanation or his in-

terpretation of the moral of the epic. The Nyanga traditionally give explanations in a very terse style for the stories they narrate. *n'erisúma rátáá katí, but excessive callousness*: the idea of excess is rendered in Nyanga by the expression *rátáá katí*, lit., which throws away (or which buries) the branch/tree/stick. There are two possible ways to interpret the connection between the terms. When clearing the forest for cultivation, the Nyanga do not put much care into the cleaning operation: after the banana stipes have been planted, trees are cut down and left on the spot without burning, thus giving the banana grove the appearance of neglect and negligence. To carefully remove branches, and so on, would indeed be a form of excess and might be considered to be inspired by some evil plans. The expression may also be related to current ideas about the secret activities of sorcerers. The verb *itáa* means to throw away, but also to bury. Sorcerers are said to bury certain vegetal or other materials in order to cause evil. Excess and evil, toughness and disregard for established patterns of behavior are all evoked by this expression. *buma-kíma/kinship solidarity*: lit., the state of being one; one of the terms that currently designates kinsmen. *Kaʃékúmbúka kúrikangá nti maramyana hó/So, the world is but made of mutual aid*: lit., so the world is seated being mutual saving (healing). *Kingship is the stamping (of feet)* . . . : that is, there is no chief without people and a chief can only have a multitude of people if he is a generous protector of them. *murai ráréngá irénga biné/a hero (so as) to surpass the others*: lit., a hero, in a way that surpasses to surpass the companions (the congeners, the age-mates). *wámushée kisondángé we/who could turn against him what he was looking for*: lit., who could show him the thing that he is looking for. The Nyanga have a profound dislike for boasting and megalomania. For this reason they dislike making subjective evaluations of the relative moral or physical qualities of specific individuals. In most of the epic, the hero Mwindo behaves like an arrogant boaster, blindly believing in his own power. For the auditors, the hero's attitude caused reactions of uneasiness and sarcasm. Yet, there was an excuse for the hero as long as he was the victim of his father's unjust decisions and actions. The personality of the hero would ultimately have been unacceptable to the Nyanga if a moment of crisis and restraint had not come into his life. The moment came, after Mwindo had found his father, when the lightning spirit acting as a *deus ex machina* carried him away to the realm of Rain, Moon, Sun, Star to be castigated by them. The hero's incapacity to be successful in all circumstances made him acceptable to the Nyanga. In a great many of their stories, the Nyanga manifest strong fatalism and skepticism; even the sacred chiefs are limited in power and intelligence by superior beings, sometimes by the creator god himself. The statement, then, conceived as one of the morals of the epic, is in its wording both euphemistic and elliptical. The narrator means to say that there does not exist an individual so great as to surpass all others; even the Nyanga hero is not immune, but is subject to limitations set by superior forces and by immanent justice. Grammatically, the statement is to be considered as part of a cryptic dialogue between two individuals: one provoking the other and the other saying: "Beware, you look for trouble, and trouble you will get!"

NYANGA TEXT

Kwábéséngá mwamí ųmá nti ngí shé-Mwindo.[1] Íngo mwamí wáhįmba ubúngú nti ngí kuTubondo, múcǔo cámwiHímbí.[2] Shé-Mwindo nti wabútwá ná mwįsį'ábó ųmá nti ngí Įyangura.[3] Nǎ ndo ubúngú rwáshé-Mwindo nti rúrí mó ndushú sirínda sábea bé.[4] Íngo mwamí shé-Mwindo wábinga bomína barínda.[5] Shé-Mwindo wakíé wamakįnd'íbingǎ mbo bomína bé barínda, wásonja ébea bé bátį: banúnké n'ébea bakwákare, bahanį, bakungú n'ébarųsį.[6] Ábatį ba wárįa bó mukįbų.[7] Bákíé įyé bárí múkįbų shé-Mwindo wárįka nkatį-nkatį na bó, wábíkíra muréngé, mbu: bǎnų bomína bé, íngu wabútí mwáná-muỹú mubǎnų bomína bé barínda, iwé nti wamuỹi, bǎnu bátį cáhundá mwéndįyo bǎnų mubútánge bǎna bámukárį bara-ara.[8] Mwíkįnd'įéca émwǐkó o, wįrekera múma-nųmbá ábakárį, nti wecáa ndásį kúrí bakárį bé. Mǔmbo bomína bé nti bárí mó ngantsį ná nya-kashómbé. Nya-kashómbé nti wahįmbírwá kubukoné hírare, ná bámpé bomína bé nti bárí múmwangantse, munkatį ỹérúbúngú.[9] Kwákíé kwámetá matų ântswá, bakárį mbo barínda bárįére ná makúre mongo.[10]

Kwįhį n'erúbúngú rwáshé-Mwindo nti kúrįkangá rǔsi rųmá nti rúrí mó įrįba, nǎ ndo įrįba nti rírí mó mukįtį mįné-márįba.[11] Kwárį-kángá Múkįtį mwírįba, wárúkíra mwasį, mbu kunandá n'é kúrí mwamí uri ná mwįsį'ábó ngí Įyangura, unyényanga búrí masįa ámwǐshí bų-shwá éríhunda.[12] Muna-Mukįtį wakíé wamarúkírá ámwasį weríhunda rǎngo kikumí Įyangura, wámwende mubingo kámukóhe.[13] Mukįtį wéya kuTubondo, shé-Mwindo wámusámísha mwicumbi.[14] Bákíé įyé murųsįsį, bámakįnd'įrengera biỹó, Mukįtį wére shé-Mwindo, mbu: ǒngo įnyantįré, mubįtų'abé ngu Įyangura ngí cásįngwá iwé wéya kúno kúrí ǒngo.[15] Shé-Mwindo wakíé wamakįnd'írúkíra, wáshee Mukįtį mpéné ỹákabųsá nti ngí nceo, wére ná Mukįtį, mbu wé wǎkusúbíéyo mukǒmá.[16] Mukįtį wéba, mbu: aé titá shé-karųo, nashįmá.[17] Bákíé ébųtú wámǎca, múmukomá-kómá Mukįtį wíkía na búrí kanyero kânkó mwímbara, nti wambará bisumbó-sumbo múmabóko na múmǐndí n'émukóbá wénkéngé, nti warįá n'erįsįa híỹ'ǒmųntwé.[18] Ákwárįkángá shé-Mwindo ná mwįsį ábó Įyangura, nâ bó bímónya hó tu mwímbara.[19] Mukįtį na shé-Mwindo bákíé básúngana, Mukįtį wére ishíbé, mbu: ébasi, héyerěyo aní kǔno ntí nénkį nasúngáná na mubįtų'aní.[20] Shé-Mwindo

mwírúkírǎ bo, wásonja bana-cé bátį, ábakungú n'ébarų́sį, wénda na bó
námá.²¹ Shé-Mwindo wére bana-cé, mbu: émwĮhwa weyáyo kǔno, nti
usondáa mubį́tų'aní, ná bǎnų múmúsúbíe ke. Bakungú n'ébarų́sį mwírúkírǎ bo, bárįsja, mbu: cáhundá múshwei kása Mukį́tį Įyangura.
Béta n'Įyangura kúrí Mukį́tį. Mukį́tį wakíé mbu wásungé Įyangura
búkókóbócáángé we, wįshį́sha múmutíma, mbu: réro ntí-ngí ǔngu, uri
búrí ntsémbe.²² Įyangura nâ wé nti wambará ncangį́ síbí sámasingure,
sásįngúrwá mó ukarú ná makų́ta ámbéa.²³ Bákíé básúngana, Mukį́tį
n'Įyangura, bókane múmakų́ba ábábábí, bákéána. Mwį́kį́nd'įkéána,
Įyangura wére Mukį́tį, mbu: mbéti unganyé hó, ǒngo Mukį́tį? Mukį́tį
wámwĮre, mbu: angá įsįmįka tu émuréngé, ǒngo mukárí, súnga búmį́-
nį́rengí aní kumongo búrí kintsênyá, niseéngi na múmatéma.²⁴ Mukį́tį
n'Įyangura bákíé bámasúngáná bo, ébakungú n'ébarų́sį báshé-Mwindo
básúbíe Mukį́tį, mbu bó báshįmá ǒngo Mukį́tį múkinwa cábé, į́yé
wendaa kánonka, unonka bĮngí, unonka bikeké, nti į́yé ǒngo'nonkéngi
bó.²⁵ Mukį́tį wakíé wámerírwá bo, wákų́rų́ke kurwé, nti émutíma
wámámusįka.²⁶ Mwį́kų́rų́ke kurwé bámuraa bįndį birínda byerį́rųsha
ébehe.²⁷

Mukį́tį wakíé į́yé uri kurwé, wásonja bana-wé, wére bó, mbu wé
utúkáa kakóha, iwé wakerwá bihumbi mwendá ná mpéné ÿámwěru,
ná ÿámutonye, ná ÿákabų́sá, ná ÿákįbį́mbí, ná ÿákisha, ná ÿanya-
mwį́sí, ná ÿábasike.²⁸ Bakungú n'ébarų́sį bákíé bárúkirǎ bo, bákóngóta
múmįne, mbu bó báshįmá, ǒngo nyeré-kurwábó, ibó bátákocé įrúka
éndįkǒ ÿa ÿébehe, bųshwá ínco kikumí ntí cį́tárwa mo.²⁹ Ématų arínda
ákíé ámakį́nd'į́sį́ra, múmukomá-kómá Mukį́tį wásúbíra éndįko, ná
bana-cé bámusį́ere kųrųma, bénda kwáshé-Mwindo kámurįkure. Mwítúka kurwé, wénda karéré mûbúngú rwában'Įyana.³⁰ Ban'Įyana bá-
mushee kihárábúté. Bana-Mukį́tį ná Mukį́tį wįsį́né báincira ná kuró
nti bárí búrí mbúhá bųshwá ámasíkúté.³¹ Múmukomá-kómá Mukį́tį
wásį́mána, wénda kirúndá mûbúngú rwábana-Mitandį; bana-Mitandį
básheere Mukį́tį mpéné, wáincira kuró.³² Bákíé múmukómá-kómá
wįsįca kwįkúra, hįma ná bana-cé, wénda ná keyá kwábishíbé kuTubondo kwáshé-Mwindo.³³ Bákíé béyá kuTubondo, shé-Mwindo wáshée
bó icumbi reríincira mo, wáshee na bó mpéné ÿábúhárwa. Bákíé į́yé
múmurusį́sį, Įyangura wáhúÿe moké meca, bénda kwishúá o mongo.³⁴
Mwį́kį́ndį kwishúa, bį́sįngo ukarú, bátáríe na hánkingo, Įyangura
wákinduca ná moké mwĮndi.³⁵ Mumukomá-kómá, kwábe mushibo.³⁶
Shé-Mwindo wátuma bana-cé bátį, bátékére ná hįmá muntéko. Bákíé
bámakį́nd'į́tékére, bana-shé-Mwindo bátį, Mukį́tį wásáa n'éndįko, wásįca ÿó bishíbé. Bishíbé báshįma na ÿó ngųrų. BámwĮre, mbu: kaį́ nó'-
ǒngo wábǔme ukeráá byǎra.³⁷ Bákíé bámakį́nd'į́tį́ngírira éndįko, bana-
shé-Mwindo bére Mukį́tį mbu wákųrųké kǔkwé, ibó bâmuhérúcíéyo
mukárí.³⁸ Mukį́tį mbu wárukiré bo, wéba, mbu ebį́tí byongó-byongó
byara-ara, cásúmá nti érítimwa. Wákų́rų́ke kurwé; Mukį́tį wakíé į́yé

uri kurwé, wákárísha bana-cé biyó bịngị, bụshwá mbu iwé weshánge
benj. Ákwásịángá shé-Mwindo kurwé, wakíé wasúnga Múkịtị waréré
wendá, múmukomá-kómá wáhénd'imutụ́ca, bénda kahérúcá Ịya-
ngura.³⁹ Mwịenda rábó ndo, ébahérúcịi bárịa Ịyangura, kịro ịnanta
kwantsí muketo ntícá mumeca.⁴⁰ Bahérúcịi bákíé béya n'émuhérúkị
kwáMúkịtị, Mukịtị wáshée bó icumbi, bárịka mó. Bátịngịre bó nkókó
ỹámùme ỹeríshúrúra éměno.⁴¹ Múnụmbá njo ỹerícumbi bárịkeca Ịyangura mukitụ́mbị cŏtébe.⁴² Wakíé ịyé urịkịre, Ịyangura wáshaísha
écăra cébuntu cákusímbúrá mŏ we múmwăbó kurwábó.⁴³ Bárísa có
báná moké Mukịtị. Moké wakíé wamarísá mụ́kibírá ca cébuntu, bá-
túkă ha bárụ́ịre tŭ bo buntu wámatekere.⁴⁴ Ébuntu wématekere wákíé
ịyé búrí émunụmbá, bére Mukịtị mbu wárịké mukitụ́mbị cŏtébe, ná
mukárị kitụ́mbị cŏtébe, n'ébuntu bárịkeca bó munkatị-nkatị ỹábábí.
Bákíé bámatékére, bére Ịyangura mbu wábuké katoré kábuntu mwị-
kasa rékumaryó, wárishé bo moké hịmá na múnyényị sényama.⁴⁵
Ịyangura wábúka kitoré cábuntu, wárísha moké co; ná moké wátúnja
kitoré cábuntu, nâ wé wárísha có mukárị. Bákíé bámakịnd'ịrísa ébuntu,
moké na mukárị, ábakungú báMúkịtị báshee shé-Mwindo kímása
cánkambụ́.⁴⁶
   Bákíé bámakịnd'ịrísă nco kímása cénkambụ́, básúbíe Mukịtị, mbu:
émwán'ịtụ́, ŭngu umánubinga, angímukíayo mó nya-turịco, nya-
mirémbe, angímukíayo búrí mufúkú wịkóra mirimo.⁴⁷ Bámakịnd'ịébă
bo, múmukomá-kómá báhend'ịenda, nti bámakósórwá mianda irínda
ỹábutéá na Mukịtị.⁴⁸ Ébahérúcịi bákíé béyá kuTubondo, báshịma ná
ngụrụ hịmá n'émwamí wabó shé-Mwindo. Kwásịángá Múkịtị ná
bana-cé, ná mukárị Ịyangura, wábíkíra muréngé, mbu: bănụ bana-cé
bátị, múmasúngáyo otụ́ rụmá mwea wahítá nă ndu rŭsi, nti múmu-
kongora erịkụ́a rémongo, bănụ bana-maká, bana-birúrumbá, bana-
nkomó, bana-tụbụ́sá ná bana-mpongo; ịna éntsě nji ỹawéndéndé érŭsi,
ngí éntse nkịrị ỹerịéta mó ébea bátị.⁴⁹ Wakíé wamecá émurémbe wesá-
ntse sé síbị bo, na múbúngú rwé ndo nti kúrịkịré shé-mwamí wé
mukịrị nti ngí Kasịyémbé, Mukịtị wére émutambo wé ngo mukịrị
Kasịyémbé: ŏngo, wendayo ŏngo'rịkáa ná mukárị ngu Ịyangura héndé
érịrịba, nâ wé Mukịtị wěndá urịkáa háno hásịkéngí ésántserya sịtị,
n'émyoo ịtị háréenga ỹo munkatị n'erịrịba.⁵⁰
   Kwárịkángá shé-Mwindo kuTubondo hịma ná bakárị ná bana-cé
bátị básíma ná kuró, énkúrú ỹé ỹénda ínku nă nku múcŭo kịtị.⁵¹ Ématụ́
ákíé áměta, bakárị bárịkangă hó n'émakúre, otụ́ rụmá mutúbá múba-
kárị bé bịkokora, bábúta băna bámukárị bara-ara;⁵² ụmá mubó, nya-
ngantsị wásịa usingánge n'ébukúre. Nya-ngantsị wakíé wamasúngá
babịné bámabúta, nâ wé ngí wasịá n'ébukúre, wénda wịongánge, mbu:
réro cásúmá nci, aní hó ngí narandwá na búno bukúre, nakíí ke búnị?
bịtụ́ narịérénga na bó makúre mongo, ibó bámakịndị kwịkokora, n'âní
ngí nasịá na bó, réro mwatúkí ké nkị mubúno bukúre?⁵³ Wakíé wama-

149

kíndí kwíanikirǎ bo, mbu wásisimuké áhárí we, hámyango nti íyé hárí
kika cânkúnį, nti ntíwosí kútúkángé co; kaí émwǎna wé uri kumund'-
ĕbura nti ngí wamámurųshíé co.⁵⁴ Kwákíé kwétá kashángí, mbu wákaí
émunųmbá nti íyé muri įréá rámeca, nti ntíwosí kútúkíréngí ro, rísíné
ngí rírųsha múmunųmbá. Kwákíé kwétá kashángí, mwéya tú isúsa
ribísi; nya-ngantsį mbu wásungé ro, wáshįshara ngųrų; kaí émwǎna
uri ékumund'ĕbura nti ngí uronjánge étushįngįshį tųtį nto.⁵⁵

Ábárįkángá mûbúngú bákíé básúngá nya-ngantsį warésingé hó
n'ébukúre múmwe, bénda bámúseángé, mbu: íngu nǎ wé wabútí ké
mwaní matú? Ákwárįkángá ámwǎna múbura wína, wíshįshįrįsha múbura, mbu wé utákocé įsáíre kumb'ŏmubi wína, bųshwá báméndáyo
bámúseángé, mbu wé mwǎna wámumína; iwé utángáhųná n'įsáíre na
múbŭnu wína, bųshwá báméndá bámúseángé, mbu wé wasárwángá
búrí munkondé.⁵⁶ Ébukúre wákíé íyé búángé, mwéya bakúngú bébaríkį,
bakárí bébakungú, béya mó nya-ngantsį nti íyé usingánge n'ébukúre.⁵⁷
Ákwárįkángá émwǎna múbura, wátáӱa n'ébura, wábiruruka n'émŏbó,
wénda ná kasáíré na múmųnwe wémuróta. Abakúngú baríkį bákíé
mbu bámúsúnge íyé unyaírée ékwantsí báshįshara, mbu: cásúmá nci,
émwǎna wahingá kě tú įna!⁵⁸ Bákíé mbu bámúsúngíre hântsí, bámushemba, mbu: mwǎna nkí? Bįma múbakúngú baríkį bárįsįa, mbu,
mwǎna wámuӱú. Ábakúngú bįma múbaríkį bábúrǎ mbu bábikiré
múbutara mbu kwábútwá mwáná-muӱú. Bįma bátįna, mbu: angá
ųmá wabíkírá mbu mwána-muӱú ngí wabútwá, bųshwá mbu shé-
Mwindo wǎkíé wámarúkíra mbu mwáná-muӱú ngí wabútwá nti wa-
sêmuӱa. Ákwárįkángá ábakungú hįmá n'émwǎmí shé-Mwindo bábíkíra,
mbu: kwábútwá mwǎna nkį ko? Ábakúngú baríkį ábárįkángá émunųmbá bábįba, bátásúbyé. Mwįkįnd'ibútwa rémwǎna, ábaríkį bámunínka n'érįna ráMwindo, bųshwá mbu ngí mwǎna wámuӱú watųcángá
bǎna bámukárí bara-ara mwíbútwa rábó.⁵⁹

Ímo mwákubútwángá émwǎna, nti murįkįre kitúndúkútú ékumi-
hįmbo.⁶⁰ Ákwárįkángá shé-Mwindo, wakíé wamakįnd'íbúsa mbu
kwábútwá inyé mwǎna, n'ébaríkį bámafúnd'ímusako, muna-kitúndú-
kútú wátúka mwákubútwá émwǎna, wénda keré shé-Mwindo, mbu:
ŏngo mwamí kwábútwá mwǎna wámuӱú ínku, érįna ré ngí Mwindo;
ngí cákusįngwá bátákúsakú ábárí mó. Shé-Mwindo wakíé wamarúkírá
mbu nya-ngantsį wé wabútá mwána-muӱú, wásúbíra n'erįtųmo, wátį-
ranya ró mwíhíkiro, wáhíke ró; wéta na ró kwákubútwá émwǎna.
Wakíé mbu wákangikí ro émunųmbá mwírungú, émwǎna wábáráka
hárįkįré we, wéba, mbu: érįtųmó ndi rénda réyéréngí hįtįn'ĕndúí,
ríténdí réyéréngí kúrí ábakúngúmbi bárįkįré múno bébaríkį, rítéyéri
na kúrí įna.⁶¹ Shé-Mwindo wákáso mó érįtųmo mbíso mutúbá nti
réyéréngí hó hándúí. Ábakúngú bébaríkį, bákíé básúngá ákashįngįshŏ
ká, bátúrúka émunųmbá, bábéka, mbu bó báméndá kakwíré mo. Shé-
Mwindo wakíé wamáruhárúhá n'erísįnga-sįnga n'erítųmo ré, wákų-

rúká bukwáté weríȳa Mwindo, wére ábakungú bé, mbu bátịmé ákabụ́rị
bákịsé mo Mwíndo, bụshwá mbu iwé utángáhụná isúnga mwáná-
muȳú. Ábakungú bákíé bárúkirá ékinwa cányere-kurwábó, bátámúaȳí
bátịma ékabụ́rị.⁶² Kákíé kámakịnd'ịrị́sa, báringa émwăna, Mwindo;
bámubétábeta, bénda ná kámukjsá múkabụ́rị.⁶³ Mwindo wáráka
kumund'ĕkabụ́rị, mbu: é titá, rwâkwí hó ŏngo rŭndo, usúngí kása maé
mịngí.⁶⁴ Shé-Mwindo mbu wárukiré tu ékikoé cákátáwá, wáfine bana-cé,
mbu báhụmbị réro ékabụ́rị.⁶⁵ Bana-cé báringa mitámbá, bárịa ȳó hịyo
n'e; n'ehábásirw'ĕmitámbá bárịa hó oto rwịngí.⁶⁶ Mwindo (kaí) mwî-
bútwa ré ndo, múntambị ȳa, wábútwa ná conga nti wahátá co múkubóko kwé kwábŭme;⁶⁷ wábútwa tu ná mbasị nti wahátá ȳo múkubóko
kwémarémbé;⁶⁸ wábútwa tu ná kaku kámushụmbú waKahómbó, nti
wambará ko bukíko n'é múháro rwákurémbé; ékakúka nti kárí mó
murị́ more kumund'akó;⁶⁹ Mwindo wábútwa nti useánge, nti webáa
nákubá.⁷⁰

Bákíé ébụtụ́ wámakịnd'ịsị́ra, ábárịkángá múbutara, mbu básungé
hákutáwá Mwíndo, écăká nti kírí ho búrí hásanéngí mwïshí, bénda
keré ábábŭme; nâ bó béya, básúnga hó, bátárịkị́ na hó kashángí ká-
rehyánị́, bụshwá écụ́ká kịngí kírí búrí kashá nti kíshikángé bo.⁷¹ Kása-
ngá bákíángé, ío wéta wásúsa hó éméso nti wahúngá na.⁷² Bákíé ịyé
múmahombekerera, ébea bátị ịyé báréré, Mwindo wátúka múkabụ́rị,
wénda kịkị́mị́yá muri ịna.⁷³ Mwindo wakíé ịyé unyaïréngi émunụmbá
muri ịna, kwárịkángá shé-Mwindo, mbu wárukiré búriréngí émwăna
mwanya-ngantsị, wáshịshara ngụrụ, mbu: réro ákításúngwáa cású-
ngwa; ịyé murirê tú mwáná mu! Mbéti mukárị́ wamabútá kĕ tu úmpé
mwána!⁷⁴ Shé-Mwindo wákwa mamụ́ma erịsị́mána, bụshwa ébŏbá.
Múntsịnga-ntsịnga sébŭme, shé-Mwindo wásịmána, wénda mwámu-
kárị́ mwanya-ngantsị, nti wendáa kantsóka, kịro ịráca nkịndo. Wéya
mó, wárúngúrira; mbu wátaé mó rịso, wásúnga émwăna nti waincírá
hântsí; wákịme mó, wáshịsha mukárị́, mbu: kúnị́ kútúkángé tu émwănă
ngu, mbéti úkusịángá úmpe múbura, ngí wamabútá tú ŏngo? Mukárị́
wámusúbíe, mbu: Mwindŏ ngu uri múno.⁷⁵ Hárịkángá Mwíndo hântsí
wịkóbére. Shé-Mwindo mbu wásungé ékananganŏ ka, ébŭnu wámu-
bimba, wátúka émunụmbá nti ntíwasúbyá tu kímpé kinwa.⁷⁶ Kwétángá we, wénda kásịmó ébakungú. Mbu wéyé ko, wére bó, mbu: kírí
nku ngí kírí ko, cábịshịsharo.⁷⁷ Wére tŭ bo, mbu: mukŏmá ébụtụ́ wá-
kíáyo wámacá, nti mwéndáȳo kákerá wásịngá ȳamutí, nti múbasă ȳo
mó muhoró wángoma, nti murịa n'ékihú cémukaka ékụsi nti cátamba.⁷⁸
Bákíé ébụtụ́ wámăca, ébea bátị básonjanya-sonjanya, bénda kasúngá
Mwíndo múnụmbá mwịna; Mwindo wásịra ná misúngánó-sungano.
Bákíé bámakịnd'îmusúnga ébakungú báhíta ékumundụra kákerá écụ-
ndá cémutí cémuhoró wéngoma.⁷⁹ Béya ékubusará, bákera có, bákú-
rúke na có kumbúka. Mbu béyé ékumbúka bábasa-basa có, bátóbóra
na có, cábe ná muhoró. Bákíé émuhoró wámarịsa, báringa tu Mwíndo;

bámubétábeta, bámukịmịya ná kumund'ěmuhoró wéngoma. Mwindo wéba, mbu: réro titá usịra ịsásị, kabóntsó-bóntso kájịrịrịsịwa![80] Banashé-Mwindo báringa n'ékihú céngoma, bákángátia na có hábásirw'-ěngoma; bábambire na có ho.[81] Shé-Mwindo wakíé wamasúngá wámarịárwá musike wé kumund'ěngoma, shé-Mwindo wábíkíra murénge múbea bé bátị, mbu wé usondánge bịndamị báruundú bábí bịshúị bêndáyo katáá éngomǎ nji mwịrịba rahákítabinduka.[82] Ébịndamị bébịshúị bákíé bámashékána báháta éngoma, ébea bátị bákúka na mûbúngú, bénda katáá Mwíndo. Bákíé béya hịrịba rahákítabinduka ébịshúị bákịmịre n'éngoma mwịrịba ékǔsi bịshúángé; bákíé béyá munkatị ỹérịrịba, bábíkíra muréngé, mbu: méti túmúkíríe háno? Ábárịkángá ékumishi bátị bárịsịa ná mongo, mbu: hǐha, mukásịngwá-tu-íyo wákụrúka.[83] Báreke n'éngoma munkatị ỹérịrịba, ỹákịme n'ékumunda.[84] Ábarịnga bịrịnga na hábásirwa hákukịmịré éngoma. Ébịshúị bákíé bámakịnd'ǐmutáa mwịrịba, bákụrúke ékumishi. Shé-Mwindo wáshịma na bó ngụrụ, mbu mukórá murimo. Wánịnka kíra mwịshúị kikumí; ábábábí ba bákịndị n'íbinga, bụshwá érúhémbo rwémaruho ábó.[85] Mótụ ndo rwákutáwá Mwindo, ékwantsí n'ékwịyo kwákụmánana bụshwá émbụra nịngị, ỹéca ná mitabero irínda ikenga, émaụwú nti átátúkáa ékwantsí; émbụrǎ ỹa ỹárụsha ná rwǎka rwịngí kuTubondo.[86] Bákíé bámakịnd'ịtáa Mwindo, bákụrúke kuTubondo. Bákíé béya ékumbúka, shé-Mwindo wáhie mukárị nya-Mwindo, mbu utáhícé ná mintsórị mbu uriréngi musike wé; wámare, iwé nti wǎmubungúshá kwákutáwá musike wé. Érótụ nǎ ro nya-Mwindo wábíndúke ná nyakashómbé.[87] Mwífúnd'ịre, nya-Mwindo wénda ushéshémúkwáa busabusa, angá ná kámuntsórị kábiririo.

Kwárịkángá Mwíndo mwịrịba, kwátáwángá we, wakíé íyé uri ékumund'ěmeca múmịsịe wáhuhume kumund'ěngoma, wáhanda émụntwé múngoma, wáhúrúkírire; wéba, mbu wé, érịenda kumbo'érǔsi ná ntíwaraá ịshé ná bana-cé bátị bákumutáanga, bárúkíra ěmukúbú wé wémuréngé, kaị nti ntí wé ngí Mwíndo.[88] Kwárịkángá éngoma kumund'ěmeca múmịsịe, ỹábáse hábásirw'ěmeca ỹịsịné. Ỹakíé ịyé iri hábásirw'erịrịba munkatị ỹaró, ỹárịka na hó, itáhítí n'érǔsi itátáí na ró na.

Kwárịkángá ébea ékumbúka kuTubondo kwátúka mukónga wábikumí, byénda katúkó meca ékǔsi hítúkúriro.[89] Bákíé béya ékǔsi, mbu bárekeré émẽso munkatị ỹérịrịba, básúnga éngoma hábásirw'ěmeca, nti itịmbéngi hó; bábúsánya, mbu: é bana-kịtú, twahụmánáná, éngoma ỹatáwǎyo na Mwindo ngí iỹá! Kwárịkángá Mwíndo munkatị ỹéngoma mwịrịba, wéba, mbu kaị iwé wámafúnd'ísímba, ímbu búrí ébikumí mbi háno, búkírí bútúkóngí bo émeca ékǔsi, kaị iwé nti wǎrụká íngu wǎtụrá ámwasị ékumbúka kúrí ịshé kuTubondo.[90] Ébikumí byákíé byárengeka mwítúko émeca ná bákurérwá hó éngoma, Mwindo kwárịkángá we kumund'ěngoma mwịrịba wárekera énderị kubụnu, wásímba:[91]

Karáni̧ uendo![92]
Niraánge shé-Mwindo
Niraánge shé-Mwindo
Ntsêkwá bi̧ra[93]
Katitá kántáa múngoma
Ntsêkwá Mwindo
Bakungú bábéka shé-Mwindo
Bakungú bábíndúkí ntserya[94]
Bakungú báshé-Mwindo
Bakungú báshé-Mwindo
Bakungú báréserá i̧hano
Katitá kashé-Mwindo
Katitá kántáa múngoma
Ntákwí na kárami[95]
Kábingúrá Yangura
Kábingúrá I̧yangura
I̧yangura mubi̧ty̧ washé-Mwindo.[96]

Ábǎna bémukárí̧ bákíé básúnga búsímbángé Mwíndo kumund'-ěngoma mwi̧ri̧ba, bátáÿa ékumbúka bátibícáángé, nti bámasi̧á ámaréá ékǔsi bunyy̧mé-nyy̧me busantsaara.[97] Bákíé béya ékumbúka, ébábǔme mbu básungé bo básáa ékwi̧ky̧ra bátibícáángé, ébábǔme básúbíraa ématy̧mo, nti báhakángé mbu bári̧ki̧tányí̧wángé ná kihuká.[98] Ébikumí, mbu básungé ématy̧mo, báráke bi̧shé, mbu: tǒto, twendánge kábuty̧ré mwasi̧ wákuri̧ká éngoma ÿatáǎyo bǎny̧ mwi̧ri̧ba; isímbánge, mbu bakungú báshé-Mwindo, bakungú báréserá i̧hano, bakungú bábíndúkí ntserya. Shé-Mwindo wakíé mbu wárukiré bo, wére ébikumí mbu bíti-mángé: éngoma twaréré twatáǎÿo mwi̧ri̧ba, wafúká tu! Ébikumí byári̧si̧a, mbu: uri hó ho Mwindo. Ibó bákumusúngá ná mĕso, ná ukírí uri hó ho. Shé-Mwindo wakíé mbu wárukiré bo wásonja bana-cé báti̧ na, érúbúngú rwási̧a ná busa, ábáti̧ báti̧te n'ékǔsi nti báhátá maty̧mo ná myampú ná kashá.[99]
Mwindo kwási̧ángá we ékǔsi, wákíé wamasúngá wámáti̧té ébikumí ékumbúka, nâ wé wáreke kása érísímba, wéba mbu wé wǎsímba tú nti ébea báměya, by̧shwá mbu ébikumí bǐmbi byámasúngá éki̧shi̧sharo cáé. Ébea báti̧ berúbúngú, bǎna bany̧nké, bakúngú n'ébasike, bomína, bákíé mbu béyé ékǔsi, mbu básungé éngoma munkati̧ ÿéri̧ri̧ba, bákera n'éntéko básísírísángé éngoma. Mwindo wakíé wamasúngá bo bámatécá ékumishi wárekera énderi̧ kubǔnu, wásímba:[100]

Niraánge shé-Mwindo
Ntsêkwá bi̧ra
Bakungú bábéka shé-Mwindo
Karáni uendo!

153

Bakungú bábíndúkí ntserya
Kâkwí na Kárami
Kábingúrá Iyangura.[101]

Mwindo wakíé wamakį́nd'îsímbǎ bo, mwįraa įshé ná bana-shé-
Mwindo bátį, éngoma ỹį́kį́mį́ya n'ékumund'ěrį́rįba; ébarį́nga bį́tįmba na
hábásirwa. Kwárįkángá shé-Mwindo ékumishi ná bana-cé, báshįshara
ngųrų; bátenja émįntwé, mbu: réro cásúmá nci, kwâbútwí ke kátá-
bútwáa![102] Bámakį́nd'îsúnga ákananganį ká bákų́rų́ke ékumbúka
kuTubondo.
Kwétángá Mwindo kumund'ěmeca, wátáÿa n'érǔsi kunand'âró,
wénda katángíré ro háncókó ÿérǔsi kwáKįnkųndų́rį.[103] Wakíé mbu
wéyé kwáKį́nkųndų́rį, wásáme kuró; wéba mbu wé ubungúránge
Iyangura, isínkárį́ wé, kwétį́ré we; nti wamakį́nd'įtų́rį́rwa mwasį́ na
Kahúngú.[104] Wátánja uendo, wábungura sínkárį́ wé Iyangura kumb'-
órǔsi; wásímba:

Mungaį́ tántúkíré muntse
Įkųkų́hį ntátúkíré muntse
Utúkocé Mwíndo
Mwindo kábútwa-kénda
Nibingúránge Iyangura
Kabų́sá ntátúkíré muntse
Utúkocé Mwíndo
Ná Mwindo kábútwa-kénda
Canta ntúkíri muntse
Canta utúkocé Mwíndo
Nabungúrá Iyangura sínkárį́
Mutáká ntátúkíré muntse
Utúkocé Mwíndo
Nibingúránge Iyangura sínkárį́
Kitorų ntátúkíré muntse
Óngo'súngá nabingúrá Iyangura sínkárį́
Narimbura mbu
Mushengé ntátúkíré muntse
Utúkocé Mwíndo
Súnga nabingúrá Iyangura sínkárį́
Iyangura mubį́tų washé-Mwindo
Nya-ruí ntátúkíré muntse
Ná Mwindo kábútwa kéndayo
Nabingúrá Iyangura sínkárį́
Mubį́tų washé-Mwindo
Caÿo ntátúkíré muntse
Óngo'súngá nabingúrá Iyangura sínkárį́

Mubítu washé-Mwindo
Súnga utúkocé Mwíndo
Mwindo kábútwa-kénda
Áwamutáyí mo ngí wakwírí muntse.[105]

Mwindo kásángá ukíánge wéya hárí kikúro, nti wébá mbu kímútúkíriri
émuntse, bátámúkocé, iwé wendánge kwísínkárí wé Iyangura. Mwindo
wakíé wéya kwáCáyo, wáincira kuró; múmukomá-kómá wáhénd'-
iyenda, wásímba:

> Ntsúká ntátúkíré muntse
> Óngo'súngá nabingúrá Iyangura
> Óngo'súngá utúkocé Mwíndo
> Mwindo kábútwa-kénda
> Kirúrumbá ntátúkíré muntse
> Óngo'súngá nabingúrá Iyangura sínkárí
> Óngo'súngá utúkocé Mwíndo
> Ná Mwindo kábútwa-kénda
> Mushómwá ntátúkíré muntse
> Óngo'súngá nabingúrá Iyangura sínkárí
> Óngo'súngá utúkocé Mwíndo
> Ná Mwindo kábútwa kéndayo

Musóka motó waMukítí waréndá káríká hábásirwá na Mukítí:[106]

> Musóka ntátúkíré muntse
> Utúkocé Mwíndo
> Mwindo kábútwa kéndayo

Musóka wakíé mbu wásungé Mwíndo wéya hárí we, wátúma ntúmwá
kúrí Múkítí kebá mbu kúrí mwea kúno kúrí we, kwáMúsóka, ubungúránge Iyangura. Éntúmwá yátibite tété kúrí Múkítí; yéya kó yátúra
émwasí, mbu: kúrí mweä nku, ubungúránge Iyangura. Mukítí wásúbíe
éntúmwá ya, mbu wérenga Musóka, mbu émweä o utákundúkíngá hárí
we, mbéti iwé wamuríkécángá ha bushwá nkí? Éntúmwá ya yéya kúrí
Músóka, yátúra émwasí wákwerírwá we na Mukítí. Musóka wénda
uhangírée kí Mwíndŏ bo, nti ntíwosí mbu mwäna wámukárí waMukítí
Iyangura. Musóka wásúbíe Mwindo, mbu: Mukítí watíná mbu utétí,
íyé ébŭme wábé ngí wâkwěca; aní ŭngu, Musóka, nakítá háno, utúshéí
intse kwětá ŏngo. Mwindo wámusúbíe nti wahehéá ámuréngé, mbu:
aní Mwindo ntáhangírwánga intse, năhúmúrá mpe hákíkísé ŏngo.
Mwindo wakíé mbu wárukiré bo wítumatuma, wásía émeca hábásirwa,
wákíme n'ékumund'ěmjsíe, wénda ná kasáá nkatí-nkatí Músóka na
Mukítí. Mwindo wakíé wamasúkáná Músóka, wamahúmó émuruta

wáMúsóka, wĵamba, mbu: aní ǔno Mwindo kábútwa-kénda, ntáshe-mbwánga réro. Musóka wakĵé wámusúnga tú kumbo n'é, wĵtĵnge ékubŭnu, wéba mbu: réro émutárě ngu wákwetá ke kúnĵ? wákwetá ékwĵyo kongó nákusúngá érĵrụmbĵ-rụmbĵ ré; wêté ékwantsí kongó nákurúkírá ésánkĵndo sé![107] Musóka wĵanya ngụrụ, mbu: kaĵ iwé wǎfi-nírwáyo na Mukĵtĵ mbu wé wasúkányá mwea.

Mwindo wakĵé wamasukáná Músóka wátánja uendo rwĵenda kwá-Múkĵtĵ; wásímba:

> MwaMukĵtĵ mwaMarĵba[108]
> Mukĵtĵ ntátúkíré muntse
> Óngo'súngá nabingúrá Ĵyangura
> Ĵyangura mubĵtụ washé-Mwindo
> Mukĵtĵ utúkocé Mwíndo
> Mwindo kábútwa-kénda

Mukĵtĵ kwárĵkángá we wákĵé mbu wárukiré, wátenga, mbu nyé watíkó mukárĵ! Wátenja ékwantsí n'ékwĵyo, émurĵba ụ́tĵ wátengana. Kwárĵ-kángá Mwíndo wéba, mbu: réro twǎsíbáná rúno'otụ́ bǎte na Mukĵti n'âní Mwindo ntásúbáháa kitaba, nénkĵ ntángasúngána n'é.[109] Mwindo wakĵé warúkirǎ bo, wéba mbu: réro moké wasínkárĵ utimánge, aní Mwindo ngí nahangírwá ántse ẏakwásínkárĵ! Mwindo wítuma-tuma, wénda ná kasáíré hákĵsĵngo hĵkụnyĵé Múkĵtĵ. Mukĵtĵ wákĵé mbu wámú-súnge, wéba mbu: réro ntí ngí ǔngu, watáríké tu. Wáshĵsha, mbu: ǒngo ngí nyé? Mwindo wĵasha, mbu wé ngí Mwíndo kábútwa-kénda, mwǎna wĴyangura. Mukĵtĵ wére Mwindo, mbu: búnĵ e? Mwindo wá-musúbĵe mbu wé ubungúránge isínkárĵ wé Ĵyangura. Mukĵtĵ mbu wárukiré bo, wére Mwindo mbu: ǒngo' timánge, háno hátétánga réro mwea, wákinduké émyoǒ nji n'esántsĵrǎ ntsi, réro ǒngo uténdánga toró wĵanikira, óngo ngí ǔkundúká hó háno hárí we! Mukĵtĵ bána Mwindo bákĵé ĵyé bébánángé hó bo, na kúrĵkangá Ĵyangura kwátúka bikumí, byénda katúkó meca, kúrĵkĵré Múkĵtĵ nti ngí kúrĵkaá erítúkúriro. Ébi-kumí bákĵé bámasúngá Mwíndo bútíkóngí wátíko Ĵyangura mbu isín-kárĵ, byátibite kúrí Ĵyangura; byéya kó, bére Ĵyangura, mbu: ínku kúrí moké'ábé Múkĵtĵ, kúrí kámwea kĵma kébángé mbu, mbu Mukĵtĵ wámúreki, iwé ngí Mwíndo, iwé wendánge nti ubungúráa Ĵyangura sínkárĵ wé. Ĵyangura wakĵé mbu wárukiré émwasĵ o, wéba mbu kaĵ mwána wé o, iwé wéyé kása kúrí we. Ĵyangura wátáẏa éróu, wénda kasáíré hítúkúriro, wárúngúrira ékǔsi, mbu wé wásungé kása émwea umutíkóngi, mbu wé ngí Ĵyangura. Kwárĵkángá Mwíndo, wakĵé mbu wásungé isínkárĵ wé wěya kámusúnga, wásímba mbu:

> Nkụ́sánge Mwindo
> Ntsékwá Mwindo

Isínkárí Iyangura nti íyé uhítánge, wénda usímbángě ke nti usísírísánge
kútúkíréngí isínkárí.

Sínkárí Iyangura
Mukítі wamánkangé éntse
Nibungúráa sínkárí Iyangura
Nabingúrá Iyangura
Mubítу washé-Mwindo
Mukítі ntátúkíré muntse
Nibungúránge Iyangura
Mubítу washé-Mwindo
Mukítі titá ntátúkíré muntse
Utúkocé Mwíndo
Katítíirí na Mpúmba
Ná Rіnteá na shé-Burénda[110]
Titá ntsêkwá Mwindo
Sínkárí Yangura wáráka wébayo
Sínkárí Yangura wamúmubi.[111]

Iyangura wéba, mbu: kúti éngomǎ nji iri mó mwĮhwa wábana-Mitandį,
ýéýé háno, iwé wásungé ýo hámákako n'e. Isínkárí wakíé watíkó bana-
Mitandį bo, éngoma ýátína įkentsere kwįhí n'Iyangura. Mwindo
wíonona kumund'ěngoma, mbu réro sínkárí wé wǒsá! Isínkárí wé
wéba tú, mbu: kúti ǒngo ngoma, ǒngo mwíhwa wámusíngwa-námá,
іyá háno, kentséré kwįhí n'e. Isínkárí wé wakíé wamatíkó basíngwa-
námá bo, éngoma ýátína hó tú įkentsere kwįhí n'e. Isínkárí wé wéba
tú, mbu: kúti ǒngo mwíhwa wában'Iyana hó, iyá háno hámákako n'e.
Mwindo wakíé mbu wárukiré bo, wénda ná nti usímbánge, mwítúka
ré hírіba:

Nendánge kwásínkárí Iyangura
Iyangura mubítу washé-Mwindo
Kabáré-báré na Ntábare
Kwátéé moké babá byoo[112]
Ná mwĮsí wakóndá marámį
Ná musike mongó kakóma yo[113]
Twanánge múano
Rwánángá Babúýá[114]
Twanánge ruano
Rwánángá Babúýá
Twanánge múano
Kaséngerí umínéngi múconga
Nó'ǒngo súngánga conga cándérema[115]
Nkúróngó waréndé musúsu

157

Muhasha wakwị́ré mahúha[116]
Námatikátị́ká carwĭmbo
Cámakwá kítánkwirĭ nko[117]
Ntábonjé na ntsịra-rịna[118]
Bébérenga marụ́o Mukị́tị
Miréngé isímbánge bătе
Ná barịmị bátásibé ỹo
Ntánjnkwé mbụ́rụ́ nará bịngị
Narịka nakéndéré bura[119]
Nasúngángá múme wánkókó birangira
Nasúnga ná muntorị́ wámushemba[120]
Karangị́ kamúmpunge
Kátátiká-tíkánga
Ébụtụ́ wámăca
Nasúngá myaníkírí iỹanga
Ỹaỹángá bantsị́bị́ na nịna
Kasungú kámatúbá-tuba
Kasungú nti kásondá mwandị[121]
Warị́ré ntsúká taményera
Nti warísá mutíma mwịndamị[122]
Nya-bungé wámabungé mpetị
Nti warụ́ká n'émakụ́rụ́kịro
Nasíbángá mbu mpúnda séta
Munyohó ná mubembị hánkingo
Úmarúkírá mbu shúmbe-shúmbe
Nti émukúngú wakángá mubịre
Nirịkanga níkandíráa
Bérenga muhú na ngị́rịma
Nahíngíré mberụ́ kịrị́mụ
Ná kisakí cárụ́ka urịanga
Muhangú nya-bị́húndé mantse
Nya-mwịsị́ wámakwá na músike
Nti atúmbú ukéngi n'éntongị.[123]

Mwindo wakíé ịyé uhítáa hó n'érŭsi, ịyé ubungúráa sínkárị́ wé, wénda ná keyá na hámákako n'e, hárí we. Isínkárị́ wé wátịnge n'éngoma, bámunịnka mweré bana-cé; wábéráa n'éngoma; mbu wátunjé ékihú, wásúnga n'ébentsé-bĕntsé byákéntsé na mwĕrị. Éríhunda rémwăna rĭrá Mwindo. Mwindo wásáa na múngoma nti uri hó n'éconga cé n'émwandá wé, hịmá n'ékánkŭ ké kárí mó émurị́. Kahúngú wakíé wasúnga Mwindo ịyé usúngánáa n'isínkárị́ wé, kénda ná katụ́rá mwasị́ kúrí émutambo wanịnkwángá Ịyangura mbu ngị́ wĕndáyo umurangánge.[124] Kéya hó, kámutụ́re mwasị́, mbu: ŏngo, óngori kúno, ntí kábŭme kásáá nku, kárí ná mishịngá kakịrị́, ŏngo ukwá. Kasịyémbé

wakíé mbu wárukiré émwasí o, wéba, mbu: ŏngo ntúmwá, ŏngo we-
dánge, ŭkíá úmeyá kúrí Mwíndo, mbu utáriráni n'íéta kúno, iwé nti
wămukongórá éríkúa ré rémongo, iwé ŭno uteánge masha ná ntsoí, ná
ngembe ékwantsí; iwé kongó wásíbayo kwânantáyo wé. Katéé wakíé
mbu wásungé bo, wénda kasáé hárí Mwíndo, wámwǐre, mbu: ŏngo
Mwindo, bínú bákwêndéé námá, bákútéángé ná masha, ná ntsoí, ná
ngembe;[125] iwé katéé, ntí ŏngo'musúngaa ékwantsí, kumund'éróto?
Mwindo wámusúbíe, mbu: nankí, iwé ukusúnganga ékwantsí ngí kúrí-
kangá ŏngo. Katéé wakíé wamatúré Mwíndo émwasí wékikúbá ca
cerímutonde, wámwǐre tú mbu: wé wecá muhéngéré útukiri háno
hárikíré ŏngo, iwé wéshé na ó kumunda n'énumbá mwasónkárí'ábé,
hítína n'énguriro. Mwindo wámurísja. Mukeí wátánja itíma éróto
kumunda na ró. Mwindo wére isínkárí wé Iyangura, mbu: ŏngo sínkárí
wé sondórá, nti ŏngo wendánge kurwábé, iwé wăkukúmáná kuró; ná
ngu Kasíyémbé, ŭngu umuhiéngi ínku, nâ wé wăsúngánáyo n'e kása,
kúti nâ wé ukwée kăra, iwé nti wăsúngáná n'e. Wére ná sínkárí wé mbu:
umwírenga wítúngányanye, íngo umuhiéngǐ ko. Mun'ebué-bue nâ wé
wátúka n'ékumund'ĕmasha, wangánge émeko, wésha na ó hábásirwa
n'émasha; émasha ábe ná meko mara-ara, iwé mbu ngí hêndá háshatéé
Mwíndo hǐmpe, iwé utúnge na mun'ebué-bue, Mwindo utákocé ikwí-
rírira, nâ bó ngí bárí ko. Isínkárí wakíé wameríwá na Mwindo mbu
wásondoré mwíenda, utákíí tu ná ntíndírísí, wíire na kûkwé. Kwásíángá Mwíndo kurṇma, wéta na múndákí ỹaKatéé, wásáire ná mwa-
sínkárí wé mwIyangura, múkahómbó ké.[126] Kasíyémbé wakíé mbu
wámúsúnge, wéba mbu: Mwindo íyé uri na kúno, ná wákusáíré ke
kúní! Bísa-kuró béba, mbu bó ntí bósí kwákusáíré we.

Iyangura wakíé wasúngă musike wé Mwindo wamĕya, wámwǐre,
mbu: musike wé nénkí utárísí biỹó, wéyé kása kúno, ibó bámíné ngoma.
Mwindo wakíé wamarúkírá ébŭnu wásínkárí wé, wátúka émunṇmbá,
wásáa hárí sínkárí wé hâmbúka, wére sínkárí wé, mbu wé ŭno, wamíná
iwé ntíwarísá biỹó, iwé wăcíkáné múngomă nji![127] Isínkárí wé wámusúbíe, mbu: angá, míná hó, ŏngo musike wé, nâ wé utúnge n'é, wăkíá
kĕ tu búní, ná ngu wanínkwángá we mwímucṇnga ngí webánge mbu
úmíné! Ná twăkíá kĕ tu búní? Iyé umínaa hó. Mwindo mbu wárukiré
ékinwa císínkárí wé, wéba, mbu: támáta, namína kása, rwáka rútáỹá-
nga mwea. Mwindo wásímba, wáráka wéba:

> Kasíyémbé utúkocé Mwíndo
> Ná Mwindo kábútwa-kénda
> Kasíyémbé mbu túmíné mongo
> Sh'írungú tunínke kǐmo
> Twámakwá nti twakukwíré
> Kaséngerí umínéngi múconga
> Conga cándérema[128]

Nderánge Mpými̱mba
Mpými̱mb'aní̱ ná bisumbú-sumbú.

Mwindo wátámbáira múmasha ubéndééráa hí̱yo'ǎmasha, ang'į̱bábára
na múngembe, wétána n'eki̱tí kwákumutéángá Kasí̱yémbé angá n'į̱bá-
bára. Mwindo wakí̱é wametáná kwáki̱téíwá we, wámį̱na, wákúbánya
éconga í̱nku nǎ nku, nti usímbánge:

Katéé ngí̱ mí̱ri̱ngí̱ wantserya
Ná kantorí̱ ngí̱ shé-Biréo¹²⁹

Wásha bana-Mitandį̱ mbu:

Murésúngá naréshiá bana-Mitandį̱
Kahúngú ntwendá kasóna
Nasóná ki̱ndu kwáshé-mi̱mbo¹³⁰
Nasúngá batúká bámondo
Wásíkútá wásį̱ka¹³¹

Į̱yangura wéba, mbu musike wé wárisé réro biỹó, hákweyéré réro
wé ntíwákutúrá réro oté mwirísa biỹó.¹³² Į̱yangura wáshee musike wé
nkambí̱, wákonda ỹó. Mwîrísa, ábárí ékumishi ngí̱ bénda bárísángé
ỹo, ébikumí, iwé nti utángecá muỹó kubi̱nu mbu urísánge muỹó.
Mwindo wakí̱é wamakį̱nd'îrísa énceo ỹénkambí̱ ỹákumusheé isínkárį̱
hį̱ma n'ébikumí, Kasí̱yémbé, émubushú-búshu wé, wámwendere hó
múbingo rwį̱sasa imuỹa, mbu¹³³ í̱ngu muỹú ngí̱ wasêmufúndwa hó,
nâ wé warúkíráyo mbu watúkáyo kumund'êngoma!¹³⁴ Kasí̱yémbé
wáráke Nkúbá Mirábyo, mbu: ǒngo Nkúbá uhítanga, úberaé Mwíndo
bebe bíbí ímu muri wé, hį̱má nǎ mbi bikumí bį̱tį̱ bírí n'ě mo. Mwindo
wakí̱é mbu wárukiré búhiéngí Kasí̱yémbé wámuhie, wére ébikumí
bį̱rį̱kį̱ré n'e múni̱mbá, mbu bárį̱ké uháro ri̱mǎ n'e, bi̱shwá mbu
Kasí̱yémbé usasį̱re imuhície nkúbá. Mwindo wáhie muna-Nkúbá, mbu:
ǒngo Nkúbá, ǒngo'hítánge, uhítenga muháro ri̱ma rwáni̱mbá, ang'-
íhíte múháro rúrí mo Mwíndo. Muna-Nkúbá mbu wárukiré émuréngé
wáKasí̱yémbé, wáhíte na múni̱mbá muri Mwindo. Mwindo wáshemba
ỹó, mbu: ngí̱ rwâkwí hó bǎni̱ rǔro, bǎni̱ mutáỹánge hó mwį̱kóngó.
Muna-Nkúbá wáhíta ngendo sirínda, nti ihítée hó muháro ri̱ma rwá-
ni̱mbá muri Mwindo, itáráráni̱ na kúrí we, ékashá kásaka múkebé
kį̱ma; ékebě ca cábindúke ná moté mwara-ara. Kwárį̱kángá Į̱yangura
isínkárí̱ waMwindo, ébiririo byámutúke múměso byámuhíte na mú-
m1ndí̱, iwé mbu kaí̱ musike wé wakwá, iwé nti ntíwamusúngá shu!
Mwindo wáśáa émuni̱mbá hį̱ma n'ébikumí, wí̱kange múntéko ỹébea,
wí̱asha, mbu wé ǔno, kábútwa-kénda. Wére isínkárí̱ wé, mbu wáke-
ntserí kúrí we, iwé wámwíri. Isínkárí̱ wéya kwį̱hí̱ n'e. Mwindo wá-

mwĩre, mbu: angá tú įre, ŏngo isínkárį wé ngí cásįngwá Kasįyémbé wámwĕca hó mó ékashįmbŏ mbu, nâ wé múbųtų wámukŏmá, nâ wé ntíbámusúngáyo kása, kaį nti ntí wé utųnge na Mwindo.[135] Wére isínkárį wé, mbu wé wĕndá kása ukóhyánge, érįhųmbe ráKásįyémbé nti įyé ríshíréngí.[136] Kwárįkángá Kásįyémbé, bákíé mbu básisimukí, érį-hųmbe ráKásįyémbé rábunga na mó kashá, érúmįnį rwéya na mú-mwănyá, ásândá sįtį n'étuhuká tųtį kásángá túrįkįré múmųntwé n'e, étųtį twátįnda na. Bákíé básúnga érįhųmbe ráKásįyémbé įyé ríshíréngí, bana-cé waKasįyémbé básubukia káringá meca múmaréá erįrįmya ékashá ékumųntwé na Kasįyémbé. Bákíé mbu béyé ékumaréá, béya kó nti kúsįrá meca, áátį nti ámakámé múmaréá, nti angá tu n'įtondį rírí muó. Báhúnge ékubesé byesámpókó, béyakó nti byákukáma, angá na n'įtondį mubyó. Béba, mbu: éo, múturiri émųntwé mûnté! Ásânté sáhina múbea bátį, émŏnu ábó árụka maté.[137] Bákíé bámasúngá bǔbó, béba, mbu: Kasįyémbé ngu wasêkwá, mwêndi kámukaíré kwányeré-kurwábó, kwáMúkįtį ngí kúrįkangá murįba. Béta kó. Mbu béyé ko, bákųmána Mukįtį ékibabárį n'émintsârį nti ngí imutįmbánge mó, nâ wé nti wákukámírwá n'émeca, émurįba ųtį nti wákukáma, angá na n'įtondį. Isínkárį wakíé mbu wásungé ca, wénda karákíríré kúrí musike wé, mbu: kokórá émutíma, ŏngo musike wé wamúmubi, mwăna ųmá, weyángá kĕ kúno kúrí we nti ŏngo wendáa kĕ tú kahéndá bo, sįcá ému-tíma, úború moké hįmá n'émutambo wé ngu Kasįyémbé, úramyé bo, ang'įshųnáne tǔ bo.[138] Isínkárį wakié wamakįndį kwįtóndóora kúrí musike wé, Mwindo wásįca émutíma, wásįmo Kasįyémbé nti umubutée éconga cé, wásímba:

> Wéndángá toró nasímuka
> Utúkocé Mwíndo
> Mwindo kábútwa-kénda

Simúká ke múconga cé kíno cándérema:

> Wendángá toró nasímuka
> Kaenga ncaténgi múconga

Bákíé mbu básisimuké, Kasįyémbé wárama. N'émaréá, émeca ákų-rúke tú muó; n'ébesé byémpókó bįtį byábe tǔ mó meca; nă nku kwá-rįkángá Múkįtį, émeca ámukúrúke tu, érŭsi rwárįsa na. Bákíé mbu básungé ékashįmbŏ'ka, báshįshara ngųrų, mbu kaį Mwindo wábǔme nâ wé.[139] Kasįyémbé wánįnka Mwindo, mbu: karamo karamŏ ka é Mwindo. Mwindo wárįsja ná, mbu aé. Mwindo wakíé wamecá ákashį-ngįshŏ ka, wére isínkárį wé, mbu wé mukómá nti wé wendá kuTubondo kakwáná n'įshé, bųshwá mbu įshé wamutáángá mbíso sįbį, nâ wé wĕndáyo kása kasúngáná n'e. Isínkárį wámwĩre, mbu: é titá utúkocįyo

kuTubondo kwásó, ǒngo mwǎna wémwioroyo, ubútwǎyo tété-tétéyo,
ngí ǔkocá kuTubondo, ubúngú rwándushú sirínda![140] Iwé Iyangura
wákutúnjǎyo kumunda n'éngoma, iwé utǔnge n'Iyangura, iwé watǐná
ngyry, ang'íyo jenda tu kwísiné; éntse ýakwísiné itákóndánga. Mwindo
mbu wárukiré wébángé isínkárí wé wítiníre, wárírībanya isínkárí wé,
wísímbíre. Isínkárí wámwǐre, mbu: ǒngo mushúkira wé, ibúta rámuyú
iruhuka, ang'íyo ikwánayo na só; kúti wěnda-hó-yo, nǎ wé nti wěndáyo
na bé kasúngá búkúbáá-báángé isó. Wére n'ébikumí mbu bárongí
ébisheke byé, kongó ibó béndayo na Mwindo, byshwá mbu éntse ýakwí-
sìné ntíyahundá, itásíanga, ikúmána kikáí cámúyá mwea. Bákíé ébytú
wámǎca básímbúre érúendo rweríkúrúke kuTubondo. Mwindo wénda
himá n'isínkárí wé, hima n'ébaombé, nti bámúrisíángé. Mwindo
wásímba:

> Ntírirí wabíré mubánga
> Ná musará wabíré mukéndo[141]
> *Karáni uendo!*
> Nendánge kǔndu kuTubondo
> Ntsékwáná kǔndu kuTubondo
> Ná Tubondo makúra arínda yo
> Twebánge bira
> Sínkárí nkané ihano
> Ntakwáná na bákumbo
> Báhátá matúmo ná nguba
> KwiHímbí kwárikángá Bírori
> Ntsékwa Mushymo
> Kuntsurí kwárikángá Rúronga
> Munongo kwárikánga shé-Cǎra
> Bitúmbí byashé-Mené Ndyra
> Ná bakúngú bákwáne mushuri
> Kumbare kwárikángá Kárai
> Wabéséngá shé-mutúro wábinwa
> Bámbáré bárí n'Irímwe wabó
> Tunkundú bárí na Ntéko ýabó
> Natíkó Mabúra Bányore
> Kwábó bakóyo
> Kabotyó Munyá-ngoro
> Nya-buké Kamwíkoti[142]
> Cámwǐndí wákínda kuMpúrwa
> Ná kikoshú wákínda kuKámuri[143]
> Bytú wákucá nebánge
> Bérenga nkandá mukúki[144]
> Ébytú wákǔno búcírengá ntambi
> Nti émuandá watéká rytúnda[145]

Mikéré bárí na Mbórụ wabó
Ná Batoị bárí na Túa'bó
Inyé ngịra Bụ́kụca kwáNgara
KuMbụhị kwáMútatéa bó bána Mwindo
Kirambo cáMámboréo[146]
Bịsa-Ntándá bátịsaní nyama
Bábíkángá mumína ukíenga
KuMpíngá Buróngo
Ná kuNkásá kwábó Buróngo
Bána Mwindo
Batémbó bátịsaní nyama
Bábíká Mutụ́mba ná Kunju[147]
Ná Biréré byáRúkoba-kóba
Ntáróbí na Bároba
KuBuráẏa kwátukwa
Ná kentsé cábịngị́té isumba
Ná Batịka-Rúkari
Maéré kịsị́ kaRúkunja
Maéré urịré kě nki wěyá
Ntárịré káréngáná ngụrụ
Narịré mpéné kishángịre
Nará ná musúsa bútara
Nti úrịséré mịsịe ná nkondị
Kakundá úmaser'ịsaka
Katịtị wámúsịére itindi
Nkụ́róngó sakúno sásuma
Nkụ́róngó sámasúngá bea
Sárera matindi
KuKúmbú-kúmbú kwáBátobo
Kwárịká Ntsúrú na Rúkari[148]

Mwindo wásímba:

Karánị uendo!
Nendánge na sínkárị
Kárére károngé
Eé titá káramúk'ịenda
Twará twendánge băte
KwáMúnkondé ban'Ịyana[149]

Mwindo wakíé ịyé wendánge hó n'isínkárị wé bo, érịoró-óro rénda kámukụ́máná kwábịnyantịré ban'Ịyana. Wásáme kuró nti bámámukeréré mpéné ẏánceo. Wakíé wamakịnd'írísa émpéné ẏa hịmá n'isínkárị wé ná baombé bísínkárị wé, Mwindo wére bịnyantịré, mbu wé wendá-

nge kakwáná na shé-Mwindo kuTubondo; múmwése, bǎnu ngí běsi bébi-
ramba, bǎnu binyantįré.¹⁵⁰ Ban'Įyana béba, mbu bó básêkwěsa. Bá-
mwambica biráto byácǔma cara-ara ná pantaró ỹácǔma, bámwěse ná
shimíshi ỹácǔma, ná nkobíra ỹácǔma. Bámwĩre, mbu: ngí cásíngwá
ǒngw'endánge kakwáná na só, ématů́mo êndá ákúrúndángé bo, nti
énda ákéngí múcúmǎ nci kírí múmubi. Binyantíré bákíé bámakínd'-
įmwěsa, béba mbu bó bátákocé tú įsía, ibó béndángé na bé, béndí
kasúngá wásêkukámá bo. Múmukomá-kómá Mwindo wátínge múendo
hima ná binyantíré, n'isínkárí wé Įyangura, n'ébaombé bísínkárí wé.
Mwindo wénda nti usímbánge, wáráka wéba:

> Ntsékwáná kǔndu kwáshé-Mwindo
> Sánkambú sábíká shé-Mwindo
> Síkumané Mwíndo
> *Eé karáni uendo!*

Bákíé básond'įya kuró, íyé báráráméé kuró, isínkárí waMwindo wére
Mwindo, mbu: eé titá túkurukį háno, kaé wákíá kǔndu kwásó nkú-
ngúshá, kǔndu kuTubondo ubúngú rwámakúra arínda, kúrí bea bįngí,
kǔndu básêtushírísha. Mwindo wásúbíe isínkárí wé mbu: aní Mwindo,
ntásúbáháa kitaba nénki ntángakwána na có, nisondánge kása nteréká
shé-Mwindǒ ngu, wabíshíé ngúru émuhao.¹⁵¹ Mwindo wéta usímbánge:

> Twendánge kǔndu kuTubondo
> Kwáríkángá shé-Mwindo.

Bákíé béya hámunkobóngó, mbu: túsamé kǔno. Isínkárí wáráka
wéba, mbu: twǎsámé hání, háno hásįrá nų́mbá, kaé Kírúká nya-mbúra
waměya, nya-mbúra itáhumba.¹⁵² Isínkárí wáráka wéba, mbu: eé titá
twǎréré hání, émbura ỹamárururuma, munyeré uri búrio.¹⁵³ Mwindo
wakíé mbu wákai, wéba, mbu wé usondánge manų́mbá; ámanų́mbá
íhimba na. Mwindo wéba, mbu binyantíré émutangá o, n'isínkárí wé
éúmpé mutangá ó, nâ wé Mwindo énų́mbá ỹé ỹíhanda munkatí na
bó. Isínkárí wáráka wéba, mbu: aé titá Mwindo úramé ná manų́mbá
ítú, kaí ná shé-Mwindo warébútá muraj; Kahómbó titá, nakunínkí
buntu. Twíirí na karánj wįtú, karánj wįtú wáramé nkúbá ná mirábyo.¹⁵⁴
Shé-Mwindo warébútá muraj utásúbáhánga, ná Mwindo wísıné mu-
raj.¹⁵⁵ Bákíé íyé bárí hákibíká mpo, émanų́mbá ámakíndí kwíhimba,
isínkárí waMwindo wámwĩre, mbu: eé titá Mwindo, túkururké, utúkocé éngencě nji ỹábea iri kuTubondo. Mwindo wéba mbu wé usêreka
kása. Įyangura isínkárí waMwindo wámwĩre, mbu: eé titá Mwindo,
twárísá kě nkí, kaé basokontíré bĩmbi kakíri kabó, n'âní Įyangura niri
ná mukónga wábea, nó ǒngo Mwindo, óngo'ri ná basij ná basímbį,
énkúmo ítį ỹa ỹárísá nkí? Mwindo wakíé warúkira wámámwĩré isínkárí

wé, wárįsįa, iwé mbu: ntíutimá, ŏngo sínkárį wé, iwé wasúngá énkúmo
įtį iri na bó nti ÿamakįnd'ļkwá rwǎka. Wákae ékwįyo, wįshįsha mbu
wé usasįre iringa kása ébiÿó bįtį bírí kǔndu kuTubondo bímúkųmáne
háno, kongó iwé wákwánayo na bó nti įyé byámakįnd'îmukųmána.
Mwindo wásímba nti įyé utútúráa ébiÿó bírí kwįshé. Isínkárį wáráka
wéba, mbu: eé titá tusêrísá kįnkį? Mwindo wáráka wásímba, mbu:

        Émantu árí kuTubondo
        Ámantu ákųmané Mwíndo
        Mwindo kábútwa-kénda
        Ányama sírí kuTubondo
        Nyama síkųmané Mwíndo
        Sányama sábíká shé-Mwindo
        Nyama síkųmané Mwíndo Mbórų
        Mwindo kábútwa-kénda
        Nkųnį sábíká shé-Mwindo
        Eé titá síkųmané Mwíndo Mbórų
        Ná Mwindo kábútwa-kénda
        N'ékashá kábíká shé-Mwindo
        N'ékashá kákųmané Mwíndo
        N'émeca ábíká shé-Mwindo
        N'émeca ákųmané Mwíndo Mbórų
        Maréá árí kwáshé-Mwindo
        Maréá ákųmané Mwíndo
        Mwindo kábútwa-kénda
        Ásáncangí sírí kwáshé-Mwindo
        Sáncangí síkųmané Mwíndo
        Mwindo wendánge kakwána
        Ásántengį sírí kuTubondo
        Sántengį síkųmané Mwíndo
        Eé titá kábútwa kéndayo
        Kínyihíré ihima
        Ásántangé sábíká shé-Mwindo
        Ásántangé síkųmané Mwíndo
        Ná bįbo byábíká shé-Mwindo
        Ná bįbo bíkųmané Mwíndo
        N'émukwa wábíká shé-Mwindo
        N'émukwa úkųmané Mwindo
        Kábútwa-kénda[156]
Ngí wébángé Mwíndo bǔbo!
        Ná nkókó sábíká shé-Mwindo
        Ná nkókó síkųmané Mwíndo
        Baréngé-réngé bárérana
        Bárįkangá nti báréraná kare

Baréngé-réngé bárérana
Bárérané nkatį-nkatį kebútara
Kâkwí na kárami
Kákumané Iyangura háno
Iyangura mubįtu washé-Mwindo
Ásámpéné sírí kwáshé-Mwindo
Ásámpéné síkumané Mwíndo
Ásánkambú sírí kuTubondo
Sánkambú síkumané Mwíndo
Ásánkambú sáráka séba
Mbu eé titá túkumané Mwíndo
Ásámbíbi sírí kuTubondo
Sámbíbi síkumané Mwíndo
Sámbíbi sáráka séba
Mbu eé titá túkumané Mwíndo
Twarįká twakokórá nįnga
Búrí batįmį bámasha
Masambú árí kuTubondo
Masambú ákumané Mwíndo
Ná taba úrí kwáshé-Mwindo
Ná tafa úkumané Mwindo
Mukúsá wámįná mitúta
Tumbotįá túrí hámutíma
Ná mbarį sábíká shé-Mwindo
Ná mbarį síkumané Mwíndo
Matųmo árí kwáshé-Mwindo
Matųmo ákumané Mwíndo
Sámbasį sírí kwáshé-Mwindo
Sámbasį síkumané Mwíndo
Mikúshu iri kwáshé-Mwindo
Mbu eé titá mikúshu íkumané Mwíndo
Báruké ná umá uhínganga
Marokó árí kwáshé-Mwindo
Marokó ákumané Mwíndo
Karokó kahára mbúbį
Karokó kákumané Mwíndo
Turųo twábíká shé-Mwindo
Turųo túkumané Mwíndo
Báruké n'úmá uhíanga
Inku sábíká shé-Mwindo
Ná nku síkumané Mwíndo
Éngembe sábíká shé-Mwindo
Ná ngembe síkumané Mwíndo
Kúruké ná umá ubéwanga

Butéá wábíká shé-Mwindo
Eé titá butéá
Búrįké búkụmané Mwíndo
Kúrụké nǎ ngu umbaranga
Ntsáro sábíká shé-Mwindo
Ná ntsáro síkụmané Mwíndo
Kúrụké nǎ ngu umbaranga
Mimbo ÿabíká shé-Mwindo
Ná mimbo íkụmané Mwíndo
Kúrụké nǎ ngu utúnganga
Bǔsa wábíká shé-Mwindo
N'ébǔsa búkụmané Mwíndo
Kúrụké nǎ ngu ukóÿanga
Sámpų́ká sábíka shé-Mwindo
Mbu eé titá mpų́ká
Síkụmané Mwíndo
Kúrụké nǎ ngu ukákanga
Nyungú sábíká shé-Mwindo
Ná nyungú síkụmané Mwíndo
Kúrụké n'ų́má utékanga
Mitúndú ÿabíká shé-Mwindo
Mitúndú íkụmané Mwíndo
Kúrụké nǎ ngu uhítanga
Mumangá wábíká shé-Mwindo
Mimangá íkụmané Mwíndo
Kúrụké n'ų́má utóréranga mįnį
Tuané kwaruano
Runaáná Bábuÿa
Bisárá byábíká shé-Mwindo
Bisárá bíkụmané Mwíndo
Kúrụké ná ụmá usáríenga
N'émuba wábíká shé-Mwindo
N'émuba úkụmané Mwíndo
Kúrụké nǎ ngu wésanga
N'ényondo sírí kwáshé-Mwindo
N'ényondo síkụmané Mwíndo
Kúrụké nǎ ngu wésanga
N'ébě̌sį bábíká shé-Mwindo
N'ébě̌sį bákụmané Mwíndo
Kúrụké nǎ ngu wésanga
Nkéndo sírí kuTubondo
Nkéndo sábíká shé-Mwindo
Nkéndo síkụmané Mwíndo
Kúrụké nǎ ngu ukéndanga

Mabondo árí kwáshé-Mwindo
Mabondo ákųmané Mwíndo
Kúrųké ná ųmá ukéndanga
Ná utéanga
N'éngoma sírí kuTubondo
Mbu eé titá ngoma
Síkųmané Mwíndo
Kúrųké nǎ ngu umínanga¹⁵⁷

Mwindo ná bįnyantįŕé n'ísínkárį wé n'ébaombé béyángá na bó, basímbį n'ébasij, bákíé mbu básisimuké, ébikáí bítį byárįkángá kuTubondo kwáshé-Mwindo byákųmánana bó mpo hárįkįŕé bo. Isínkárį waMwindo wakíé mbu wásungé ébikáí bítį bya, wére musike wé Mwindo, mbu: eé titá, ǔhingánáyo n'ébikáí byábené mbi bísonjángé ǒngo. Ábárįkángá na Mwindo hákįbíka bákwa ná mbįhe ỹerísúkúta ébiỹó, bátákwí tu ná mpóỹá, écuká cákųmánana bó. Béba mbu, kaí Mwindo wábǔme utébánga bushųkį-shųkį, mbu wé ngí kábútwa-kénda, kárįkįŕé kínyihíŕé,¹⁵⁸ áwamutáỹí-mo ngí émuberé wakwírí múntse nkįrį; ntí mwea wíshoshįwa na. Mwindo wakíé wamasúngá ébikáí bíshé byámámukųmána, wébá, mbu įshé wasįá kǔndu nti įyé kihuhúru cábusabusa. Wére isínkárį wé, mbu wé usasįrį mbu bįnyantįŕé básondoré kása, béndi kása kakwána, nâ wé Mwindo n'isínkárį wé básįé kása háno hákįbíka, kongó iwé wǎsúngá kása bútįngengá bįnyantįŕé bátįnge ékǎra kábó. Wakíé wamatúmíshá bįnyantįŕé bo, mbu béndí kakwána, bįnyantįŕé bénda ná kakwána, nâ wé wásįa hįmá n'isínkárį wé hákįbíka. Kwétángá bįnyantįŕé, bákwáne ékwantsí n'ékwįyo, ná bįsakuTubondo béba, mbu: bǎnų mutǔkerí ro rúno'otų́.¹⁵⁹ Bákíé mbu básisimuké, bįnyantįŕé waMwindo báshíríra na, bákwa; bįsa-kuTubondo báshírísha bó. Ųma múbįnyantįŕé waMwindo wíshunura munkatį ỹébįtá nti įyé mubándé, wábéke kúrí Mwíndo katų́rá mwasį, wéyakó mbu: ínku kwákwetá bǎte [ntí na bo] bįsa-kuTubondo bákutuhima, ébea bátį basokontįŕé bákusįka. Isínkárį waMwindo wakíé mbu wásungé éntúmwá ỹa, áncáma ỹákumurįsá émubi ų́tį, mbu wárukiré n'émwasį wákusįká ébea básįka, wįtáte, mbu: eé titá Mwindo nakwiréngá mbu, aní mbu utúkocé bįsa-kǔndu kwáshé-Mwindo, ǒngo mbu kįro; sombó kása énkébé ỹá, énkórį ntsondorį; kaé wámashírírá bó.¹⁶⁰ Mwindo wére sínkárį wé mbu: n'âní něnda kása kéreka ngí cásįngwá bįnyantįŕé báshíríra ábátį, nâ wé shé-Mwindo ntíwasúngáná kása n'e, kaį nti ntí wé ngí Mwíndo. Isínkárį wé wámwíre, mbu: eé titá Mwindo, kǒko, ǔsįngwá énkúmo įtį ỹéyǎyo ná bǎte ỹáshíríra, úmashoshá bįsa-kǔndu kuTubondo nti twakwá bǎte bátį. Mwindo utárúkírí ébǔnu wísínkárį wé, wéba mbu wé wendá kakwána, ǒngo sínkárį wé, sįá n'émwandá wé ǔngu, n'ekákú ké kárí mó murį; nâ wé Mwindo wendá n'éconga cé nci. Mwindo wéta. Kwétángá we, wénda

katáríé kuTubondo. Bị̃sa-kuró bákíé básúnga Mwíndo wárembera
hị̃kụ́ra bámushemba, bére shé-Mwindo mbu: súnga kámwea kị̃má
kikáa kásáíré ékwị̃kụ́ra kwátúkăyo ébị̃tá. Shé-Mwindo wásúbíe bana-cé
mbu: méti ákámwea kị̃má ngí kásêkíá búnị̃, nákị̃ro kéya nti twăkerá ko
érị̃kotị̃, nti kákwa. Bana-cé bámusúbíe, mbu: kúsáángé bị̃sị̃-bị̃sị̃ nti kwâ-
sáí hó mabárị̃, ákámwea kị̃mă nki kámátutámbyá kŭno nti ntí twakíá
ko búnị̃. Shé-Mwindo wásúbíe bana-cé mbu: kámushị̃rě nki kéndí kába-
mbáré kumarare. Mwindo wárembera mwị̃kụ́ra nti usímbánge, nti
ukúbánge éconga ínku nă nku. Mwindo wakíé wéyá kuTubondo,
wéyere hánkatị̃ kébutara, wére bị̃sa-kuró, mbu wé usondánge ị̃mị̃na
ngoma. Bị̃sa-kuró bámusúbíe, mbu: utúkocé ngoma sákŭno, ŏngo
kámushị̃re. Mwindo wásúbíe bó mbu nkondé ÿa, iwé utárindáa hó
kása wáruhuka.¹⁶¹ Bị̃sa-kuró bámwîre mbu kúsị̃rá ngoma kúno. Mwindo
wére bó, mbu ésángoma sáséěya. Mwindo wénda webánánge nă bị̃sa-
kuró bo, nti ị̃shé nti uri múbukị̃té wé. Mwindo wásímba:

Iwé utáríéngi kŭno KuTubondo
Iwé wendánge kakwáná na shé-Mwindo

Wakíé ị̃yé usímbánge wénda utóndóóráa, mbŭ nki kâkwí na kárami
kábinguranga Ị̃yangura. Wátárísha émuréngé ékwị̃yo, wásímba:

Ákátángakwá na kárami
Mbu eé titá kábinguré Ị̃yangura
Ị̃yangura mubị̃tụ washé-Mwindo
Kóÿo aní nya-mwako¹⁶²
Mbu eé titá kâkwí na kárami
Kábinguré sínkárị̃
Mubị̃tụ washé-Mwindo
Boto ná bababá bâní
Munkụ́mánanga
Ákátâkwí na kárami
Kábinguré Ị̃yangura
Sínkárị̃ mubị̃tụ washé-Mwindo
Mukú waní ị̃yá
Kâkwí na kárami
Kábinguré Ị̃yangura sínkárị̃
Mbu eé bakóÿo mwěyé
Ákátâkwí na kárami
Kábinguré Ị̃yangura sínkárị̃
Nankwá bị̃ra
Céwángá nti céwi-tu-ị̃yo
Ntakwáné kŭno kuTubondo
Ná Tubondo makụ́ra arínda

Bakungú bátíká-tíká shé-Mwindo
Kâkwí na kárami
Kákумané Ịyangura sínkárị́
Bakungú bábéka shé-Mwindo
Kâkwí na kárami
Kákумané Ịyangura sínkárị́
Nkúbá mịra'aní ubúránanga[163]
Tumbotịá túrí mutíma yo
Nakíí namíÿangé rịko
Áwasokí muró wacíkíriri
Naráke Ịyangura sínkárị́
Ịyangura sínkárị́ ukasananga[164]
Mwindo wáráka wéba mbu:
Tumbotịá túrí mutíma yo
Mịra'aní Nkúbá ubúránanga
Ntsêkwáná kǔno kuTubondo
Ná Tubondo makụ́ra arínda yo
Tubondo kǔno nkúbá sirínda
Ntsêkwáné kǔno kuTubondo
Nabụná nkúbá sirínda yo
Mwindo wásúbya múmisóná:
Bakungú bábéka shé-Mwindo
Bakungú báréser'ịhana
Bǎnụ ngí mubíndúkí ntserya
Kǔsi
Katitá kántáa múngoma
Ntsêkwáná kǔno kuTubondo
Tubondo kúbindukí ntserya
Sara-ara
Bakungú bábéka shé-Mwindo
Bakungú báréser'ịhana
Bakungú bábinduké ntserya
Mịra'aní Nkúbá ubúránanga
Tumbotịá túrí mitíma yo
Naráke sínkárị́ Ịyangura
Kâkwí na kárami
Kábinguré Ịyangura
Sínkárị́ mubịtụ washé-Mwindo
Katitá kashé-bushụ́náné
Katitá kántáa mwísinda
Titá wásíba mbu ntsênịnke
Katitá kántáa mwísinda
Katitá kásíbǎ mbu ntsênịnke

Úmasíbá mbu băna bámukárí bea
Mbu eé titá nti bátíngé behe[165]
Múno mutíma webángá mbu ébăna bémukárí ngí bea kúrí we, bámu-
réngá; nó'ŏngo ùsíbá ke rúno'otú.
Bámukárí bea
Mbu eé titá nti bákéngí behe
Tubondo nkúbá sirínda
Mwindo wáráráme ébutú, weba:
Míra'aní Nkúbá
Kǔno kuTubondo nkúbá sirínda

Mwindo wakíé mbu wáraramí ékwiyo, wáshée-kó-éconga. Ékwiyo
kwáNkúbá kwátúkwa na, kwásáa ná nkúbá sirínda, sáhíte ná kuTubondo kumbúka. Kutubondo kwábungukara na, n'émufufu wóka na,
ábátj bárjkángá kuró bábe ná mukungú mwara-ara.[166] Kwárjkángá
shé-Mwindo ékubukíté wáráka, mbu: réro kútárindirwí kǔno. Wamakínd'ĳébă bo, wáhíta na hámukukuru, wáhúnga na. Kwábékéngá we,
wénda keyá hárí kikŏka, wákúra có, wákímíre na hítína racó. Mwindo
wakíé wamáhimá kuTubondo, wítata hánkatí kébutara, wéba, mbu:
rérŏ kwe íngu unitáÿange mó, áwjhárá-hárá kúrí aní, mwjkwána n'aní,
nti uruhée busa. Wénda webángě bo n'ébĳnda byábinyantíré ábyátá-
ngírángá jkwá, nti íyé bíbŏngí. Mwindo wáhíte hásĳángá sínkárí wé
hákjbíka, mbu kongó ibó bísúmbe hákabásj. Wéya kwísínkárí, isínkárí
wámubúsa, mbu: mahyó nko kútúkángé ŏngo.[167] Mwindo wámusúbíe
mbu kuTubondo kwáshá. Wére na bó mbu: ĕo túbasí kuTubondo ngí
kwákangámá, tútuké háno hákjbíka.[168] Isínkárí wábúra mbu wárongi-
rongi ébikáí, Mwindo wámuhange, wámwíre, mbu: síá ébikáí, bísĳné
byâtukúmáná kǔndu kuTubondo. Wamakínd'ĳébă bo, wéta na, n'ísínkárí wé wámutúca hĳma n'ékikémbé cébaombé céyángá na bó. Bátáríe
kuTubondo, béya kuró. Bákíé íyé bárí kuTubondo, ébikáí byákusĳángá
bo múkjbíka byákúmáná bó. Mwindo wéba, mbu wé utákocé jtúca jshé
kúti ntí nénkj wafúcá bjnyantíré. Wásĳmo bó nti usúndákánge bó
éconga, ná nti usímbánge:

Áwendángá toró nasímuka
Mántíre kóÿo usimukanga
Nashiángá ban'Ĳyana
Mántíre kóÿo ngése[169]
Shé-Mwindo utúkocé Mwíndo
Mwindo kábútwa-kénda
Mántíre kóÿo ngése
Ŏngo mwĕsĳ wábiramba

Mwindo wákịnd'ịsịmo ná bịnyantịré bátị, báťúka na. Kwábékéngá shé-Mwindo, wénda nákubá nti ịýé wịcábíránge, wénda ná keyéré na kwáMúisa, ínku kútánóntwáa ékashá.[170] Kwárịkángá Mwíndo kuTubondo n'isínkárị wé ná bịnyantịré n'ébaombé bé basịmbị n'ébasij, Mwindo wére bó mbu: túbunguré shé-Mwindo kwétịré we kwáMúisa, túmwêndí mubingo. Isínkárị wé wámusakia énkǔ ýé iri mó émurí, wámusakia n'émwandá wé, n'éconga cé nti wahátá hó co mịné-co. Mwindo wére isínkárị wé mbu: ǒngo sínkárị wé sịá kǔno kuTubondo ná bịnyantịré bímbi n'ékikémbé cébasịmbị n'ébasij béyángá n'ịtų́, bụshwá mbu bǎnụ murísánge biýó byákumbúka, mutúkocé étushịmbo tų́tị n'ébiburá bísúngángé we ínku kwétángé we.[171] Mwindo wére tu sínkárị wé mbu: ǒngo sínkárị wé, ǒngo'sịánge kǔno kurwịnų́ kuTubondo, émurí ngí ǔno, sịa ná cụ̌ndá kịma, utịngíriraa có, nâ wé wábinguré ịshé kwábékéngá we kwáMúisa; ukíí umarúkírá émurí úno wámabịba, kúti útángátenga tú, ákwétángá we nti utútéí tǔ ko ámaté, kaị ékashá nti kárịmá, iwé nti wakwá. Wamakịnd'ị́ébǎ bo, muna-kantorị wáhíte hárí we, wámwîre mbu: eyá kúno ntákuhaná éntse ýakwétángá só na hákịmịréngá we hịtịn'ǎkikǒka, bụshwá mbu isó wakíángá wabéka, nâ wé kantorị nti uri hábásirw'ǎmambịyo; isó wábéka ná nti wé umusúngánge wịcábírángé we. Mwindo mwịenda ré, kantorị wamakịnd'- ịmutų́re émwasị, wáraa isínkárị wé, wátịnge múcụ̌ndá cémurí n'ísínkárị wé wásịa watịngírírá mucų̌ndá kịma. Mwindo wírekera mwịkų́ra. Wa- kíé wěya hákikǒka, hákịmịréngá ịshé, nâ wé wákúra ékikǒka, wákịmịre hịtịna racó, wéta na, wénda ná kasáíré hítúkúriro; wakíé mbu wěyé ho, wákų́mána hó mwịsị waMuisa Kahindo.[172] Kahindo wámukókére mbu karíbǔ nko Mwindo. Mwindo wárịsja, mbu aé. Iwé Kahindo nti usámbánge binyóra, ébinyórǎ byá nti byárétúkíré múrịno byéya na múnkúkúnyú, byáhíta n'émíndí, byéya na múmpandá sěbisando.[173] Mwindo wakíé mbu wáteané, Kahindo wámuhange mbu tǒto. Wá- mwîre, mbu: ǒngo wendánge kúnị́? Mwindo wámusúbíe, mbu wé wendánge kwáMúisa káshaká ịshé, bụshwá mbu ngí kúrí we kǔndu kwáMúisa. Wámwîre tú mbu: tíndira kása háno hárí we, kǔndu kwá- Múisa kútétwánga, nó'ǒngo ngí wětá hó kuró búnó-bǔno, n'émuhao ų́tị? Kahindo wére Mwindo, mbu: ǒngo ǔngu wendánge kwáMúisa, ǔkíá úmeyá kuró, úmakịmé hárǔshú, úmasúngá cábǔme kikịrị kere nákubá, cịondóndé múmoté hárịko nti ngí Múisa ǔo; ná wámakukéa, wámebá mbu: makangura áa, titá, nó'ǒngo nti úrịsjá mbu: aé titá; ná wǎkíá wámakusịéré kitų́mbị, nti utịnǎ co, nti úmwîré mbu: kǒko titá, émụntwé wịshé mwea ngí wábése tu ékitų́mbị! Wǎkíá wámaku- sakíá kákisha kámaụ mbu úrisé ko, nti utịna, nti úmusúbié, mbu: angá titá émwea nákịro wábíndúke mwǎna nti ngí cásịngwa wárisa hó émashu wịshé mwea! Muisa wǎkíá wámakukenjá bo, nti wákunịnká: karamo karamǒ ká Mwindo; nó'ǒngo nti úmurịsjá, mbu: nó'ǒngo karamo karamǒ ká titá. Wǎkíá wámakunịnká buntu mbu úrisé bo, nti úmu-

súbié mbu: nákįro mwea wábése mwǎna, nti ngí cásíngwǎ hó mwea
wárísa tųbí twíshé mwea!¹⁷⁴

Mwindo wakíé wamasúngá Káhindo wamámwiré ébinwa byá-
hundá-húndá bo, wíire mbu wé utákocé jenda ntíwashúá ébinyóra
byáKáhindo. Mwindo wátųmíka ushúánge ébinyóra byáKáhindo,
wátendea na byó mwįkųto ébikókó bítį byébinyóra. Mwindo wakíé
wamakįnd'îshúa ébinyóra byáKáhindǒ bo, wamakíndí n'íramya na
byó, Mwindo wámusúkána, wénda katáríé kwáMúisa; wéya kuró,
wéyere hárǔshú. Muisa mbu wámúsúnge, wámukéa, mbu: makangura
áa, Mwindo. Mwindo wárįsįa, mbu aé titá. Muisa wísubukia, mbu:
bánįnké Mwíndo ékitųmbí wárįké mucó.¹⁷⁵ Mwindo wámusúbíe, mbu:
tǒto eé titá, émwea nákįro wábése mwenį nti ngí cásíngwa wárįkere
múmųntwé wíshé! Muisa wéba tú mbu wé wákusíá kákisha kámaų̌
mpe, kía ntákukųbų́ré tukeké? Mwindo wéba mbu: kǒko titá, nákįro
mwea wábése mwenį nti ngí cásíngwa wárísa émashu wíshé mwea!¹⁷⁶
Muisa wéba, mbu: karamo karamǒ ká titá. Muisa wéba tú mbu: bá-
kúrų́į twábuntu eé Mwindo? Mwindo wámusúbíe mbu: tǒtó titá, émwea
nákįro wábése mwenį nti ngí cásíngwa hó wárísa tųbí twíshé! Muisa
mbu wásungé ca, wámwíre mbu: karamo karamǒ ká Mwindo. Muisa
mbu wásungé Mwíndo wamáramá ábinkú bya, wére Mwindo mbu:
endá ná káruhúká móo mwámwįsí'įnų́ Kahindo.¹⁷⁷ Mwindo wéta mó.
Wakíé mbu wéyé mwaKahindo, mbu wásusí mó mĕso, wásúnga Kahindo kumund'ĕnųmbá, Kahindo nti wákwikíá na búrí kanyero kânkó
mwįmbara ná kwísįngo ukarú ná makų́ta ámbéa. Mwindo mbu wámúsúnge, wábúrǎ mbu wákųrųké manyųma, bųshwá érísúnga ébentsé-
bĕntsé kumunda n'énųmbá. Kahindo mbu wámúsúnge, wámwíre mbu:
karíbu eé Mwindo.¹⁷⁸ Mwindo wéba mbu áwasíá kurųma wásįtaré,
mwįsí'įtų́. Kahindo wakíé wasúnga Mwíndo wamakímé munųmbá,
wíire, mbu kaí Mwindo wakwá rwǎka. Wamabángúka na, wamendá ná
káronjá twábuntu túrehě mpe twámoté.¹⁷⁹ Wakíé wamakínd'įrúa tó,
wárųshje bó Mwíndo mwíremeso ré.¹⁸⁰ Muisa wakíé wasúnga Káhindo
wárųshjé Mwindo ébuntu, wákányáhe tété mwámwįsí wé, wénda karún-
gúrírá muri Mwindo, wére Mwindo, mbu: eé titá Mwindo ǒngo'rí-
sánge ébiỳó mbi, mukǒmá úhend'įramuke kámuhíngé mubísi, úteté
bukurá, wĕké n'esâmpókó, úkondé na, úkasé na, úsarií n'esâmpóko, úsekí
na tó; úrųshé n'ékihumbé. Úmakínd'įronja émirimo ítį ỹa, nti wé wasíbǎ
ke ikunínka isó.¹⁸¹ Muisa wakíé wamakínd'ííre Mwindǒ bo, wámwíre tú
mbu ǔkíáyo wĕndá kahínga, iwé nti wákusakia ná mwea ųmá kasísírísá
búhíngángé ǒngo. Wakíé wamakínd'įébǎ bo, wátúka hámyango, wákų́-
rųke hárǔshú rwé. Mwindo kwásíángá we émunųmbá wátųmíka urísánge ébuntu. Bákíé ébųtú wámakínd'įcá, múmukomá-kómá Mwindo
wásúbírá émukúshu, Mwindo wénda kahínga. Muisa wátúnja mwea
ųmá wátíndíkįa Mwindo ékwihínga. Bákíé béya ékubusará, émwea
watúnjángá Múisa wáshée Mwindo ntata nįmá iri mó mangó. Mwindo

mbu wásungé éntată ẙa, wásínja émikúshu hântsí, ẙ́sĭné ẙéca n'émi-
kandá; ẙamakĭndá émukandá, ẙátéta.[182] Mwĭkĭnd'ĭtéta, ésâmpókó
sĭeka sĭsĭné. Mwĭkĭndĭ kwĭeka kwesâmpókó, Mwindo wáhícíe kó kitumo
cámyandá; émyandá nâ ẙó ẙákĭndĭ nĭkonda ẙ́sĭné. Mwĭkĭndă ha,
wáhícíe kó kitumo cámikúshu; émikúshŭ ẙa ẙéta n'ámubísi nti ika-
séngi.[183] Kwárĭkángá émutĭndĭkĭĭ wáMwindo, wákẙrẙka kúrí Múisa.
Wakíé mbu wêyé ko, wátẙre Muisa mwasĭ, mbu: réro ntí muhíngĭ,
íngu urĭ nku, uri murwatété, muhíngĭ wábĭshĭsharo, ntíwákutẙráná
mucŭma, ébyŭma bĭsĭné bíhíngángé n'ĭkonda, n'ĭkase. Wámakĭnd'-
ĭtẙre Muisa émwasĭ, wákẙrẙke tu kúrí Mwíndo ékumubísi. Kwárĭkángá Mwíndo, émikúshu ẙakíé ẙamakĭnd'ĭkase, ẙákera byoko; ébyoko
bĭsĭné byáséke n'esâmpókó. Mwĭkĭnd'ĭséke ésâmpókó ébyoko, ékihumbé cáse na. Émutĭndĭkĭĭ wátibite katẙrá mwasĭ kúrí Múisa. Wéya
kó, wére Muisa, mbu ntí mwea urĭ nku, wákuhíngá érótẙ ro, ésâmpókó
sámêta na, n'esâmbú ĭyé mbuẙa na.[184] Wére tu Múisa mbu ékihimbé
kĭcá Mwindo ĭyé uri keyá na có. Muisa wakíé mbu wárukiré bo, wéba
mbu: kaĭ émuẙúngu wĭtúnjá tŭ nku kubusará, iwé waréré wamutimáyo
kása émwĭoroyo wĭshumurayo, wáramayo ébikúbá bya, na rúno'otẙ
iwé wákumwereka tu, ngí ŭngu wendáa tu kárama. Muisa wakíé
wamáshĭsháré Mwíndŏ bo, wátúma kó ékarémba ké kesántsimbí;
wérekó mbu: ŏngo karémba ké, óngw'endánge kwáMwíndo, ŭkíá
úmamusúnga nti úmukẙnyaá na, nti úmuhanda n'ébŭnu hântsí. Karémba kákíé kámarúkírá bo wérírwá e na nyeré-kurwábó, kénda n'ékumubísi. Kákíé kásúngá Mwíndo ĭyé utengánge émutengo wesâmbú
úrí mó mbuẙa, ékukisambú, kéya na hárí we, kĭhẙmba na kúrí we,
káfúírisa ná Mwindo, kámusĭmata, kámuhanda n'ébŭnu hântsí, érú-
fúmba rwátúka na; wárẙka nă mbu wásêtúnjá we émuká; émashu
n'étẙbĭ twárana, érúfúmbá rwátúka na; wárẙka nă mbu wásêtúnjá
we émuká; émashu n'étẙbĭ twárana, twárẙka nă ngu wăhíhá to. Éconga
cáMwindo cákíé cámasúngá nyeré-kurwábó warẙká bukwáté wĭtúnjá
we, éconga cásubukia, cĭhẙmbá-hẙmba hámẙntwé na Mwindo; Mwindo
wásárá-sara wákáso éríkĭshé, wákaisha émêso ékwĭyo; wákando émêso,
wásĭmánya ó, wákae mpômpó. Mwindo wakíé wamásĭménýĭwá n'ékarémba káMúisa, émurí wábobera na, útátengí tŭ na. Isínkárí wé kwá-
sĭángá we kuTubondo, kwásakírírángá we múcẙndá cémurí, wísúnda
n'ékwantsí, iwé mbu kaĭ musike wé wakwá. Wábíkíra émuréngé émwĭhĭ
n'émore. Mwíbíkíra ébashẙmbẙ, wéba mbu: íngu watúkí ko ngí
mwăna.[185] Kwárĭkángá Mwíndo wakíé mbu wákẙkẙmé émêso wásímba:

Muisa wamashúrá Mwíndo
Ntsêkwá bĭra
Muisa utukocé Mwíndo
Ná Mwindo kábútwa kéndayo

Mwindo mwîsímba ré bo, wásubukia isínkárí wé, mbu: ǒngo'rí nko
kuTubondo, iwé ákwasá umarúkírá émurí wé ntíwákutenga, wáku-
bobera, bushwá mbu Muisa ákwasá wamǎmusimenya, nti wákumu-
kandá búrí kitu câmbú; ína, ang'íkwá tú isírí ínko kúríkíré ǒngo, bushwá
mbu émurí wé wámákusubukia, iwé wamárama, éconga cé ngí cámá-
musímánya. Mwindo wakíé wamakínd'írebeka isínkárí wé émuréngé
mwímusubukia, nâ wé wárebeka éconga cé kúrí Múisa ékumbúka,
mbu: ǒngo conga cé, ǔkíá úmeyá kúrí Múisa ékumbúka nti úmusimata
ná ngururu, nti úmuhanda n'ébunu mwôto, érwǎmi nti rwákíme n'ékumunda n'erôto; ná ǔkíá iwé utángakúrúka, utángéyâ nko kumbúka,
nti utúngámureke. Éconga cábirira na; cákíé mbu céyé kúrí Múisa
hárǔshú, cámusimata na, cámuhanda n'ébunu hântsí, érwǎmi rwátíma
n'erôto; émashu n'étubí twárúka ná mpúngá, nǎ ngu wasêhíhá to
wárúka na; émuká wárúka nǎ nku kwásêsáíré o.[186] Kwásíánga Mwindo
ékukisambú, wáronge éburusi wesâmbú hímá n'esâmbuÿa. Wákúrúka
n'ékumbúka. Wakíé mbu wákaishé éměso hárǔshú, mbu wákaí Múisa,
érúfúmbá rwákumusáá múbunu na múměmbé. Kahindo mwisí wa-
Muisa, mbu wásungé Mwíndo, wásanguhe kúrí we, wámwîre mbu:
ǒngo weyánge, ishé ntí[ná bo] kúno wákukíndí réro isúsa! Mwindo
wásúbíe Kahindo mbu wé wendángá kúno nti wé usondánge ishé, íyé
munínke ishé kúno, kongó iwé wákúrúkayo n'e. Kahindo wámusúbíe,
mbu: tángiri kása iramya ishé, kongó wásíba ikutabure isó, kongó
wákunínka wé. Mwindo wásímba mwísimo Muisa:

> Wendángá toró nasímuka
> Muisa utúkocé Mwíndo
> Ná Mwindo kábútwa-kénda
> Kahómbó kábútá Múisa
> Shé-kwísea
> Muisa mutúkocé Mwíndo
> Kaÿó karǎme kanahangírá rwímbo[187]

Wendángá usímbángě bó Mwindo, ná nti urúndákáa Muisa éconga
múmuntwé, mbu wásimuké. Muisa wakíé wamásimuka, wamárama,
wéba mbu: ǒngo Mwindo kaí nó'ǒngo wábǔme. Muisa wére tu Mwíndo, mbu: ǒngo mwǎna, uhéndiyo ienda kámukundúré ébǔki wé mbu
búrí múmutí mpe. Mwindo wíanya, mbu: réro nakwíré ke.[188] Mwindo
wakíé wamashéíwé ébúkí mbo na Muisa mbu wáhend'íkundo bó,
ébutú wásíra. Kahindo wárúíre Mwindo buntu, Mwindo wárísa bó.
Mwíkínd'irísa ébuntu bénda mútoró. Bákíé ébutú wámǎca, múmukoma-
kómá, Mwindo wamakósórá émwandá, wametá n'ékubusará kákundó
ébǔki; wáháta n'ékashá. Wakíé mbu wéyé hítína rémutí, wátáÿa n'émutí,
wénda ná kabásé na hámǎu hárí ébǔki; wábíkíra, mbu: hánǒ eé? Bá-

muríṣia, mbu, hǐhá; mbu kaí wasêkocá bo. Mwindo wákúmányie bó
kashá. Wákáso émwandá múmutí, wásímba:

> Nkundóngi bůkị mwaMuisa
> Kabúmbú urembéngi múnembe
> Nya-bárí-mwĭrí múrukiré
> Wébángé nya-késị kábinwa[189]
> Míra'aní Nkúbá ubúránanga
> Tumbotía túrí múmutíma yo
> Katitá kántáa múngoma kǔsi
> Titá wásíba mbu ntsênịnke.

Kwárịkángá Múisa ékumbúka, wéba mbu kaí émweǎ ngu wasêkíndá
hó ikundo ébůkị mbu. Muisa wátúma ékarémba ké, kénda ná kásịmátá
Mwíndo múmutí, kámuhanda n'ébǔnu múmpịtị ỹémutí, émuká wá-
fúndị n'íṣáa, émashu n'étụbí twámurara na.
Kwárịkángá isínkárí wé Ịyangura, émurí wámusubukia, wéba mbu
kaí musike wé wakwá: émurí, ǔngu wámábobera tu. Kwásíángá Mwíndo éconga ékwantsí, muna-conga wásubukia mbu kaí nyeré-kurwábó
wakwá, cátáỹa kúrí we, cénda kịhúmbáká-húmbáká múmụntwé na
Mwindo. Mwindo wákáso éríkịshé, wákụkụma émĕso, n'ekámǔká
kásáa mó kakeké. Mwindo wéba mbu: kaí nirịkíre ékwịyo, kaí ákwǎsá
nakwá. Wakíé wamákandó émĕso, wáráke míra wé Nkúbá, wásímba:

> Míra'aní Nkúbá ubúránanga
> Tumbotíá túrí hámutíma yo

Mwindo wakíé íyé usịkánge ékwantsí, wáráke Nkúbá, wákae ékwịyo,
mbu: míra'aní Nkúbá nikwánge. Nkúbá wakíé warúkira émuréngé
wámíra wé Mwindo, wáhíta na múmutí, wábenga na ó bebé-bebé.
Míra wé Mwindo wásịka hântsí nti usịra angá na ná kihúrú. Wakíé
íyé uri n'émutúndú wébůkị hântsí, wátáỹa n'ebůkị ékumbúka kúrí
Múisa, wéya kó, wámusịca émutúndú wébůkị, mbu ébůkí bǔmbu, ína
iwé usondánge mbu úmúnínke ịshé. Muisa wakíé mbu wárukiré bo,
wátúma muỹú kákaé hábíséngá wábíse shé-Mwindo. Émuỹú wéya hó
nti shé-Mwindo nti usịra tǔ ho; kaí Muisa nti ngí wákutondéngá shé-
Mwindo mbu wábekeri kwáNtúmba. Émuỹú wakíé wamasóná ákwasá
hịbíṣá shé-Mwindo ná wamakínd'ịkae hó hásịrá mwea, wákụrúke kúrí
Múisa, ná Mwindo wéya hó, wére bó mbu: bǎnu murịkịre kúno shé-
Mwindo wákubéka, usịrǎ mpe héndá hárịkángé we. Kahúngú wéya,
wátúre Mwindo mwasí mbu: mínú ngu Muisa utimánge, iwé ngí wákutondéngá só mbu wábeki kwáNtúmba, mbu ǒngo usúmá ngụrụ.[190]
Kahúngú wakíé wamatúré Mwíndo émwasí bo, wíokere tu múmwǎnyá.
Hásíángá Mwíndo na Muisa, Mwindo wátítịa Muisa, mbu: munínke

jshé kúno, ákwámubįsángá ŏngo musháíshe, iwé wĕndí n'e; kaį ngí
búrí ŏngo bŭbo, ŏngo kindĕsa, ubúrángá mbu iwé wámakuhíngíré
mubísi wábé, wámakukundúré n'ébŭkį nti úmunįnká įshé; iwé usondánge úmúsháíshe éno-mpéná, éróté rútákámí na ntíumusháíshá.
Muisa wakíé mbu wárukiré búmútįtįáá Mwíndo wákóhyá-kohya átwá-
mĕso, wéba, mbu réro émuŷú ngu wanibįmbyá bura kúno kurwâní.¹⁹¹
Mwindo wakíé wamasúngá Múisa ntiwasháíshá įshé, wárúnda ná
Muisa éconga hántato n'émųntwé, Muisa étųbí twámurande na háma-
táo, wáhúhúka na; émashu ábíndúke ná karámbá ékwantsí; érúfúmbá
rwámutúkíre múmĕmbé na múmĕso, rwárįsa n'ékwįtánge, wáshée
n'ébyŏndó ékwįyo, wánanuke na búrí mukúsá.¹⁹² Mwindo wéba, mbu
sįa nákubá nă bo, ŏngo mbíbi, iwé wakuramyi nti wé wamakųrųkángá
kwéndă we. Mwindo wéndere įshé mubingo kwétángá we kwáNtųmba.
Mwindo wénda nti usímbánge:

> Ncakánge shé-Mwindo
> Mwétángá shé-Mwindo
> Shé-Mwindo wabékéngá mwaNtųmba
> MwaMuisa
> Ncakánge mwaNtųmba
> MwaMunundu
> Ntųmbá ndįndųrį
> Shé-Mwindo wakįtá mwaMunundu
> Shé-Mwindo wabéké mwaNtųmba
> Ncakánge titá shé-Mwindo
> MwaNtųmba mwaMunundu
> Ékentsé cábįngįtá isumba
> Ncakánge shé-Mwindo
> Shé-Mwindo wabéká mwaNtųmba
> MwaMunundu
> Katitá kánitáa múngoma

Mwindo wáráke Nkúbá mbu:

> Mįra'aní Nkúbá ubúránanga
> Tumbotįá túrí mutíma yo
> Katitá kashé-karųo yo
> Ncakánge titá mwaNtųmba
> MwaMunundu
> Mįra'aní Nkúbá ubúránanga
> Tumbotįá túrí mutíma yo
> Ntsondánge katitá kashé-karųo
> Katitá kántáa múngoma
> Katitá kashé-mųngó wábea

Katitá kándása kŭsi[193]
Ntúmbá ndjndúrj
Ntsondánge katitá kashé-karúo

Mwindo wakíé íyé utjmbá-tímbáa hó éríkoí rémurjmba ráNtúmba
muri jshé, ná Ntúmba wákuhusá ékumunda, Ntúmba wásjme shé-
Mwindo, mbu: nti ŏngo wendánge, ákábŭme kárí hámyangŏ mpe
kákarámá, nó'ŏngo ŭngu óngo'súngáa búsánánángé we hámyango
n'eríkoí.[194] Shé-Mwindo wakíé mbu wárukiré wíkarámyá musike wé
hamyango ÿeríkoí, wéba, mbu ékámuÿú kéyá nti kásuá. Wére míra
wé Ntúmba mbu wé wabéká. Shé-Mwindo wénda ná kabéké kwáshé-
Burúngú. Kwárjkángá Nkúbá ékwjyo, wakíé warúkira émuréngé wámíra wé, wéba mbu míra wé wamáruhá réro umurákéngi. Nkúbá
wáhíca ná nkúbá sirínda, sáhítíra na múmunundu weríkoí ráNtúmba;
wábenga na mó tobé-tobé, éríkoí rábíndúke ná mukungú mwara-ara,
émufufu wôka na. Mwindo wakíé mbu wásungé míra wé Nkúbá wamá-
bengáá éríkoí, Mwindo wárjndo n'érubj, wákíme n'ékumunda n'ému-
nundu, wásonda-sonda jshé ínku nǎ nku kumund'ĕmunundu, utámú-
súngí. Wákúmána Ntúmba ékumunda, wámwíre mbu: ŏngo Ntúmba
umecá jshé kúní, kúní ngí kwámámubísá ŏngo. Ntúmba wábjbjra búrí
ntíwarúkírá. Mwindo wámutúre oté, mbu: tukǎ ho, ŏngo kjsjrá cábŭme;
kaí, iwé ákwasá uruhánge hámyango mbu murjndúrj, utína, ŏngo
úkwé mushúha. Ntúmba wakíé wamasúngá búmwírírírángé Mwíndo
kúrí jshé mbu wé ngí wákumubécanga, wére Mwindo mbu: ŏngo'-
súngánge wámabíhá énumbá ÿé n'émirimé ÿé ítj; iwé wǎkíá-kĕ-yo
búní? Mwindo wéba mbu: ŏngo mushjre, ang'ínyunca tu émuká kúrí
we, kaí ngí búrí ŏngo bŭbo. Kwárjkángá Káhúngú ékwjyo, wásjka,
wénda katúré Mwíndo émwasí; wéya hó, mbu: ŏngo'sí, ŏngo Mwindo,
Ntúmba wákubécá isó, isó wákubéké na kwáshé-Burúngú. Kahúngú
wakíé wamakínd'ítúre Mwindo mwasí, wíokere tu ékwjyo. Kwásíángá
Mwíndo kwáNtúmba ébusíbúké n'ékiruhó-rúho, wére Ntúmba, mbu:
ŏngo Ntúmba ngí rwâkwí hó ŏngo rŭro, ang'íyo rôtú jshée ná biÿó
múcŭo cábé kíno. Wamakínd'ímwírĕ bo, wénda kwétángá jshé, wámwende mubingo. Kwásíángá isínkárí wé Iyangura Kutubondo, wénda
wíaníkíránge, mbu kwétángá Mwíndo kwâsjkí mutíma ntwarêya.[195]
Wásísírisa émurí wáhátá we, wéba mbu kaí Mwindo ukírí wendéréngi
hó jshé mubingo kwétíré we. Mwindo kwátúcángá wátúca jshé, wámwende mubingo n'ébusíbúké bútí nti wákumukanda, wénda keyá
híkúra na kwáshé-Burúngú; wákúmána hó banúnké, bámunínka makangura, mbu: méti usimúká eé Mwindo.[196] Mwindo wárjsja bó, mbu
aé. Banúnké bákíé bámakínd'íkéa Mwindo, bámwíre mbu: ŏngo
Mwindo ang'îtukunduka háno, twakwá rwǎka, tukóngánge biÿó.
Mwindo wáráke isínkárí Iyangura mbu wámúrebéke biÿó, ábǎna báshé-
Burúngú bákwá rwǎka. Mwindo mwíkónga ébiÿó kúrí isínkárí wé
wásímba. Mwindo wáráka wéba, mbu:

É titá kwásíángá Iyangura
Mubítu washé-Mwindo
Nihunáa bishá birínda[197]
Ŏngo'súngáa kwétángá Mwíndo
Nkúsánge rwăka
Sínkárí Iyangura
Nihunánge nyama

Wámabúrá Mwíndo:

Nihunáa bishá birínda
Óngo'súngáa nákuhénd'íramuke
Kwásíángá sínkárí
Nahuná bishá birínda yo
Sínkárí namábuná nyama

Mwindo wakíé wámaráké isínkárí mbu wé uhunánge mantu arínda
ná nyama ámúkúmáne ímpe hárí we hima n'ébăna báshé-Burúngú,
wakíé mbu wákaí émantu nti íyé árí na hárí we, átúkángé kúrí isínkárí
wé Iyangura. Ébiyŏ byákíé byámakínd'íya, Mwindo wáninka byó
ébanúnké. Ábăna báshé-Burúngú bátúmíka bárísángé émantu ná
Mwindo nti watékésá bo.[198] Ábăna bákíé bámakínd'írísa, Mwindo
wákúrúca tu ébíbo kúrí isínkárí wé Iyangura mbu wátamburé byo,
kongó iwé wásíba itáríe kwáshé-Burúngú nti ébibya byámakínd'íkú-
rúka.[199] Mwindo wákúrúca ébíbo nti usímbánge:

Nakúrúcá babíbo ná ntengi
Mahíme sínkárí Iyangura[200]
Nakúrúcá babíbo ná ntengi

Wakíé wamakínd'íkúrúca ébíbo n'esántengi, wénda katáríe kwáshé-
Burúngú, n'ébanúnké bámutúca.[201] Wátáríe kwáshé-Burúngú nti
usímbánge:

Shé-Burúngú ŏngo
Ncakánge shé-Mwindo
Shé-Mwindo wabútángá muraí
Mbu wábuté kábútwa-kénda
Shé-Burúngú
Ncakánge shé-Mwindo
Katitá kashé-karúo

Shé-Burúngú wáráka wéba mbu:

Eé Mwindo mbu túresé mongo[202]

Ná Mwindo wáráka wéba mbu:

Eé titá shé-Burúngu
Ncakánge shé-Mwindo

Mbu:

Eé Mwindo túresé mongo

Ná Mwindo wáráka wéba:

Mbu eé titá ntámbésé shé-Mwindo
Katitá kántáa múngoma
Katitá kántáa kŭsi
Banụ́nké mbu ntáresá na bó
Banụ́nké ntángáresa na bó

Mwindo wakíé wamịtóndóórá kúrí shé-Burúngu, mbu shé-Burúngú
wámúnịnke ịshé, shé-Burúngú wámwịré mbu: ntákocé ikunịnka só;
nihụnánge túresé kása mongo, kongó nasíb'ikusiburire só, kongó usíb'-
ịkụ́rụ́ka n'e. Shé-Burúngú wakíé wamakịnd'ííre Mwindŏ bo, Mwindo
wámusúbíe, mbu: bambá bo ékwantsí, iwé utâkubéki, ŏng'osí ébikúbá
byámoswá we.[203] Shé-Burúngú wakíé wamarúkírá wámasúbịwá we na
Mwindo, wáringa ékiráko wábamba có hântsí, wáringa n'éwikí wịséa
wámubúyá. Shé-Burúngú wáshia, mbu: ŏngo Mwindo, úmamurása nti
urịá só, n'ébutéá bŭmbu mianda ishátu, úmamurása nti urịá bo. Mwindo
wáshia mianda ishátu ỵ́ábutéá. Bakíé bámáshiáná ébikáí bŭbó, shé-
Burúngú wátángír'ikúka éwikí. Wakíé mbu wákuké bo, érịberé wárása
ná Mwindo ébutéá wé. Mwindo wáshia ésâmpéné sásị́ángá kuTubondo.
Shé-Burúngú wákúka tu éwikí, wárása tu Mwíndo ásâmpéné sịtị. Mwindo wáshia n'ébikáí bịtị n'ísínkárị́. Shé-Burúngú wákúka tu, wárása
ná Mwindo ébikáí bịtị n'ébea n'ísínkárị́.[204] Mwindo wásịa hó na wịsịné
n'éconga cé, mịné shé-Burúngú nti wamakịnd'îmurása ébikáí bịtị,
n'ébea bátị bárịkángá kuTubondo. Mwindo wakíé wamakịnd'íráswa
ébikáí byé n'ébea bé, wáshia éconga cé. Shé-Burúngú wakíé mbu wákuké, nâ wé wáhina. Mwindo wákúka, wárása shé-Burúngú ébutéá
wákushiá we. Shé-Burúngú wáshia tu, Mwindo wákúka tu, wárása
mináni. Ábyákushiángá shé-Burúngú, Mwindo wárása tŭ byo.[205] Shé-
Burúngú wáshia ébikáí byé bịtị n'esánkambú sé. Mwindo wákúka tu,
wárása tú mináni, wárása n'ébikáí bịtị byáshé-Burúngú: bea, mpéné,
nkambụ́ . . . Mwindo wátuma na; shé-Burúngú wásịa hó na wịsịné
bụróbo.

Kwárịkángá Kántorị́ na Kahúngú, béya hárí Mwíndo, bámutonde,
mbu: ŏngo Mwindo eyá tété, isó usasịrị tú ịbéka. Mwindo wakíé wamakịnd'îrúkíra émwasị́, wáreke n'éwikí, wéta na tété-tété, wénda ná ka-
kụ́máná ịshé hákisambú cáshé-Burúngú. Wakíé mbu wámúsúnge,

bámuhára mó byăra.²⁰⁶ Mwindo mbu wásungé jshé, wámushísha mbu: eé titá, ŏngo ngí ǔno? Shé-Mwindo wárjsja, mbu wé ngí ǔno. Mwindo wáshísha tú jshé mbu: ee shé-Mwindo, ŏngo ngi ǔo? Shé-Mwindo wárjsja tú, mbu wé ngí ǔno, ŏngo musike wé. Mwindo wakíé wama-tíngé jshé bo, wákúrúka n'e, wábáse n'e kwáshé-Burúngú. Mwindo wére shé-Burúngú mbu: ŏngo shé-Burúngú, ákwasá ŏngo'bjsá-bjsánge jshé, jshé ntí ngí ǔno? Mwindo wére tu shé-Burúngú mbu: ŏngo shé-Burúngú, iwé utángáhuná tu ébikáí byábé bjti byákurásángá we, jyé sja n'ébikáí byábé bjtj byákurásángá we, iwé ǔno wendá n'jshé. Mwindo wakíé jyé usasjr'jkúrúka n'jshé, wáraa shé-Burúngú ná bana-cé bátj, mbu: eé titá shé-Burúngú [mbu] karamǒ nko. Shé-Burúngú wárjsja mbu: aé nó'ŏngo Mwindo, wendaa usúmá hjmá na só shé-Mwindo. Mwindo wakíé wamakjnd'jraa shé-Burúngú, wákúruka nti jyé usímbánge:

> Rúkira waNtúmba Munundu²⁰⁷
> Wendángá nakúruka

Mwindo wátenja émurí, wásubukia isínkárí. Na kwárjkángá isínkárí wé, nâ wé nti warérembéá émurí mó ntsúmbo. Mwindo wásímba:

> Wendángá nakúruka
> Ŏngo'súngáa nirjte shé-Mwindo²⁰⁸

Mwindo wjrekera kwáNtúmba, wéya mó nti Ntúmba wamakjndá tú jhjmba. Mwindo wásímba:

> Nkandíráa mwaNtúmba Munundu
> Écǔo mutáká²⁰⁹
> Wendángá toró nasímuka

Mwindo wáíre Ntúmbá, mbu nkj ngí cásjngwáá jshé, iwé ǔno uri n'jshé. Mwindo wásímba mbu:

> Ntúmba utúkocé Mwíndo
> Ná Mwindo kábútwa kéndayo
> Nashúré múno mwaNtúmba yo
> Súnga nirjte shé-Mwindo
> Katitá kashé-karúo
> Shé-Mwindo mukú wjyangura
> Shé-Mwindo ngí wabútángá muraj
> Sínkárí Jyangura nikúrúkánge
> Mwindo kábútwa-kénda
> Nirjte katitá kashé-Mwindo
> Katakwá kumb'ŏmikómbj²¹⁰
> Usúngá naréshiá ban'Jyana

Mwindo wakíé wéya kwáNtʉmba, wére Ntʉ́mba ákarʲsóró kátʲ, wámwíre mbu: ǒngo Ntʉ́mba uhemúkéngá busa. Ébikáí bítʲ byáNtʉ́mba:
éróto n'émasambú n'ébea, ébʲtʲ byákʉ́rʉ́ka na. Mwindo n'ʲshé shé-
Mwindo básáme kwáNtʉ́mba. Mwindo wakíé wamakʲ́nd'ʲramya ébikáí bítʲ byáNtʉ́mba, Ntʉ́mba wére Mwindo, mbu: wendanga, ǒngo
mukwákare, iwé utákútíkónga, iwé usʲra na bé mwěbé. Mwindo wakíé
watúka kwáNtʉ́mbá hʲmá n'ʲshé, wénda usímbánge, mwísubukia isí-
nkárʲ́ kuTubondo:

> Wendángá nakʉ́rʉka
> Muisa
> Mbu ébʉtʉ́ wácere[211]
> Mbu émǔme wánkókó birangira[212]
> Ná muntorʲ́ wámushemba
> Mwindo wasêyá mwaMuisa
> MwaNyárʲre
> Ntúkánge mwaNtʉ́mba
> MwaMunundu
> Muisa mutúkocé Mwíndo
> Ná Mwindo kábútwa kéndayo
> Bǎnʉ ngí muhemúké busa
> Súnga nirʲte shé-Mwindo
> Muisa mutúkocé Mwíndo
> Ná Mwindo kábútwa-kénda
> Súnga nirʲte shé-Mwindo
> Nikʉ́rʉ́kánge kuTubondo
> Kwásʲ́ángá sínkárʲ́ ʲyangura
> ʲyangura mubʲ́tʉ washé-Mwindo
> Sínkárʲ́ kabúto ʲyangura[213]
> Narírí mukʲbo ná ntengʲ
> Nti neyá kuTubondo[214]

Mwindo wakíé watúka kwáNtʉ́mba hʲmá n'ʲshé shé-Mwindo, wénda
kʲ́rekérá mwaMuisa. Mwindo wakíé ʲyé uri mwaMuisa, Kahindo wéya
kúrí Mwíndo, mbu: ǒngo'súngánge ʲshé ǔngu, émakʉ́a é árérʲsʲ́á mutú-
ndú, iwé wǎkíá-kě-yo búnʲ́? Cáhundá úramyé ʲshé, ang'îmusʲa bǒbo,
musʲmó, ʲshé wásimuké, bʉshwá mbu ngí émwǎmí wébea bátʲ. Kahindo
wakíé wamakʲ́nd'ʲ́íre Mwindǒ bo, Mwindo wásʲmo Muisa, wásímba:

> Wendángá toró nasímuka
> Titá Muisa
> Wendángá toró nasímuka
> Súnga
> Bǎnʉ

Ngí muhemúkéngá busa
Súnga
Nirįte titá shé-Mwindo
Muisa
Wendángá toró anasímuka
Muisa
Mutúkocé Mwíndo
Mwindo kábútwa-kénda
Shé-Mwindo wabútángá muraj
Nendánge kwásínkárį Įyangura
Įyangura mubįtų washé-Mwindo

Mwindo wakíé įyé usįmóngi Muisa, wénda umusúndákánge éconga cé, ná nti umwiréngi mbu: bǎnų muhemúkéngá busa, mwįrengécángá na Mwindo, ná Mwindo nti kábútwa-kénda, kátárísánga biỹó byáku-mbúka; n'erótų rwábútwángá we ntíwarérísá múmabére įna. Mwindo mwįkįnd'įsįmo Muisa, Muisa wásimuka na, wáfúka. Muisa wakíé wamakįnd'îfúka, Mwindo wámwîre mbu wé weswángá ná bįnyantįré ban'Įyana; émubi wé wárįsá cǔma cara-ara, nó'ǒngo Muisa utúngá-musúnga hé, ngí cásįngwángá umutáỹa mó? Muisa wáshįsha Mwindo, mbu: ǒngo Mwindo, ubútwángá kása búnį ǒngo; mbéti ǒngo'ri ná busháké ngí búkwénjangá? Mwindo wámukandure ékandokó kémwasį wábútwángá we. Wámwîre mbu: ǒngo Muisa, kaį ntíurérúkírá kása mbu wé watúkíréngá múmųnwe wįna wémuróta; iwé ntíwabútwángá búbútwanga abâmpé bǎna, iwé wabútwángá nti webánge, nti wendánge nákubá; ǒngo Muisa ntíurérúkírá mbu wé watáwángá mukabúrj, bárįa na mó mitámbá, iwé wáfúfúka tu; įshé wámurekera tú kumunda n'é-ngoma, wámurekera ékǔsi, watúka tǔ ko; ntíurérúkírá ke étushįngįsho tųtį tó, ǒngo Muisa, ngí cásįngwángá umushata mó!

Mwindo wakíé įyé uri kwáMúisa, wátenja émurį kwásįángá isínkárį wé kuTubondo, wámusubukia. Įyangura wére bįnyantįré waMwindo ban'Įyana mbu kwétángá Mwíndo warékįnd'įtįnge įshé, įyé ukųrų-kánge n'é. Mwindo, mwįkųrųka ré kuTubondo, wáraa Muisa wásímba, mbu:

Ǒngo Muisa
Usúngá nti įyé nendánge
Ǒngo Muisa murįa-byábene
Kwásįángá sínkárį Įyangura
KuTubondo
Wendángá nakųrųka

Muisa wakíé wasúnga Mwíndo įyé wendánge, wámwîre mbu: eé Mwi-ndo ǒngo musike wé, cáhundá úbingé Káhindo wé ngu. Mwindo wá-musúbíe mbu wé utákocé ibinge kúno; iwé wabingírí kuTubondo kwáshé-Mwindo.

Mwindo mwîtúka kwáMúisa, wátánja uendo, bán'jshé bákụrúka, bénda ná kasáíré hákịmịréngá we hákikǒka. Mwindo na shé-Mwindo bákíé básáa hịkụra rákuTubondo, ábárịkángá ékumbúka, Ịyangura ná bịnyantịré waMwindo, bárubuka n'ékumbúka búrí mintsuntsu, bénda kakókéré Mwíndo bán'jshé hịkụra, bákụmána na bó.[215] Ịyangura ná bịnyantịré waMwindo mbu básungé Mwíndo, bámukụkụma n'é- kwịyo, bámurịa na múntóngá-ntóngá sémịne. Bákíé bárembera múbu- tara wákuTubondo, Mwindo wére bó mbu bámúsịcé. Bámusịca na hánkatị kébutara, báringa kitumo cántsóngá-ntsóngá sématụmo ngí sárịkere mó Mwíndo, nti ngí sírí búrí ékitụmbị cerútébe; bịnyantịré nti ngí bámámweréká bǔbó, mbu kúti émwịhw'ǎbó uri búrí hó mbu wámwesángá bo. Mwindo wakíé ịyé uri hịyo ékitụmbị hánkatị n'ébu- tara, wátụre isínkárị mwasị kútúkángé we n'ǎmbu wákwánángá we nti usondánge ịshé; wásímba:

Nakíé nahíta n'áshịnga
Sínkárị
Nakụmánaná Kahindo
Kahindo wáráka wéba
Mwindo ntákurerá binwa
Úmasúngá Múisa
Mbu câbúrá Múisa
Ǒngo nti utịnǎ co
Mwindo mbu
Nendá kumbúka kubutara
Kúrịkaa Múisa
Námasíngwá
Kúrịkaa Múisa
Nakíé něyá kumbúka kwáMúisa
Muisa wáráka wéba
Muisa wákụto kitụmbị
Mbu eé Mwindo tárịká mpe
Mwindo wáráka wịonga
Mbu mụntwé wábé Muisa ǔngu
Muisa wáráka wéba
Bakungú múmbési twámaụ
Ntanịnká to Mwindo
Ná Mwindo wáráka wịonga
Mashu ịshé mwea átárísánga mwǎna
Muisa mbu túkwané mongo
Nakámángá Múisa
Nará nendánge[216]
Neya mwáNtụmba
MwaNtụmba mwaMunundu

Ntúmba mbu túkwané mongo
Nakáma Ntúmba
Aní nakámángá Múisa
Nó'ŏngo Ntúmba utúkocé Mwíndo
Mwindo kábútwa-kénda
Anú nakáma Ntúmba naruha
Nará nirungúkánge mwashé-Burúngú
Nakíé néyǎ mpe jkúra kwáshé-Burúngú ongo[217]
Banúnké báráka béba
Mbu eé Mwindo twakwá na rwǎka
Aní natúmjré mantu kúno
Banúnké bárísa ná mantu
Nará nendánge kwáshé-Burúngú
N'ébanúnké mongo
Shé-Burúngú mbu túresé mongo
Aní mbu shé-Burúngú ŏngo
Utúkocé Mwíndo kábútwa-kénda
Káfúndísángá Múisa na Ntúmba
Naráka njonga
Aní mbu mbése titá kúno
Shé-Burúngú wáráka wéba
Mbu Mwindo utúkocé wikí wáshé-Burúngú
Wárásángá Bụtú n'Oto[218]
Twakúka múmbaj
Mwindo wáráka wéba
Mbu shé-Burúngú utúkocé Mwíndo
Ntámbési shé-Mwindo
Usúngá namákurása
Kahúngú watondéngá Mwíndo
Kahúngú wáncée shé-Mwindo
Aní ngí natjnge shé-Mwindo
Katitá kashé-karúo
Twará tukúrúkányánge
Shé-Mwindo twêndí kumbúka
Túbasirí kuTubondo
Kwásjángá sínkárj Jyangura
Cákórángá shé-Mwindo
Nabásíre kuTubondo
Ongo'súngá nirjte shé-Mwindo
Nirjte katitá kashé-karúo

Jyangura wátúre musike wé mwasj mbu ngí cásjngwá ŏngo úó umeyá na só, murje kása émunúmbá mwjremeso wáruhukj mo.[219] Bárja shé-Mwindo mwjremeso wárjka mó. Mwindo mwjshee jshé wámukere, êmpéné ínji itánenánga itáshubánga na, bátéke ÿó ịshé ná mumpunge.²²⁰ Wére ịshé mbu: ésâmpéné sábé sǐsa, ŏngo ngí uhemúkéngá busa, uhe-muke Mwindo kábútwa-kénda, mbu utúngáhụná bǎna bábaÿú, ŏngo'-hụnánge bǎna bámukárị; umwiririsa wásasá ŏngo;²²¹ kaị nti ntíóngo'sí karamo kémukịsa wáMwíndo.²²² Mwindo wakíé wamakịnd'ịshee ịshé biÿo, Ịyangura wére Mwindo mbu: ŏngo musike wé, ibó bêndí hó bárịkanga múmurárá úno bịsịné kịro bâmpé bea, iwé Ịyangura, iwé usondánge mbu úramyé kása ébea bátị bárịkángá kǔno, bâkíá báma-kịnd'ífúka, iwé nti ngí wasíbǎ ké ibúsa musike wịtú shé-Mwindo, nti wámutúre múmyasí áwákíángá we, ébụbí bútị wákuronjééngá we. Mwindo wárúkíra ébǔnu wisinkárị wé werịramya ábákwángá. Bịnya-ntịré ban'Ịyana bámusiire ésángoma, nâ wé Mwindo nti umịnánge bụshwá ésángoa sịshé, serímusúnga. Básímba:

Sínkárị wáráka wéba mbu:

> Titá shé-karamo kábea²²³

Mwindo mbu:

> Eé titá mbu ntáramyá bea
> Aní mbu wendángá toró nasímuka
> KaMwindo kábútwa-kénda
> Katitá kántáángá múngoma
> Shé-Mwindo utúkocé bea
> Mịcó ÿábea ÿasúmá
> Katitá kashé-mụngó wábea
> Kánisuríréngá mintsuntsu
> Ÿákịndị ná mwǐshí
> Narúkịre ÿó bukwáté²²⁴

Mwindo wakíé íyé uramyánge ábákwíréngá kuTubondo, wénda ukíánge wéya mwịkúa rámwea wásúnda hó éconga cé, émweǎ o nti wasimúká na. Mwîfúca bó bo:

Kíntsí íngu wakwángá ná bukúre, nti wafúká n'ébukúre wé!
Kíntsí íngu wakwángá utangírwánge ná bukúre, nti wafúká nti utangírwánge!
Kíntsí íngu wakwángá nti urúánge, wáfúka nti urúánge!
Kíntsí íngu wakwángá nti unenánge, wáfúka nti unenánge!
Kíntsí íngu wakwángá nti utéánge, wáfúka nti utéánge!
Kíntsí íngu wakwángá nti urumánge, wáfúka nti urumánge!
Kíntsí íngu wakwángá nti wesánge, wáfúka nti wesánge!
Kíntsí íngu wakwángá nti uhíngánge, wáfúka nti uhíngánge!
Kíntsí íngu wakwángá nti ubúmbánge nyungú ná maréá, wáfúka nti ubúmbánge!

Kíntsí íngu wakwángá nti ubasáa ntengi, wáfúka nti ubasánge!
Kíntsí íngu wakwángá nti ubangánáa na míné, wáfúka nti
ubangánánge!
Mwindo wáshibana mitebero ishátu nti uramyanga hó bea, wákwa ná
bikango byébiruhó-rúho. Ébea n'émanymbá áti, kírǎ o mwea wafúká
nti wíhandá na múmwe.²²⁵ KuTubondo kwárísána nákubá n'ébea
n'esâmpéné, bambíbi, bankambý, bankókó, érúsiké-síke n'erúkumí,
ébitásá n'ébaÿú, bǎna n'ébanýnke, bakúngú bebábǔme ná bébomína;
munkatí n'ébea bátī ba, ábarúsi n'ébakungú, n'ábatwá, bandírabitambo
ábáti; ábátī ba nâ bó bíhanda. Ésángandá síti sárikángá kuTubondo
sáfúka na, sábe tu kásángá búrí to, kíra mweǎ o wakwángá nti uri ná
bikáí bírí burebé, wáfúka ná nti uri hó n'ébikáí byé.²²⁶ KuTubondo
kwábése tǔ na murungu wámakýra arínda. Ébea bákíé bámakínd'ífúka,
Iyangura wábíkíra muréngé munkatí ÿéngence ÿébea, mbu: ǒngo shé-
Mwindo musike'abó, munkatí ÿecǔo kíti cábé kíno, rákirá mau míngí
ná nkambý nâ mpéné, ábátí bákymananêyo kǔno kuTubondo, nti
twasíbǎ ké isóntsómora ébinwa bíti n'ítúngányanya byó mukíby. Shé-
Mwindo wakíé wamakínd'îrúkíra émuréngé wĪyangura mwisí'abó,
wábíkíra émuréngé more n'ámwĪhí kúrí bana-cé bátí, mbu básonjé
mau.²²⁷ Kwákíé kwámetá kasembé kima, ébikángá bíti byécǔo báhíka
ná kuTubondo hima n'émau n'esányama. Cébindi munáné múmukomá-
kómá bátumane múkiby ébea bátí besâmbúngú síti sécǔo cáshé-Mwindo.
Ébea bátí bákíé bámakínd'îtumana, bǎna ná banýnké, n'ébakwákare
n'ébakúngú, Mwindo wímbarica, wábíndúka na búrí kanyero kânkó;
isínkárí wé Iyangura nâ wé wíkímía ná mǔntsi sakwáMúkíti ésáncangí;
ishé shé-Mwindo nâ wé wámbare ákwantsí n'ékwiyo: tuhúhuma túrí
mó ngora, bamafýta âmbéa, bandorera, bamasia;²²⁸ nâ wé wábíndúke
na búrí kanké. Ébea bákíé bámakínd'ítékére múkiby, ábafúkú bára-
mbika biráko ékwantsí, kwásêtá Mwíndo n'ishé n'isínkárí wé. Múkiby
mó ébea bátí bákóba na mbú pi! Kábe ná kabībi.²²⁹ Ímbi bentsé-běntsé
bíshátu: Mwindo n'ishé n'ísínkárí wé básáa múnymbá, bénda hâmbúka
hákiby, nti bákonángé busa-busa. Ábárikángá múntéko ÿékiby báhé-
mba bó měso, ákúsáíréngí bo bárérwa kó; bima mubó bámbuka, mbu:
ébasi mbéni shé-Mwindo wabútwá ké tu n'ompé musike? Bimá mbu:
shé-Mwindo uri hó n'émwamí washé-Kwábahingá hima ná mukárí.
Bimá mbu: angá, shé-Mwindo uri mpe ná mwisí'abó, mukárí waMukíti ná Mukíti wísíné. Ábasindú-síndu béba mbu shé-Mwindo uri ná
mwisí'abó Iyangura mukárí waMukíti hima ná musike wé Mwindo,
kábútwa-kénda, shé-mishíngá mingí, íngu kásángá uirírísíwánge n'ishé.
Shé-Mwindo ná Mwindo n'Īyangura bénda kirambí kima mwísáa
munkatí ÿéntéko hákiby. Mwindo wárekera muréngé kwámíra wé
Nkúbá wímukónga bitýmbí bíshátu byámiríngá. Nkúbá wáhíca byó;
byákíé íyé bírí kwihí n'ékwantsí, íyé bírí keyá hântsí byárímbe ékwiyo
métero isáno múmwǎnyá itúkíre hântsí.²³⁰ Mwindo n'ishé n'ísínkárí

wé bátáríe ékwįyo múbitų́mbį́. Įyangura wárįka munkatį́ n'ebábábí,
shé-Mwindo múháro rwakwábŭme ná Mwindo múháro rwámarémbé.
Ébea bátį bákíé bámakį́nd'įtékére múkįbų ná bámakį́nd'įkóba, Mwindo
wásį́mána múkitų́mbį́, wátárísha émĕso ékwįyo, wáráke Nkúbá, mbu:
ee mį́r'ȳaní Nkúbá uhángenga ébųtų́.²³¹ Wamakį́nd'įébă bo, wáhíca
émĕso ékwantsí múngence ȳébea; wéba, wásínja bó, mbu: músaruké
bănų bămí. Bámurįsja, mbu aé. Wéba mbu: bănų bakungú músaruké;
mbu aé. Mbu: bănu batambo músaruké; mbu aé. Mwindo wásínja
ékįbų nti wahátá n'ébikáí bįtį byábútwángá n'e: conga, mwandá, kâkú
kárí mó murí. Wáháta ná nkóma ȳékibúȳá ȳerísínja ákįbų.²³² Mwindo
wakíé wamakį́nd'ísínja ábárįkángá múkįbų, wábíkíra muréngé, mbu:
múndŭshú sirínda sírįkangá kŭno kuTubondo, íro rŭshú rúrįké ntéko
ȳaró, n'ébămí n'ébatambo bamúsímpé mbúngú, nâ bó bárįké ntéko
ȳăbó. Mwįkį́nd'jébă bo ébea bítúngányanya na, kíra rŭshú ná
ntéko ȳaró. Mwindo wábíkíra muréngé mbu bįna bátį ábarínda bárįké ntéko ȳăbó, Įna nya-Mwindo, įna wamubútá, wįshį́ke kakeké ná
bįna banúnké. Wamakį́nd'įébă bo, bįna bíshį́ka muntéko ȳăbó, įna
wamubútá wįshį́ka kákananí kakeké kwįhį́ ná babį́né. Mwindo wábíkíra muréngé, mbu: ĕo ŏngo įshé ukóro rwábé ro, tų́re ábămí mwasį́
ácánihųnyį́éngá ŏngo; kúti nakukángángá, nakuhųnyje byábé, naku-
báka byó, tų́re ébămí mwasį́ bárukiré. Hárįkángá shé-Mwindo wábo
na, ésántubano sátúkíre na múmpandá ȳémŭme, sátáríe na múma-
bíndú, sénda ná keyá mútéó rwémųntwé; múntsįnga-ntsįnga sébŭme,
shé-Mwindo wásį́mána. Múnkene nįngí múmĕso na shé-Mwindo, utá-
sínjí tŭ na ébămí, wéba nti íyé utįtį́mánéngi, n'ekákakóhóró kárįka na
hángongo ȳémuhú kábutúrá-túra, nti ntíwarané ko bųshwá ébųbí
wásúmá wébubíshá-bísha.²³³

Shé-Mwindo wéba mbu:
Bănų bămí bátį muri háno; iwé ntíwatúná ébųbí bų́tį wákíángá we
wákííre éríbúta ré ndi, musike wé; Įna iwé wecángá hó émwįkŏ bo
kúrí bakárį́ bé munkatį́ ȳéntéko ȳébakungú n'ébarų́sį, iwé mbu
áwabútí mwáná-muȳú mubănų bakárį́, iwé nti wamukerá hįma
n'ámwána wé. Múbomína bátį, mutúbá mubó wábúta băna bámu-
kárį́ bara-ara, ná nya-ngantsį wé ngí wábúta émwána wémuȳú.
Nya-ngantsį wé wakíé wamakį́nd'íbúta émuȳú, iwé wámushómba
na, mukárį́ nya-ngantsį wábíndúke ná nya-kashómbé, iwé wénda
umukaírée ná kumunda n'ébisando. Múbusíbúké bų́tį bo, wásúbíra
įtúmo, iwé wákáso ró múcarí ngendo mutúbá, iwé nti usasį́r'iȳa
ámwăna hįmá n'įna. Iwé wakíé wasúnga émwăna ntíwakwá, iwé
wárįsjenya n'ébakungú n'ébarų́sį, ibó bátáa ámwănă ngu múkabų́rį;
ibó bákíé mbu básisimuki múmukomá-kómá, mbu bó básimuké,
básúnga émwăna nti íyé unyaírée tú muri įna. Iwé wakíé mbu wásungé ca, wíshį́shį́rįsha múmutíma, iwé mbu kaí wámaremé ntíwaȳá

íngu mwăna, kaí ntiwamukų́tų́ múkitų́mbí cé céwămí; nâ wé ŭngu
wamasúngá ébịshịsharo bị́tị bíbíáángé we; kaí íngu mwăna wamu-
kókérí ukị́rị, iwé wámurʃa ke múngoma, wámurekera n'ékŭsi. Kwétángá émwănă ngu, iwé wásíba kí mbu umuiríísánge, kaí nti umu-
súmyángĕ ke. Ngí hátúkíréngá n'ebusíbúké wémwănă ngu; wakíé
wamatúká ékŭsi, wámweyere na mó, wámuhénda na kúno kuTubondo; ngí hátúkíréngá na wé, iwé wábéka, nti ébea bátị bámá-
mushíríre. Kwábékéréngá we iwé wámóa mbu wé waramá, ákwé-
ndángé we ngí kúrí ákaramo, kaí nti wé wị́rekéránge mumenké
ÿerị́támbá-tamba écŭo kị́tị iwé nti wantsánge ématị́na émití, iincira
hányará, ịrá biÿó byêmá;[234] ngí hǐha hámwendéréngá ná musike
wé múbingo, wénda kámutúnjá mwị́rịba rébịbị́-bịbị́ bị́tị bísúngángé
we, wénda kámutịngị́ré hêndé écŭo, iwé nti warékámá búrí buria;
ná ngí bŭmbu wéyá we kŭno kuTubondo; kaí éríbúta rébaÿú ríramé,
ngí cásị́ngwá iwé wásúnga wácá ébụtų́, n'erúmóo rų́tị rwerísúnga
tu écŭká cébea n'ecébikáí bị́tị byákŭno kuTubondo.
Ịyangura wére ébábŭme bárịkángá múkịbụ mwị́tị́tʃa musike wăbó
íngu (shé)-Mwindo:[235]
Iwé mbu ngí ŭno isínkárí waMwindo, bănụ bămí, bănụ murịkịre,
iwé musike wabó ngu shé-Mwindo wamubingíshángá kwáMúkị́tị,
iwé wámenyera na kó, n'émwínyihiro wámoké,[236] bụshwá émirimo
ÿé n'erị́rịsịenya n'é, moké wámurʃa n'ékwịyo, wámwanye ná ịrénga
ébomína bátị́ bábingá we. Ngí hǐha, bănụ bămi, iwé utábúruhyí, utá-
búrị́í ná kore-kore mumuróró wábinwa bị́ngí. Iwé wakíé mbu wákai,
émwănă ngu wásáa kwárịkángá we, Mukị́tị nti ʃyé usasị́rị imuÿa
bụshwá mbu nti ntíwosí mbu mwăna wé, n'éwĕnge wé n'émanko
é ngí ámuramya.[237] Ngí hǐha hámísányángá namísánya n'e kámu-
haná éntse ÿakwáshé-Mwindo, n'ékikandí cerímusúnga. Ngí hátúkíréngá ná Mwindo wákwána n'ịshé, bụshwá ébusíbúké wébịbị́ bị́tị
byámukóréngá ịshé. Wáhima ná kŭno kuTubondo, ịshé wábéka na.
Kwábékéngá we, Mwindo wámwendere mubingo, mbu ịshé wamé-
ndáyo kakwíré múbisú.[238] Wakíé mbu wámúkų́máne, wámutị́nge,
ngí bŭmbu wákų́rų́cá Mwindo wésha tú ịshé kŭno kuTubondo; ngí
bŭmbu búrí băte múnkų́mánano íno ÿékịbụ cébămí.
Wéba tú mbu:
Ŏngo shé-Mwindo ukórángá bụbí hịma n'ébakungú bábé n'ébarų́sị.
Ábesí mukungú ngí watúkíréngá mo erị́hanŏ ndi reríiririsa Mwindo,
kongó wamákerwá háno hákịbụ; ịna umáramé nti ŏngo wịsị́né ngí
utúkíréngá mo erị́hanŏ ndi. Ubíshángá, ŏngo shé-Mwindo, útobo-
rora ébána, mbu hárí bịma bêmá na bámpe báhundá, ná nti ntíóngo'sí
kírí múbura wámukárị́'abé, ácánịnkwángá ŏngo na Ongo, usúnga
có nti cémá, écŏngó cábíndúke cêmá; kaí ékumbúka kúsịra ná cŏngo;
ịna twamáshịmă ke, bănụ bábŭme, áwámáhandírá tú băte kŭno

kuTubondo, Ina shé-Mwindǒ ngu nti wakórángá kinwa camúharú; kongó kwáshírírángá bea kúno, nti shé-Mwindǒ ngu ngí washíríshángá bo. Aní Iyangura nashúre nendě mpe.²³⁹

Iyangura wakíé wamakínd'Iéba, Mwindo nâ wé wásímána; wásínja ékibu; weba mbu:

Wé utúnge na Mwindo, shé-mishíngá mingí, kábútwa-kéndá, iwé usira ná buÿongwá n'ishé; ishé ngu utákwí ná kashírá mbu wé uri hó n'é busíbúké; angá; iwé usira n'ishé busíbúké. Ábyákórángá ishé wámukóre, na byákóréngá iwé wákóre ishé, ébítI bya byámakínd'-Iéta, íyé túntsontsomoré ábyásêyayo, ábyêmá n'ébyongó-byǒngó; wâtángírí-tu-íyo itánja mubó bábí, ngí wabíshi, n'ebábǔme bátI mbi nti bákaéngí. Íyé túrIké shu n'écǔo kítú, túremberé n'ébea shu.

Shé-Mwindo wábíkíra muréngé, mbu wé utúnge na shé-Mwindo éríbúta rísira mo rányará; iwé ǔno urIkíre háno, iwé ntí mwamí tu, íyé Mwindo ngí wasíá múcando cé; íngu wakambí Mwíndo múcǔo kíno, nti wakóngótérwí mumIne ÿabábǔme.²⁴⁰ Mwindo wakíé warúkira émuréngé wíshé, Mwindo wámusúbíe, mbu wé: ǒngo ishé, rIká hó múkitúmbí cábé céwǎmí, iwé utákocé ibé mwamí kúti ǒngo'kírí uri hó, iwé nti wakanúká kindI ná mwIshí. ÁhárIkángá hó ébakungú n'ébarúsi, básímíra Mwindo, bére shé-Mwindo mbu: musike'abé ntíwebá bubí, banyá écǔo mbíso síbí: musike'abé wárIé cǔndá nó ǒngo cǔndá, bushwá mbu ǔkíá úmamusibúré ékItI, nti umukwírí tú monó mukírI, n'émonó o nti wârushí hó tú runtsaka-ntsaka mukíno cǔo. Shé-Mwindo wéba mbu: angá, bǎnu bakungú n'ébarúsi, iwé usira mǔbya, Ina iwé usondánge mbu musike wé ngí wábesi hó mwǎmí, iwé wěndá utúmíkée kuruma n'é. Ábakungú bámwÍre mbu: ǒngo shé-Mwindo, banyá écǔo cábé mbíso síbí, ǒngo cǔndá ná musike'abé cǔndá, bushwá mbu karekare kásángá ǒngo wébanga mbu ǒngo wísiné hó ngí wábǔme irénga bámpé, ná cébá ǒngo nti cétá, ngí cásíngwángá ibó básúnga ébinwa bítI mbi, ibó bárúka intse ÿeríkuaÿa, bushwá érúsúbáhwá rwábé; kaí émwǎmí wámafúnd'îaÿjwa nti burúngé wásúmá. Shé-Mwindo wéba mbu: ngí cásíngwá, bǎnu bakungú bé n'ébarúsi bé, mumeba ékinwǎ ca, íyé nabanyá écǔo mihango ibi: Mwindo cǔndá n'âní shé-Mwindo cǔndá, bushwá érúsúbáhwá rwínú, Ina rina ré nti wé ákwǎsá usasír'- isíére Mwindo écǔo, nâ wé nti wěndá urísáa múbiÿó nti íyé uríree mubyó kuruma ná musike wé Mwindo, bushwá mbu iwé wasúngá nkene nIngí kúrí musike wé na kúrí ébea bátI.²⁴¹

Shé-Mwindo wakíé wamakínd'Iébǎ bo, wásibure musike wé éwǎmí, wíkúngúra ébikáí bítI byéwǎmí kásángá bíríté we: éncangí ÿemasingure, n'émirí ibi ÿémibungo; wámunínka tú butéá wátukúshi werímbare múmabóko, mwítuma ésányama sébsebse, n'ébutéá wémíndí; wámunínka tu ncámbi; wámunínka tú kataba; wámunínka kembo; wámunínka n'eróhú rwémwěru.²⁴² Shé-Mwindo wámbica Mwindo ébikáí bítI byá Mwindo nti usíméne, bushwá mbu émwǎmí wambicwanga

ébikáí nti usíméne. Ábakungú báringa ékitựmbị cásịngúrwá mo ukarú
ná makựta ámbeá, bánịnka có shé-Mwindo, shé-Mwindo wárịkeca
mucó Mwíndo; shé-Mwindo wásakia Mwindo énkóma ÿéburíngá-
rínga iri mó bitetéra byébibámba ÿasịngúrwá mó ukarú ná makựta
ámbéa. Wamusakíángá byá nti íyé urịkịre múkitựmbị. Wakíángá usị-
méne, ịshé wámusakia tú nkokú n'ébutátí; wámunịnka n'ébửku búrí mó
misúngú.²⁴³ Shé-Mwindo wásakia ná musike wé éBatwá, wámunịnka
ná bandírabitambo: mwamíhésị, mushonga, mubéị, mushumbịá, mu-
hérị; shé-mụmbo, bakungú, barựsị.²⁴⁴ Bámwambícéngá ébịtị bya mwí-
cumbi. Shé-Mwindo wakíé wamasímíkíshá musike wé bo, Mwindo
wábíkíra muréngé, mbu wé wamasíma, iwé utángáhụná wákíángá ịshé
mbu ékubutara kúrịké uandá rụmá bụróbo: ésángandá sịtị sírịké múcửo:
kúbutwé mwăna muÿú ná mwăna mumína, kúbutwé ná kirựmbự
n'ébiréma, bụshwá mbu cửo kítárựkáa biréma.²⁴⁵ Shé-Mwindo wakíé
wamakịnd'ịambica musike wé ébikáí byéwămí, wábanyie ébămí bárịkángá ho émaụ n'esányama; kíră ca kikémbé cárịa maụ ná mpéné ná
nkambự. Bánịnka n'Ịyangura nkambự nịmá ÿerịkựrựka n'e kwámoké
Mukịtị. Ábămí n'ébakungú bárịkángá ho béba mbu bó Mwindǒ ngu
wásịé kửno kuTubondo ná shé-Mwindo wéndị kárịká muímpé ntata.
Shé-Mwindo mbu wárukiré bo wákóngóta n'émịne, wáshịma ná ngụrụ.
Mwísímíkwă ra ráMwíndo bịnyantịré ban'Ịyana bámunịnka kikumí
kịma, ná shá-mwămí nâ wé wámunịnka kịkumí kịma; ịshé waMwindo
nâ wé wámunịnka kikumí kịmá nti Katobororo, n'éBatwá bámunịnka
kịmá.²⁴⁶ Mwindo mwísímíkwa ré wanịnkwángá bikumí bịnye bụróbo;
wendángá wíbingíréngi wịsịné nti íyé utámbánge múcửo. Kíntsí ímpe
hásángá hánụntsánéngí we nti watúnjă ho kikumí.²⁴⁷ Mwísímíkwa
ráMwíndo ábárísángá ébiÿó báruha, bịmá mubó mánenere na mútu-
kúcá. Mwindo wakíé wamakịnd'ìsímíkwa, ékịbụ cántsóntsóbana: kíntsí
íba bátúkángá ko bákựrựke kó; ná shé-Mwindo nâ wé wátịnge mutundu wé, wásịére musike wé kuTubondo.²⁴⁸ Ịyangura isínkárị waMwindo
wakíé wakựrựke kwámoké, wásịngo Mwindo wăngá munkatị ÿéntéko,
mbu:

> eé Mwindo, karamo;
> wăngá búnu, karamo;
> isó wámakutáá mwísinda, karamo;
> utúrịkịngá ná bushựnáné, karamo;
> úsingiriré, karamo;
> uramanga, úkasanirwé, karamo;
> ná só na ntsoko karamo;
> úbuté băna bare-bare bábaÿú ná bámukárị;
> úsumé titá, kúrí aní kúsịră tú kinyomá, karamo.²⁴⁹

Mwindo mwísịána n'ịshé, ịshé nâ wé wámunịnka hó tú wăngá. Mwindo
wásakia n'ísínkárị wé bakungú bábí bímutịndịkịa; wámunịnka ná

mpéné sínye, ná mukósóro wámitúndú makúmị ábí ỹámumpunge ná
matóngá ásánu ânkókó.

Mwindo wakíé kwámetá matụ̀ ântswá wasímíkwá, wábúrǎ mbu iwé
wamakwá meru ỹámpunú ỹírísa muỹó; wáhíca ébatwá bé múbusará
kahía. Ábatwá kwêndángá bo múbusará, bákíé ịyé bárí mûntúka-kúnị
na mwịenda-kúnị, báruha; básáme munkatị ỹantse.²⁵⁰ Bákíé múmukomá-kómá báhénd'ịramuke. Kwáramúkéngá bo, bákụ́mána mukandá
wámpunú, bátụ́ca ó; bákíé mbu bátuké búrí háno na háa, bákụ́mána
tó; báshurịa tó mbu sábéká, bana-mbíbi bịrása ná mutó.²⁵¹ Bákíé mbu
bákunduké turambo túbí, bákụ́mána katuku kịmá nti ịyé kákurángé
émabịndú, bámurúnda mó nkékị. Muna-katuku mbu wé ntí mukịrị,
wáshée ébyǒndó ékwịyo, ỹákwa;²⁵² bábụso na ỹó híha-hǐha. Kwárịkángá bo múmingụ́rụrụ́, bákíé ịyé bábụsóngí émpunú, Kirịmu wárúkíra ékihuhumo cábó.²⁵³ Kirịmu wéba mbu: ébasi, kúno bea tu; niha-
kanga mbu anísịné nirịkanga kúno, kaị nti kúrí hó tú beá nku! Kirịmu
wénde na bó kantsóka. Wakíé mbu wéyé kwịhị na bó, wísúnda mubó,
wábáka na hó batwá báshátu, wámịna na bó. Ụmá mubó, múbatwá,
nti ngí Nkụ́róngó; wáshunukara, wábéka; n'esâmbíbi sámutụ́ca, sábéka
n'e. Kirịmu wéba mbu wé ényamǎ nji ỹémpunú ịsịé háno, iwé watéérí
ho ésâmbíbi hịma n'émutwá, íngu wákubékanga. Kirịmu wábúnde
ná hịma n'ékịnda cémpunú. Kwábékéngá Nkụ́róngó, wakíé mbu wéyé
búrí háa, wịkébéra, wéba mbu: kaị bịtụ́ bákusịrịrịrwa, bákukwá.
Wakíé mbu wáhembị co émẹso, wásúnga nti kírí ná mịntwé irínda ná
mahémbé arínda, ná měso arínda. Wéba mbu: réro butúmámbǎ mbu,
réro Mwindo ukocanga bó utâkocịyǒ ngu mwịkwána n'e.²⁵⁴ Ákámutwá
nko kákíé ịyé kárí híy'óburambo, kákókúa, mbu: nabéká e! Kárịa byó
hánkoto; kábéka, n'esâmbíbi sámutụ́ca na. Wénda kasáá ékumbúka
kuTubondo nti ịyé uri kabéréká n'ámwehu; wéyere ná mwaMwindo.
Wakíé wamáruhúká kashángí kare, kámáhwíré nyungú ỹábuntu, Mwindo wámushịsha, mbu: buhórǒ nko kútúkángé ǒngo? Wámusúbíe,
mbu: kúsịrá buhórǒ nku, ǒngo mwǎmí waní; bǎte twahítǎyo bánye;
Kirịmu wámịna báshátu, n'ậní Nkụ́róngó níshunurá munkatị na bó
hịmá n'esâmbíbi; ịna ntí kirịmu, kírehe ná bụtụ́. Mwindo wakíé mbu
wárukiré bo, wéba mbu: ébasi réro cásúmá nci, ébatwá bé éríhía érị-
beré-bére nénkị báshírire ékubusará! Wákae ékwịyo wáhíca émẹso
kwantsí, wéba mbu: eé conga câní, ubúránayo múbụtụ́ wámukǒmá.
N'erótụ́ ndo ịshé shé-Mwindo nti uri kuró. Mwindo wére ịshé mbu:
ênkókó ỹěndá ikwáa mukerị nti wé wákwenda, iwé wǎhénd'ịramuke
n'émutwá ụmǎ ngu, kakwáná na Kirịmu.²⁵⁵ Shé-Mwindo wakíé mbu
wárukiré bo, wáhange musike wé, mbu: eé titá kǒko; ang'ịendayo kó;
kirịmu cámashíríanga, cámarángá mukakụ́a ná kakụ́a kábea; úmashoshá tǔ nci kirịmu, nti utukóké ukịrị mukíno cǔo.²⁵⁶ Mwindo wére ịshé
mbu: n'ậní ntángásonda, nihéndị̣ hó ịramuke; ụsị́ayo óngw'eré ébakungú mbu nákwendá kakwáná na Kirịmu.

Bákíé múmukomá-kómá nguru-nguru, Mwindo wásúbíra éconga cé, n'émutwá wámusondore; bénda nákubá múbusará. Bákíé básáa híbáíro rémpunú, émutwá wáshemba ékirímu mbu: kicáa. Mwindo wére émutwá mbu: kía kásǎ mbu, nâ wé wásungé co. Mwindo wére émutwá mbu: ǒngo sja háno, muna-Kirímu wǎkíá wámanjmjna, nó'óngo nti ngí ǔtúrá émwasí ékumbúka. Mwindo wásúbíra nya-musísá wé muna-conga; wéndere muna-kirímu kantsóka. Wakíé mbu wásungané na có rĮso muríso, Mwindo wáshemba có, mbu: utûkerí ro rúno'otú iwé na bé. Muna-kirímu wísarma, wásímána; mbu cêndí koké Mwíndo, Mwindo wárekera émuréngé kubǔnu wásímba:

Kirímu utúkocé Mwíndo
Ná Mwindo kábútwa kéndayo
Kirímu umǎshoshá Mwíndo
Kirímu utúkocé Mwíndo
Ná Mwindo kábútwa-kénda
Shé-Mwindo wabútángá muraj
Muna-kítú utúkocé Mwíndo

Kirímu wakíé mbu wéndi kámjná Mwíndo, Mwindo wíamba, mbu réro wacúká ngu. Mwindo nâ wé wíkentsea kúrí co. Mwindo wámusúnda n'éconga cé. Kirímu wáke na hântsí buarí-ári, cákwa na. Mwindo wákubya n'émutwá wé (mó murénge) mbu wêyé wábusú muna-kirímu; émutwá wéya. Wakíé mbu wántsjntsé muna-kirímu mó éntámbí yé-mweré, Mwindo wámuhange, mbu: reké kása có bo, túbukiré bea ékumbúka, bêndí karjá co ékumbúka kongó shé-Mwindo wásúnga ébyumbé byécangǎ we. Mwindo wáráke ábárikángá ékumbúka, Mwindo wátúma éconga cé ékumbúka káringá ébea, bêndi káringá íngu Ongo wékirímu; wásímba mbu:

Eé conga cânǐ ngenderenga
Básíéré kǔndu kuTubondo
Básíéré kǔndu kuTubondo
Kwáshé-Mwindo
Shé-Mwindo wántúmíri bea

Kwétángá éconga, cákíé mbu cêyé kuTubondo, céyere na hámákako na shé-Mwindo, cíhúmbáká-humbaka hámákako n'e; n'ébea bátí berú-búngú bákúka na, bénda kákaé wísúndákángé éconga hárí shé-Mwindo. Shé-Mwindo wéba mbu éconga kítúrángé mwasí: kúti Mwindo ntí-wakwá nti Kirímu ngí wakwá. Shé-Mwindo wátúma kó kikémbé cábea, mbu:

Múkaí ékwjkúra,²⁵⁷
múbunguré Mwíndo!

Mwírungu murí bjngj,
muri ntsóka ibúrenga.
Múbunguré Mwíndo,
Kwákwetángá Mwíndo.
Shé-Mwindo wabútángá muraj.

Muna-conga wakíé wamirúndáká hámákako na shé-Mwindo, cóka ná
hjmá-hjmá n'ébea bákútóngá shé-Mwindo. Muna-conga wóka n'ébeǎ
mbo múmwǎnyá; cénda ná kásjké hárí Mwindo hjmá-hjmá n'ébea.
Mwindo wakíé wasúnga éconga cé hjma n'ébea, muna-conga wéyere
na múmjne ǧaMwindo. Mwindo wére ébea mbu bákukumé ékirjmu.
Báronja macéra, bárja Kirjmu hábásirwa. Bjmá mubó báháta émpunú
ǧashúrwángá n'ébatwá. Ábarjérj békirjmu bákíé mbu bátuké háno na
háa, émacéra acíka bushwá éburjtóhé wámuna-kirjmu. Báronja úmpé
mundára, bárja tǔ ho Kirjmu; bákukuma có; bénda ná keshá co ékumbúka. Cákíé cárembera, érúbúngú rútj rwákúka na: n'ébanúnké
n'ébanúnké, n'ébakúngú n'ébakúngú.²⁵⁸ Básjca n'ékirjmu hánkatj kébutara. Ébea bákíé básúngǎ co, báshjshara nguru bátúra ésândúrú,
béba mbu réro ébusará wâtúkwí mo. Bjmá mubó béba mbu réro wá-
kuǧá nci utámúsjá muna-cábó. Mwindo wakíé wasúnga ímbo bébángé
bo wácjnja na bó hǐhá nti bárí báshátu; bákwa na.²⁵⁹ Mwindo wére
bana-cé mbu bábengé ékirjmu; nâ wé Mwindo wásímba:

> Kirjmu wabáírwá híy'ótubondo²⁶⁰
> Shé-Mwindo wáráka wéba
> Kirjmu wabáírwa híy'ótubondo
> Kirjmu kírísangá bea
> Kirjmu cákjndjré bea
> Shé-Mwindo titá ntsúbáhe

Bákíé mbu báhumo ébura, hátúka mwea wíkúba nti ushwére; hátúka
úmpe, wásáa nâ wé nti ushwére. Bákíé mbu báhumu ébura, hátúka
úmpe wíkúba nti ushwére. Kirjmu wakíé wamakjnd'îbengwa, n'ébatwá báshátu bámakjnd'îtúka mó nti báshwéré, Mwindo wábíkíra
muréngé mbu wé utúnge na Mwindo, iwé usondánge mbu mǔkíá murísa
ékirjmǔ nci, murísanga có n'étukúa n'étukúa, nti mutútáí mutó. Kirjmu
wakíé wamakjnd'ibáwa, Mwindo wábanyie ná bana-cé báti ásányama
sjtj n'émakúa n'émakúa; wére na bó mbu wé wámasúngá kakúa mumu-
kukuru wányumbá ǧarebé, iwé nti wamuhongéshá. Kirjmu wakíé wamakjnd'ibanyjwa-banyjwa mitéko mitéko, báringa éměso acó bákáránga
ó muinga rúhúe. Kásángá hákíá hásáa kǐyo, cámabúa, nti hásáa ná
mwea. Éměso átj áKírjmu ákíé ámakárángwa, ásáa na mó bea kihumbj
kjma cábea. Mwindo mbu bea bé mbi: wánjnka na bó ntata.²⁶¹
Kwárjkángá Nkúbá ékwjyo, kaj nti warénúntsáná na Kirjmu; Nkúbá

ákwárįkángá we múbụtú, wakíé mbu wánụnkįrwé érúsangį rwámíra
wé Kirímu rwétá n'eríyuhu, étongó twámurara na múměmbé, émi-
ntsórį ẏámutúka na múměso. Wéba mbu wé wăkíá ke míra wé ngu
búní Mwindo? Wéba mbu wé usasírį kása imunubya kongó utásúbírí-
tu-íyo: năkíá námakínd'îmunubya kŭno kúkwâní, nti nasíba kě tu
imukúrúca ékwantsí kûkwé. Wéba tú mbu: kongó Mwindo wamúsí-
bánge mbu wé warésákáná na Kirímu, kongó ntíwaẏáyo míra wé
Kirímu, ná kongó iwé utâmukúrúcį-tu-íyo, kongó wăhéréyo na kúno
nti ntíwaréyá tu múcŭo cé; ná wamărame nti ntíásángá wosí mbu
míra wé.

Mwindo wásímba:

Nkúbá wameyá káringa Mwíndo
Nkúbá waringángá Mwíndo
Híyo Tubondo
Wakíé mbu wárukiré érúsangį
Mwindo wáráka wébayo
Mbu eé Nkúbá utúkocé Mwíndo
Shé-Mwindo wabútángá murai
Ná Nkúbá utúkocé Mwíndo Mbórụ

Mwindo wéba mbu:

Eé Nkúbá utúkocé ná Mwindo Mbórụ
Baréngé-réngé bárérįká báréráná kare
Miréngé isímbwánge barįmį bátásibé ẏo
Eé karánį ŏngo
Óngo'súngá nti íyé nendángeyo
Kóẏo'aní Nya-mwako
Usúngá nti íyé nendángeyo
Bakungú báshé-Mwindo
Óngo'súngá nti íyé nendángeyo
Bakungú báshé-Mwindo béyé háno
Kubí-kubí wírandá na Mwěrį
Míra'aní Nkúbá ubúránanga
Nkúbá wamáringá Mwíndo
Túbasé mwaNyárįre

Mwindo wáraa-raa ụmáụmá:

Kóẏo'aní Nya-mwako
Óngo'súngánge nti íyé nendánge
Nya-Mwindo wáráka wíonga
Ná Nkúbá nti wamárįndo
Ntsékíá búní na mwána'ani

Nya-Mwindo wáráka wéba
Nakwá nakwá na mwána'ani
Shé-Mwindo wáráka wéba
Nakwá nakwá na mwána'ani
Karúndú káhorángá bjra
Kámakwá nabíka murando²⁶²

Nkúbá wakíé wamakjnd'îrúkíra érúsangj rwámjra wé Kirjmu, nti
rútúkíréngí kwámjra wé Mwindo kuTubondo, wáhíta ná hïhá-hïha
káringá Mwíndo. Wáhíta na, wéyere na hábutara wakwáMwíndo.
Nkúbá wére Mwindo mbu: wé ukuringánge, ŏngo mjra wé, iwé usasjr'-
jenda kákuhana, bushwá mbu iwé wakusúbúké ngyry, ŏngo mjra wé,
ukíǎyo mbu úýé Kírjmu, ná Kirjmu mjra wé, nti usíba ŏngo'bíshánge.
Mwindo mwírúkírǎ bo, utjanyé bushwá mbu wendánge ná mjra wé,
jna bana-cé ngí bákwa mushjkj mbu émwǎmí wǎbó wendá n'erûtj.
Mwindo wásímba:

Tutáríee kŭndu kwáBísherya
Ná Nkúbá wamáringá Mwíndo
Natáríé kŭndu kwáBísherya
Ná Nkúbá wamáringá Mwíndo
Eé Nkúbá utúkocé Mwíndo
Ná Mwindo kábútwa kéndayo
Shé-Mwindo wabútjré muraj
Mjra'aní utúkocé Mwíndo
Nya-béndá mutújra hó o
Mbu ntjrjrj wabjré mubánga
Ná musará wabjré mukéndo²⁶³
Cábúrángá shé-Mwindo
Cârúkj wasóntsómori
Ébytý wákucá twebánge
Búrí nkandá mukúkj²⁶⁴
Nya-béndá-toró béndǐ to
Mibúbú wásjé ubíbéngi
Bakungú báshé-Mwindo
Bakungú bántáa múbinwa
Nebéré Mungúto kúWamba
Kubawé bábisumbú-sumbu
Nebángá na mjtý kátima
Kútuké mutíma nti jbera²⁶⁵
Kabáré na Ntábáré-bare
Titá
Kwátée moké wababá byoo

Mwindo wendángá usímbángě bo ná nti Nkúbá utáýánge n'e ékwjyo

mpômpó; ná bana-cé báMwíndo bárérwa n'ékwįyo. Nkúbá wáshíríre
ná kumund'ĕrútųndo hįmá na Mwindo; béya na kwáNkúbá. Mwindo
wakíé wéya kwáNkúbá, Nkúbá wámushísha mbu: ŏngo mįra wé Mwindo ubísháyo ngųrų, ukíáyo mbu úÿé mįra wé Kirįmu, ukáranga
n'éméso é, érúsangį rwámutárie, iwé warúkirǎ ro ékwįyo; kįro kongó
uhícǎyo érúsangį ékwantsí, kongó iwé ntíwasíbúkáyo. Nkúbá wére tu
Mwíndo mbu iwé kásángá ukutúnjáa múturéngwe-turéngwe, kaį íyé
óng'wįrengécánge n'e. Mwindo wakíé mbu wásaé nko kwáNkúbá,
wásúnga kó keme kįngí, n'erísúku nti rįngí ko, angá nųmbá, nti bárį-
kangǎ hó múweréré wara-ara, angá itíndíra hįma. Nkúbá wáringa
Mwindo, wátáríe n'e kwáMbúra. Mbúra wakíé mbu wásungé Mwíndo,
wámwîre mbu: ŏngo Mwindo utúshembwánga; émwasį wábé n'erísúma
rábé réburaį wábé, twarérúkírá hó émwasį wábé, įna kúno kúsįra tú
buraį wábé. Mbúra wáhíte ná Mwindo mbíso sirínda ná sirínda, wámu-
surucie ná mahúngú, wámutoca na. Mwindo wéba mbu: réro nahá-
ngábárá ke. Nkúbá wákųkųma tu Mwíndo, wénda kámutámbíshá
kwáMwérį. Mwěrį wakíé mbu wásungé Mwíndo, wámushemba mbu: réro
émwasį wábé wárétúrwa hó mbu usúmá, įna kúno kwįyo kúsįrá muhao
wábé. Mwěrį wáshika Mwindo múbutéó. Mwindo wítáte, mbu: eé
titá shé-Mwindo nkasanenga, n'éconga cání kítánítúkíngá múmįne.
Nkúbá wákųkųma tu Mwíndo, wénda katáríé n'e kwáMwíshí. Mwîshí
wakíé mbu wásungé Mwíndo, wámubamba mubíhúé-hue. Mwindo
wárúkįre ná mwishí bukwáté, émuhú wámukáma na, émbúshá ÿámu-
káma na, wákónga meca; baMwěrį mbu: angá, kúno kútárįkánga
meca, íyé ubúrenga hó múmĕno, urįanga émutíma mwírų. Mwîshí
wakíé wamabúríshá Mwíndo ébisongá bya, Nkúbá wákųkųma Mwindo,
wénda ná kámwishá kwáNkekénį. Nkekénį wakíé mbu wámúsúnge
wámushemba, wámwîre mbu: émwasį wábé wárétúrwa hó mbu usúmá
ngųrų, réro kúno kúsįrá buraį wábé. Kubí-kubí wátúmísha Mbúra na
Mwîshí. Ábátį: Nkúbá, Mbúra, Mwîshí, Kubí-kubí; ábátį ba bére
Mwindo kinwa kimá mbu: twakusúbáhíré kárehĕ mpe, kongó ushíríré
na kúno; ŏngo Mwindo ŏngo'kúrúkánge kúkwábé, ang'įÿayo rôtú
nyama ÿábusará na ÿákumbúka, ná kahuká búrí ngongo, ntsįne; twakíí
twarúkira mwasį mbú usúbírá tú iÿa kikáí kįmá mǔbya byámákuha-
ngíré bǎte, ŏngo nti ukwá, bana-cábé nti bátángakusúngá tǔ na. Bámukokota ématé mbíso sirínda ná sirínda, mbu: urúkírá? Mbu: aé, narú-
kírá.²⁶⁶ Bére tu Mwíndo mbu: Nkúbá ngu ngí mucųngį wabé, ukíí
úmaronjá bųbí nti Nkúbá ngí watúrí mwasį, n'erótú ndo nti wakubáká
rįmǎ hó, ang'įrana tu ná bana-cábé.

Nkúbá wakíé wamatámbíshá Mwíndo ékútį ékwįyo básibure Mwindo
kûkwé mbu wákųrųké. Mwindo mwįkúrúka ré, nti wamakįnd'įmana
ékwįyo mwǎka ųmá, usúngánge ébyongó-byŏngó n'ébįbí-bįbí bįtį bírį-
kanga ékwįyo. Nkúbá wákųkųma Mwindo, wákúrúka n'e kûkwé kuTubondo. Mwindo wárekera énderí kubŭnu, wásímba,

Mwindo nti ịyé weyánge
Kwásịángá shé-Mwindo
Kwásịángá shé-Mwindo
Mwindo nti ịyé weyánge:²⁶⁷

Wendángá nakụrụka
Shé-Mwindo wabútángá muraị
Kâkwí na kárami
Eé babá kákụmané Mwíndo
Mịra'aní Nkúbá ubúránanga
Niirí kuTubondo
KuTubondo kwábó bakóẏo'aní²⁶⁸
Aní nasúngá kóẏo'aní
Nahíté kǔno kuTubondo
Kwátitá shé-karụo'aní
Ná Mwindo úmashúrá nyama
Nti aní mịné-conga
Cátitá mukwákare²⁶⁹

Érịraị mbu: eé Mwindo úmashúrá nyama nti ukwá.²⁷⁰

Eé Mwindo úreri-tu-ịyo
Utịnanga nyama
Nkúbá mbu
Úrirani-tu-ịyo
Shé-Mwindo ubútángá muraị
Kịrụká-Mbụra tondé bendị
Kákíríá bamití mụndụra²⁷¹
Katitá kashé-karụo'aní
Katitá kántáa múbinwa
Rukombora nkombóre réro²⁷²
Titá wásíba mbu ntsénịnke
Wántáa múbinwa
Ịobora ngobóre réro
Ịobora ráMírábyo²⁷³
Nasímá kǔno kuTubondo
Mwindo
Tubondo ndushú sirínda
Ná makụra arínda
Áwakundúkí cébángá Mwíndo
Wakwí nkúbá sirínda
Ná nịmá nti ẏáwịtómo²⁷⁴
Bakungú báráka béba
Mbu cébịrwé nti céwa-tu-ịyo

Ná kampuku katákocé kinwa
Ná shé-mųmbo watákocé kinwa[275]
Bárérwá urérwi-tu-íyo
Ná mukúngú nti utákocé kinwa
Muhangá ngí wabíká tumpuku
Ná bawé ngí bábíká bea[276]
Binwa byánkébé mishúma[277]
Nya-mųmbo wáráka wéba
Mbu úmeyá kwáshé-Mwindo
Cábúrí shé-Mwindo
Câtųrí mwasí wakárí ho[278]
Shé-Mwindo wámabúrá kinwa
Nti wakwí nkúbá sirínda
Twarúkí nǎ ngu uhúmúranga
Bǎte
Nya-Mwindo wáráka wéba
Mbu mwána'aní wamánubá ngųrų
Katéré kakúno kásuma
N'ínabé mwea
Wáteré mwea
N'íshíbé mwea
Wáteré mwea
Kinkubú-nkubú camúsike
Cáseá cámwána múkarį[279]
Mubúyá muntánga mbúra
Wabéséngá mutábuká mame
Mubúka mame ámakúta
MwiHímbí kwítų nongóbo
Kwátúká kárįsį[280]
Kwárįkángá mukúmú
Kasįkí kámuntse ỹákǔsi
Kábengá ncangí ỹany'įénga

Nkúbá wakíé íyé ukúrúkánge na Mwindo, wénda uhítánge n'e mpômpó-mpômpó; wénda ná kámusįcá n'ánkatí-nkatí na múbutara wákuTubondo. Įshé shé-Mwindo wakíé mbu wásungé musike wé wárųshįwá na Nkúbá, wánínka Nkúbá uhémbo rwákikumí nti cámbícíwá mushee wámurínga wáNkúbá; bámunínka n'énkókó ỹényangé;[281] ngí hátúkíréngá n'erísímánike Nkúbá hǐha, wénda usímáníkírwáa kikumí n'émurínga wacó.[282] Nkúbá wakíé wamakínd'įhémbwa, wákúrúke kûkwé ékwįyo.

Mwindo wakíé wamakínd íruhuka wásonja bana-cé ébátį, béya na. Wére bó mbu: wé Mwindo, kábútwa-kénda, kashé-mįshíngá-mįngí, iwé uwiréngi émyasí kútúkánge we ékwįyo. Iwé wakíé wéya ékwįyo wásúngána na Mbúra, ná Mwĕrį ná Mwĭshí, ná Kubí-kubí, (na) Nkúbá; ábábúmĕ mbo básánu bámukabya iÿa nyama ÿábusará na ÿákumbúka, n'étuhuká túti twébusará n'étwékŭsi n'étwékumbúka; mbu érótų rwákíí natų́rána mukikáí mbu nákuÿá co, érótų́ ro nti kárį́má, nti Nkúbá wendí kániringá kįro įrana ná bana-câní, nti rábíndúkí ná hererį́. Wére tŭ bo mbu: įna nasúngăyo n'ékwįyo bisonga byásúmá-súmá ntákocé ibutų́re byó. Bákíé bámakįnd'îrúkíra ébinwa byáMwíndo ábárįkángá ho básóntsóbana. Shé-Mwindo ná nya-Mwindo, émihųmbe ÿăbó nti ÿaréndá móo búrí mihųmbe ÿámácá, ná kuTubondo nti kútébérée tú ngoma, nti kútábíkírée tu ná mŭme wánkókó.²⁸³ Érôtų́ rwásáángá Mwíndo kuró, įshé n'įna bábéįwa émihųmbe ÿăbó, n'esânkókó sákókóbįka; n'erôtų́ ro bangoma básihirwa ékwantsí n'ékwįyo.²⁸⁴

Mwindo wakíé įyé uri kurwé wásíma na wátanga. Wéca myomba kúrí bana-cé bátį, mbu:

báhingé biÿó bĮngí ná mirimé mĮ̃ngí;
bárįké ná mumanųmbá áhundá, bárįké ná mubúngú rwáhundá;
ang'íbangana,
ang'íbungura mumína'ábĕné wabingwá,
ang'įsea kiréma cétángé múbutara;
ná washámbárá ná mumína'ábĕné nti wákerwa.
Músimiré émwamí, múmúsúbáhe, nâ wé wábúsúbáhe.
Múrįsįanyé bănų bátį́ mongo; angá bushú múcŭo ná misóná mĮ̃ngí.
Múbuté ná băna bare-bare na bihí-bĮhí nti bănų mubúténgi émwămí.²⁸⁵

Mwindo wakíé wamakįnd'Įébă bo, wénda urįkáa na múbúngú rwé. Wásíma na, n'įshé n'įna, bakárį́ ná bana-cé. Wénda nkúrú nĮngí múcŭo cé, ÿénderera na múkímpé cŭo, na bámpé bea bakímpé cŭo bámushía na.

*
*   *

Mwăna usira mó wemá: wábíndúke kiréma, nákįro utábésí kiréma, nti utâtįnwį; kaį kánįnkwá mwea na Ongo kásįrá mo kêmá.

Éburaį búramé, n'erísúma rátáá katí rísúndangá, ntíca, rírųshįengá mwea nyongo nkįrį ÿákwăsá itámúsúngá mwea; kaį émwea ų́tį-ų́tį múcŭo utáhanwánga, nti warį́í tųbí; kaį ngí érísúnga cásúmá.

Érįrįsįanya ngí buna-kįmá, ná waramyí mĮ́né ntíusĮbįrwe, búrí émwamí n'étumpuku; kaį ékumbúka kúrįkangá nti maramyana hó, búrí émwămí wáramyé étumpuku n'étumpuku túramyé émwămí; wamí nkįndo, karįngįto kábea.

Émwea nákįro wábíndúke muraį ráréngá írénga bĮné, nti utángarų́kángá úmpé wamámubųngųraá, wámushée kísondánge we.²⁸⁶

INDEX

Aardvark, 14, 22, 27–29 *passim*, 103 and n. 190, 105 n. 193. *See also* Munundu; Ntumba

Ablution ceremonies, 65 n. 103, 83 n. 154

Adze, 24, 57 and n. 68, 86. *See also* Mwindo, magical possessions of

Affinal relationships, 5, 13, 16, 41 n. 1, 45 nn. 16 and 20, 49, 50 n. 40, 69 n. 110, 128 n. 247, 142 and n. 279. *See also* Marriage

Agnatic relatives, 3, 4, 12

Agriculture, 2–3, 35, 81, 85, 97 and n. 181, 98 and n. 183, 99, 109 n. 206, 117 n. 220, 119, 144–145 n. 286. *See also* Banana; Economy; Technology

Ancestors, 4, 5, 10

Animals, 18, 19, 22, 27, 31, 84, 89, 119 n. 226, 125 n. 239, 130 n. 251, 140, aquatic, 66; domestic, 119 n. 226; dramatis personae, 9, 14, 22; of the forest, 138, 143; little, of the forest, 143; of the river, 143; sacred, 9, 103 n. 190; of the village, 138, 143. *See also* Aardvark; Antelope; Bats; Birds; Boar, wild; Buffalo; Bush baby; Cattle; Chimpanzee; Dogs; Elephant; Fish; Genet; Goats; Gorilla; Hedgehog; Insects; Kasengeri; *Kihuká*; Leopard; Monkey; *Muhangu*-animal; Otter; Pig; Sheep; Snail; Snake; Squirrel, flying; Turtle

Anointment, 129 and n. 249

Antelope, 5, 9, 11, 22; bongo, 45 and n. 18; Duiker, 9; *mukaka*, 58 and n. 78

Aphorisms, 6

Apostrophe, meaning of, 36

Apothegms, 141 n. 277

Armlets, 13, 127 nn. 242 and 243

Arrows, 63, 105 n. 193, 116 n. 218, 127

Art, plastic, 5

Ashes, 95, 97 and n. 179

Assembly, 45, 47, 49; description of mass, 120–129

Associations, 5, 80 n. 144, 137 n. 264. See also *Bwami*; Mukuki

Atmosphere, 21

Attendants, 50

Audience, vi, 7, 13

Aunt, paternal, 4, 11, 19–21, 22, 23–30 *passim*, 33, 34, 50 n. 49, 57 n. 69, 61 n. 90, 62 n. 91, 65, 66, 68–70, 73, 78 n. 140, 82, 84, 87–94 *passim*, 99–100 *passim*, 106–122 *passim*, 124, 129. *See also* Iyangura

Axe, 22, 24, 27, 72, 89, 98, 101, 102, 122

Babuya (Babúýá), 16, 17, 70 and n. 114, 87, 122 n. 232. *See also* Bafuya

Bacira, 15, 16

Bafuya (Bafúýá), 17, 18. *See also* Babuya; Descent groups; Pygmies

Bafwasende, 15

Bag, 72, 86; of good fortune, 22, 24, 27, 34, 57 and n. 69, 89, 94, 122, 136. *See also* Kahombo; Mwindo, magical possessions of

Baherj, 16

Bahimbi (Bahímbí), 15–17 *passim*, 41 n. 2. *See also* Ihimbi

Bakungú, 4, 42 n. 6, 127–128 n. 244. *See also* Counselors

Bamate, 15, 19

Banabirurumba, 52. *See also* Fish

Bana-Kabákj, 15. *See also* Rare

Bana-Koumbo, 16

Banamaka, 52. *See also* Fish

Bracelet, 142 and n. 281
Brackets, meaning of, 39
Brothers, 3; junior, 16, 17; senior, 90, 111, 140 and n. 269
Bsebse-meat, 127 and n. 242
Buffalo, 11, 22, 51 n. 46, 56 n. 67, 140 n. 269
Buingo, 5, 53 n. 51
Buingo wa-Ngoma, 20
Bukuca, 80
Bunyoro, 1, 51 n. 46
Buráÿa, 81 n. 148. *See also* Europe
Burongo, 80
Bush baby, 127 nn. 242 and 243
Busuni, 12. *See also* Shrine
Butea- (*Butéá-*) money, 13, 47 n. 28, 51, 55 n. 59, 85, 86, 109, 127; rings, 86, 127 n. 242
Butinda, 16. *See also* Rureke
Butú, 21, 116 n. 218. *See also* Sky
Buuni, Amato, v, vii, viii
Bwami, 34
Byoo-traps, 137

Calabash, 47 and nn. 26 and 28; rattle, 7, 13
Capital letters, meaning of, 36
Cárwìmbo, 13. *See also* Epic; Singing; Songs
Cattle, 51 n. 46, 75, 82, 85, 109, 119–120 and n. 226, 128
Celestial bodies, 9, 10, 14; journey, 31, 134–139; realm, 33. *See also* Hail; Lightning; Moon; Rain; Star; Sun
Chairs, 96; copper, 30, 121–122 and n. 231
Characters, abstract, 9
Cheerleaders, 85, 87 n. 157, 135
Chief, 2, 4, 7–24 *passim*, 32, 33, 41 and n. 1, 42 and n. 7, 43 and n. 11, 52 n. 50, 55, 75 n. 130, 93 n. 169, 113, 117 n. 219, 119–120 n. 226, 121–128 *passim*, 131, 134 n. 261, 136–137, 139 n. 266, 140 n. 270, 141 and n. 276, 144–145 n. 286. *See also* Mwindo; Shemwindo
Chiefdom, 41 and nn. 1 and 2, 42 n. 6, 61 n. 90, 126 and n. 241
Child naming, 11, 41 and n. 3, 55 n. 59, 72 n. 124. *See also* Mwindo; Names
Children, 3, 41 n. 1, 42–43 and

n. 8, 45, 49 n. 35, 51 n. 47, 53, 55 n. 61, 56 and n. 65, 58, 61 n. 88, 69 and n. 110, 83 n. 154, 106–108, 110 n. 206, 116, 119–120, 125, 129 and n. 249, 130 n. 253, 143 n. 282, 144
Chimpanzee, 75
Circumcision rites, 5, 45 n. 19, 57 n. 68
Clothing, 45–46, 51, 84, 121 and n. 228, 127. *See also* Paraphernalia, of kingship
Cloud, 10, 14, 22, 137
Commoners, 22, 42 n. 6
Conga, 11, 22–31 *passim*, 34, 56 and n. 67, 60 n. 86, 74–78 *passim*, 89, 92–94, 99 and n. 185, 100–102, 104, 109, 113, 122, 131–133, 138. *See also* Mwindo, magical possessions of
Congo, vi, 1, 4
Consonants, symbols for, 36
Cook, 127 n. 244
Copper, 12, 121, 127, 142, 143; rings, 12, 143
Council, 30, 122; *kìbù*, 42 and nn. 6 and 7, 45–46, 122; *námá*, 42 n. 7, 46 n. 21, 122 n. 232; secret, 73
Counselors, 4, 22, 24, 42, 45–48 *passim*, 51–63 *passim*, 90–92 and n. 165, 115, 119, 122–129 *passim*, 131, 135, 137, 141. *See also* Bakungú
Courtship, 23, 43–44
Cousins: cross-, 44 n. 15, 45 n. 20, 47 nn. 25 and 26; parallel, 91 n. 163
Cowries, 127 n. 242
Crabs, 14, 25, 52 n. 49, 65 and n. 103, 66 n. 105
Cradling string, 90 and n. 162
Cripples, 128
Cultural relations of Nyanga, 2, 15–19, 62 n. 93, 119–120 n. 226
Cursing, 33–34, 104, 105, 106

Dancing, vi, 6, 7, 14, 25, 27, 46, 62 n. 92, 71, 72 n. 123, 74–75, 78 n. 139, 87, 89; masked, 57 n. 68; possession, 56 n. 67
Daughters of Shemwindo, 23–24, 42–43, 53, 117, 123
Deafness, 128

INDEX

Descent groups, vi, 3–4, 5, 13–17 *passim*, 30, 42 nn. 4, 6, and 7, 44 nn. 13 and 14, 47 n. 28, 48 nn. 29 and 30, 52 n. 50, 70 n. 114, 80 n. 147, 112 n. 213, 119–120 n. 226, 122 n. 232, 128, 143 n. 282; patrilineal, 3; royal, 42 n. 6, 126 n. 241, 140 n. 270. *See also* Kinship

Dike, 131 n. 254, 134 n. 261

Discourses, 10

Dishes, wooden, 5, 84, 119

Divers, 59 and n. 82

Divinator, 142

Divinities, 2, 4, 9–12 *passim*, 18–22 *passim*, 25, 27, 32, 43 n. 11, 52 n. 50, 67 n. 106, 76 n. 135, 99, 100 and n. 185, 105, 106 n. 195, 112 n. 213, 116 n. 217, 122 n. 231, 143 n. 282, 145. *See also* Kahombo; Karisi; Kentse; Muisa; Mukiti; Nkuba; Ongo

Dogs, 5, 8, 9, 18, 85, 104, 119 and n. 226, 130 and nn. 251 and 253, 131

Downstream, 49 n. 33, 52, 61, 65 and n. 103, 68

Dragon, 5, 10, 14, 22, 30–31, 72, 122, 130–137 *passim. See also* Kirimu

Dreams, v, 5, 6, 18, 53 n. 54, 74, 100 n. 186

Drum, 7, 24–25, 30, 32, 58 n. 78, 59–72 *passim*, 74, 78, 87, 89, 91, 102, 104, 108, 114, 118, 124

Drummers, 22, 84, 87 and n. 157, 94, 127 n. 244

Earth, 4, 5, 21; heart of, 5; and Heaven, 60, 116 and n. 218; and sky, 143 n. 284. *See also* Heaven and earth; Sky

East Africa, 1, 136 n. 263

Eating, 44 and n. 15, 50–51, 75 and n. 133, 79, 81 n. 149, 84, 101, 107 and n. 199, 112 n. 214, 126, 134. *See also* Food

Economy, 2, 3, 5, 59 nn. 79 and 82, 111 n. 210. *See also* Agriculture; Banana; Fishing; Food-gathering; Hunting; Trapping

Efe, 18. *See also* Pygmies

Elders, 8, 10, 44 n. 14, 58 n. 78, 64, 72, 77, 120–122, 125, 126

Elephant, 58 n. 78, 80 n. 143, 140 n. 269

Epic, vii, 2, 11–13, 16–20 *passim*, 23, 35, 48 n. 30, 52 n. 49, 60 n. 86, 142; content of, 14; dramatis personae in, 14; learning of, 11–12, 17; mode of narration of, vi, vii, 2, 13–14; occasion for narration of, 13; rewards for narrator of, 13, 14; song par excellence, 13, 71 n. 117. *See also* Karisi; Mwindo epic; Narrator, Pygmies

Ethnohistory, 1, 2, 9–10, 15–18 *passim*, 42 n. 4, 51 n. 46, 70 n. 114, 119–120 and n. 226, 136 n. 262, 143 n. 282

Eulogistic recitation, 8–9

Euphemism, 34, 37, 49 n. 35, 97–98 n. 181, 101 and n. 187, 102 and n. 189, 117 n. 219, 119–120 n. 226

Europe, 80. *See also* Buráȳa

Fame, 13–14, 33, 34, 53 and n. 51, 81, 141 and n. 276, 144

Famine, 24, 60

Fate, 60 n. 86

Father. *See* Mwindo, and his father; Shemwindo

Fields, 21. *See also* Banana, groves; Glen

Fire, 19, 26, 27, 57, 63, 84, 94 and n. 170, 101, 102 and n. 189; god of, 4, 19

Fire drill, 86

Firewood, 24, 53, 94

Fish, 14, 22, 24, 25, 52 n. 49, 65–66 and n. 105, 67 n. 106, 72 and n. 122, 111 and n. 209. *See also* Banabirurumba; Banamaka; Banampongo; Banankomo; Banatubusa

Fishing, 2, 5, 15, 59 n. 82, 80 and n. 147, 111 n. 210, 134 n. 261. *See also* Economy

Flute, 100 n. 186, 107, 112

Food, 6, 13, 14, 25–29, 34, 44 and n. 15, 50–51, 64 n. 101, 74, 75, 80–81 and n. 148, 84, 88, 94, 97, 101 n. 187, 102 n. 189, 107 and n. 198, 111 n. 210, 113, 115 n. 216, 117 n. 221, 118, 124, 126, 144. *See also* Eating

Food-gathering, 2, 100–102. *See also* Economy

Force, 56 n. 67, 60 n. 86, 88 and n. 158. *See also* Life force

Forest, 1, 18, 21, 28, 30–31, 51 n. 46, 59 and nn. 79 and 80, 63 n. 97, 98,

Imaginary beings, 19
Incantations, v
Inheritance, 3, 47 n. 27, 62 n. 91,
75 n. 130, 126 n. 241, 140 n. 270
Initiations, 5, 7, 45 n. 19, 128 n. 245
Injunctions, 11
Insects, 14, 69–70 n. 110; ants, red,
89; *atumba*, 72; bees, 83 n. 154,
102 n. 189, 114 and n. 215, 118
and n. 224; *bisibisi*, 89; butterflies,
77; centipede, 123, 138; cricket,
22, 24, 55 and n. 61; flies, 77; lice,
77; *ntsine*, 138, 139 n. 266; spiders,
11, 20, 22, 25–26, 48 n. 32, 73–74
and n. 126, 75. *See also* Banamitandi
Institut pour la recherche scientifique en Afrique centrale, vii
Instructions, 11
Interdiction, 23, 43, 52, 143
Invocations, 35
Iremeso-hut, 97 and n. 180, 117 and
n. 219. *See also* Guesthouse
Iron, 7, 12, 82, 98, 113
Isia- (*Isia-*) crest, 45 and n. 18
Itembe, 19. *See also* Banana
Ivory, 5
Iyangura, 21–26 *passim*, 30, 35, 41,
43–46 and n. 24, 47 n. 26, 49, 50 n.
42, 51–52 and n. 49, 63–71 *passim*,
73–79 *passim*, 82–85 *passim*, 90, 91,
100 n. 186, 102, 106, 107, 111–114
passim, 117–124 *passim*, 128–129.
See also Aunt, paternal
Iyobora of Mirabyo, 140, 141 and
n. 273
Iyúhu, 4. *See also* Divinities

Jar, 53, 77, 78, 84, 119
Joking relationships, 2, 5, 44 n. 16
Juniors, 42. *See also* Seniors

Kabaraka, 19
Kabóntsóbóntso, 32. *See also* Mwindo, epithets of; Names, epithets
Kabotyo Munyangoro, 79–80 and n.
142
Kábútwa-kénda, 11, 20, 25, 32, 57 n.
70. *See also* Mwindo, epithets of;
Names, epithets
Kahindo, 22, 28–29, 95 and n. 172,
96 and n. 177, 97, 101, 102 n. 189,
113–115. *See also* Kahombo; Yaws

Kahombo (Kahómbó), 4, 11, 14, 57
and n. 69, 73–74 and n. 126, 83 n.
154, 95 n. 172, 101. *See also* Bag, of
good fortune; Kahindo
Kahungu (Kahúngú), 65 and n. 104,
72, 73 n. 125, 74–75, 103, 106, 109,
117. *See also* Birds, hawk
Kakoma-pole, 70
Kalisia, 18. *See also* Divinities; Pyg-
mies
Kamuri, 80
Kantori, 109. *See also* Birds, sparrow
Kanyangara, v, 17
Karai, 79 and n. 142
Karamo, 34, 35, 53 n. 51, 78 n. 140,
118 nn. 222 and 223, 122 n. 232.
See also Life force; Values
Karisi (Kárisi; *kárisi*): as chief, 11,
17; as epic, vi, 11–18; as male
spirit, 12, 17; as name of bard, 12
Kasengeri, 71 and n. 115, 74
Kasiyembe, 22, 25, 26, 52 and n. 50,
73–78
Katakwa (*Katakwá*) region, 111 and
n. 210
Katee, 73, 75
Katitiiri, 69–70 and n. 110
Katobororo, 128
Kembo-hat, 127 and n. 242
Kentse (Kéntsé), 4, 22, 72 n. 124. *See
also* Sun
Kiana, 4
Kibira, 4, 18. *See also* Divinities;
Leopard
Kihuká, 63 n. 98
Kikoka-fern, 27, 29, 92, 93 and n.
167, 94, 95, 114
Kingship, vi, 127, 128, 144, 145
Kingwana, 82 n. 151, 83 n. 154
Kinkunduri, 65 and n. 103
Kinship, 3, 4, 5, 9, 12, 14, 16, 17,
21, 34, 35, 42 n. 4, 44 n. 15, 45 nn.
17 and 20, 46, 48 n. 30, 52 n. 49,
61 n. 90, 69 n. 110, 78 n. 140, 79,
80, 91 n. 163, 112 n. 213, 129 n.
249, 133 n. 257, 139 n. 268, 144–145
and n. 286; terminology, 41 n. 3,
42 n. 5, 43 n. 9, 44 n. 15, 45 nn.
17 and 20, 49 n. 33, 61 n. 90, 62 n.
94, 69–70 n. 110, 91 n. 163, 96 n.
177, 124 n. 235, 133 n. 257, 139 n.
268. *See also* Descent groups
Kirambo, 80

INDEX

Kirimu (Kirįmu), 5, 10, 14, 22, 30–
31, 43 n. 11, 130–137. *See also*
Dragon
Kiruka-Mbura, 83 and n. 152
Kiruka-nyambura, 83 and n. 152
Kisimba, v, vi, 41 n. 2; groupement,
v, 15
Kivu, 1
Knife, 130 n. 253, 132
Koutu, 16
Kubikubi-Star, 135, 138, 143
Kubusará, 21. *See also* Forest
Kumbúka, 21, 81
Kumu, 1, 2
Kumundųra, 21. *See also* Forest
Kundŭsi, 21. *See also* River
Kunju, 80
Kwirúngá, 4, 21, 63 n. 97. *See also*
Underworld

Lake Edward, 1
Land tenure, 2, 4
Lega, v, 2
Leopard, 4, 9, 63 n. 98, 127 n. 242.
See also Divinities; Kibira
Lianas, 57 n. 69, 79, 86, 136 and
n. 263; *muri*, 115 n. 216; *musara*,
136; *ntiriri*, 136 and n. 263
Life force, 34, 56 n. 64, 118 nn. 222
and 223, 122 n. 232. *See also*
Force; *Karamo*
Lightning, 4, 11, 19, 21, 27, 28, 30–
35 *passim*, 83, 91, 92 and n. 165,
105, 122 n. 231, 138 and n. 266, 140
nn. 270 and 271, 141, 144–145 n.
286. *See also* Divinities; Nkuba
Locative expressions, 20–21, 37, 38,
41 n. 2, 43 n. 12, 48 n. 29, 50 n.
43, 52, 58 n. 74, 61 n. 89, 63 n.
97, 65, 79, 129 n. 250, 130
Loin cloth, 136
Lubero, 15
Lubutu, 15

Mabura Banyore, 79
Maere, 81
Maidservants, 22, 25, 26. *See also*
Iyangura; Servants
Makangura, 96 n. 174. *See also*
Blessings
Mambasa, 15
Mamboreo, 80
Marámį, 70 n. 113

Mariba, 68. See also *Mįné-márįba*;
Mukiti
Marriage, 3, 23, 35, 44 n. 15, 45–51,
92 n. 165, 97 n. 180, 114, 121 n.
228, 128 and n. 247, 143 n. 282,
144. *See also* Affinal relationships
Marvelous event, 58 and n. 76, 98,
114
Masks, 5
Mat, 109
Mateene, Kahombo C., vii, viii, 37
Material culture, 14, 27, 35, 84–87.
See also Technology
Matrimonial exchange, 45 n. 16,
47–49, 92 n. 166
Matrimonial goods, 3, 23, 29, 92
and n. 65
Maxims, 141 n. 277
Mbai-seeds, 116
Mbea-oil, 46
Mboru, 11, 135. *See also* Mwindo;
Names, epithets
Mbúntsú, 5. *See also* Associations
Meat, 51, 106, 107, 120, 129, 134, 140
Meditations, 10, 71
Meetinghouse, 58 n. 78
Meeting place, 5, 10, 42 n. 4, 57 n.
73, 78, 95, 96, 98, 100, 101, 141
Mĕshé, 4. *See also* Divinities
Mĕshémutwá, 2, 4. *See also* Divinities
Mįné, 4. *See also* Ownership
Mįné-márįba, 32, 43 n. 11. *See also*
Mariba; Mukiti; Names, epithets
Minéntsí, 18
Mishįnga, 73 n. 125
Monkey, 127 n. 242; *mburu*, 71 and
n. 119
Monster, 5, 9. *See also* Mukiti
Moon, 10, 14, 21, 22, 31, 72 and n.
124, 135, 138, 143, 144–145 n. 286
Mother: little, 123; of Mwindo, 24,
33, 123, 129. *See also* Nyamumbo;
Nyamwindo
Mountain, 70 n. 113, 98, 128, 129
and n. 248, 134; Kabarebare, 70,
137; Mbuhi, 80 and n. 146; Nta-
bare, 137. *See also* Hills
Mourning, 50 n. 42, 143
Mpacá, 5, 10, 32, 49–50 n. 37, 143.
See also Forest specter
Mpamba, 2. *See also* Lega
Mpinga, 80

207

63, 92, 102–105, 121, 122, 134–143;
and Ntumba, the Aardvark, 27,
28, 104–107, 110–112; personality
traits of, 32–33, 144–145 n. 286;
physical traits of, 11, 18, 20, 32,
107 n. 201; and Pygmies, 31, 127,
129–133; as ruler, 29–30, 127–129,
144; and Sheburungu, 27–29 *passim*, 107–110; as sororal nephew of
the Bats, the Baniyana, 25, 93 and
n. 169, 113; and Spiders, 25–26,
73–74; subterranean journey of,
27–29, 93–114; terrestrial journey
to Tubondo, 26–27, 79–89; as
thaumaturg, 26–30 *passim*, 55–57,
76, 77, 83–87, 93, 101, 113, 119; in
Tubondo, 27, 29–30, 89–94, 114–
144 *passim*; and wives, 128
Mwindo epic: circumstances of an-
notation in, v–vi; dramatis personae in, 11, 14, 19–22, 43; European influence on, 70 n. 113, 73
n. 126, 80, 82 n. 151, 83 n. 154,
139 n. 266; as heroic model, 60 n.
86; learning of, 17; narrator's conclusions in, 32–33, 144–145; Pygmy
influence on, 2, 17–19; spatial
plan of, 20–21; synopsis of, 20–32,
35; temporal plan of, 20–21; variations of, 19–20, 30–31
Mwishi, 72 n. 124. *See also* Kentse

Nails, 32, 49 and n. 37, 50 n. 47, 109
and n. 206, 143 n. 283
Names, 8, 9, 17, 41 n. 3, 52 n. 50,
55 and n. 59, 59 n. 80, 63 n. 96,
71 and n. 118, 72, 78, 85, 95 n. 172,
137; epithets, 4, 8, 11, 20, 32, 43 n.
11, 56 and n. 65, 57 n. 70, 64 n.
101, 66 and n. 105, 67, 68 and n.
108, 74, 75, 76 and n. 135, 78, 84,
88, 90–94 *passim*, 100, 101, 102, 105
n. 193, 106 n. 195, 108, 111, 112
and n. 213, 113, 116, 117, 121, 125,
132, 135, 136, 139, 140 n. 271, 141
n. 273, 143; honorific, 32–33, 45 n.
17, 77, 78 and n. 139, 90 and n.
162, 112, 118, 124, 131, 141; nicknames, 4; pejorative, 62 n. 94, 68
n. 109, 71 n. 118, 76 and n. 134,
82, 89, 91, 99, 103, 104, 105 n.
193, 108, 111, 114, 117, 118, 133,
140 and n. 271; praise, 68, 80
and n. 143; teknonymic, 12, 21,

41 n. 1, 60 n. 87, 102 n. 189
Narration, mode of, vi, 6, 12, 13, 14,
62 n. 92
Narrator, vi, 6–11 *passim*, 14–19, 35,
37–38, 62 n. 92, 66 n. 105, 70 nn.
113 and 114, 71 nn. 115, 117, and
119, 72 n. 123, 74 n. 128, 77 n.
137, 78 n. 140, 79 n. 142, 81 n.
148, 97 n. 179, 101 n. 187, 111 n.
210, 114 n. 226, 122 n. 232, 137 n.
264, 140 n. 272, 142 n. 280. *See also*
Rureke, *Shé-kárisi*
Nderema-fibers, 71, 74, 78
Ndorera-fringes, 121
Necklace, 86
Needle, 86
Nephew: paternal, 22; sororal, 4, 6,
13, 16, 25, 46, 70, 93 n. 169, 115
Ngara, 80
Nkángo, 4. *See also* Divinities
Nkasa, 80
Nkebe-dance, 141 and n. 277
Nkebe-tooth, 89 and n. 160
Nkendo-knives, 87
Nkuba (Nkúbá), 4, 14, 22, 26, 30, 76
and n. 135, 91–92, 102–105, 121,
122, 134–140, 142–143. *See also* Di-
vinities; Lightning
Nkurongo, 31, 130–131. *See also*
Pygmies
Nkúrú, 33, 34, 81. *See also* Fame
Nkwángátiro, 7, 13
Nobles, 4, 22, 42, 45–48 *passim*, 119,
123–127 *passim*. See also *Barúsi*
Nomadism, 138
Ntande, 80
Ntumba, 21, 22, 27, 29, 103–106,
110–113, 116. *See also* Aardvark;
Munundu
Numbers: eight, 109, 120; five, 129;
four, 129; nine thousand, 47 and
n. 28; one, 139; one thousand,
134; seven, 21, 42 and n. 4, 47, 48,
51, 60 and n. 86, 65 and n. 103, 76,
78–79, 90–92, 105–107, 122, 123,
131, 138, 141; six, 55, 123; three,
133; twenty, 129
Nyabuke Kamwikoti, 79–80 n. 142
Nyabunge, 72
Nyakarúo, 45 n. 17
Nyamitondo, 19. *See also* Lightning;
Mwindo
Nyamumbo, 141 and n. 278. *See also*
Mother, of Mwindo; Nyamwindo

INDEX

Strength, 49 n. 37, 53 n. 51
Stretcher, 133
Succession, 3
Suicide, 5
Sun, 4, 21, 22, 31, 72 n. 124, 104, 118
  and n. 224, 138–139 and n. 266,
  144–145 n. 286
Supernatural, 4, 9–11, 14, 19, 20, 22,
  24, 31. See also Divinities; Religion
Swahili, 95 n. 173, 97 nn. 178 and
  179, 115 n. 216, 117 n. 220, 119 n.
  225, 134 n. 259, 139 nn. 266 and
  267, 140 n. 272
Swimming, 59–60 and nn. 82 and 83
Symbols: of beauty, 25, 32, 43, 46 n.
  22, 76, 111 n. 209, 121; of benefi-
  cence, 83 n. 154; of cleanliness, 97,
  120; of dancing, 71 n. 115; of
  elegance, 71 n. 116; of endeavor,
  99–100 n. 185; of evil, 67 n. 106,
  77 n. 136; of excess, 145; of hatred,
  66 n. 105, 67 n. 106; of ingratitude,
  97 n. 173; of malediction, 131 n.
  255; of malehood, 32, 49 n. 37,
  78 n. 139; of neatness, 45 n. 18, 97
  n. 178; of nuisance, 103 n. 191; of
  purification, 71 n. 119; of scorn,
  69–70 n. 110; of singing, good, 71
  n. 116; of straightness, 70 n. 113;
  of suffering, 101 n. 188; of tenderness, 70 n. 111; of toughness,
  102 n. 189; of ugliness, 66 n. 105

Taboos, 2, 10, 140 n. 270; on food,
  81 n. 148; on hunting, 35; on
  river, 52 n. 49, 81 n. 148
Tail: animal, 71 n. 115, 140; antelope, 22, 56 n. 67, 140 n. 269;
  boar, wild, 140 n. 269; buffalo, 22,
  56 n. 67; elephant, 140 n. 269
Tales, 2, 6, 9–10, 20, 48 n. 32, 58 n.
  76, 61 n. 90, 66 n. 105, 71 n. 120,
  72 nn. 121 and 123, 75 n. 131, 82 n.
  150, 93 n. 67, 96 n. 174, 100 n.
  186, 130 n. 253
Taro leaves, 51
Technology, 2–3, 5, 35, 41 n. 2, 46
  n. 23, 56 n. 66, 79 n. 141, 80, 84–
  87, 97 and n. 181, 98–99, 105 n.
  194, 119, 134 n. 261. See also
  Banana; Economy; Material culture
Telepathic bond, 100 n. 186
Thunder, 83

Tiri-Asa, 1, 2
Tobacco, 85
Tone, 8, 36, 62 n. 93, 83 n. 153, 107
  n. 200, 111 n. 209
Torches, 63
Toro, 1. See also Uganda
Transcription, system of, 35–36
Translation, problems of, viii, 37–
  38, 110–111 nn. 208 and 209
Trap, 111 n. 210
Trapping, 2, 5, 10, 15, 41 n. 2, 70 n.
  112, 85, 119, 130, 137, 139 n. 266.
  See also Economy
Trees, 119 n. 225, 140 and n. 221;
  ficus, 75; isea, 109; mango, 98;
  ntongi, 72; ntsembe (ntsémbe), 46
  and n. 22; raphia, 21, 41 n. 2,
  46, 57 n. 69, 87, 90 n. 162, 127 n.
  242, 134 and n. 260, 136 n. 263, 137
"True stories," 10
Tube, reed, 12
Tubi, Stephano, v, vii, viii
Tubondo, 20–21, 23, 24, 26–27, 29,
  30, 41 and n. 2, 44, 49, 52, 60, 61,
  65, 78, 79, 82–85, 87–94, 99, 100,
  106, 109, 112, 113, 114, 117–120,
  122, 124, 125, 128, 129, 131, 132,
  134 n. 260, 135, 136, 139–143. See
  also Village
Turtle, 53 n. 51
Twa, 1. See also Baremba; Batwá;
  Pygmies
Twins, 41 n. 3

Uganda, 1, 51 n. 46
Ukanga, 19
Ukaru-powder, 127
Uncles: maternal, 16, 19, 20, 26–27,
  29, 30, 34, 44 and n. 15, 69–70 n.
  110, 82, 84, 88, 89, 92–93, 94, 114–
  115, 118, 128 n. 246; paternal, 3.
  See also Baniyana; Bats
Underworld, 4, 20, 21, 27, 63 n. 97
University of Delaware, vii
Upstream, 49 n. 33, 61 n. 89, 65 and
  n. 103, 67
Utebe-stool, 50, 51, 115

Valuables, 47
Values, vi, 6, 7, 10, 14, 18–20, 22,
  23, 32–35 passim, 66 n. 105, 90 n.
  162, 110 n. 207, 119, 123, 125, 129,
  138–139, 144–145 n. 286. See also
  Generosity; Hospitality

212